ADVANCE PRAISE FOR
## Slow is Beautiful

*Slow is Beautiful* is thought-provoking — disturbing, funny, eye-opening — from the first to the very last page. Cecile Andrews has a vision for life far more compelling and rich than the toxic myths flogged by the cheerleaders of corporate consumer society. If you lead the kind of time-impoverished life so many of us do, this book will provide an antidote — dare I say it will set you free?

— JAMES O'REILLY, editor of *Stories to Live By*

She's a critic...she's a comedian...she's a wise philosopher... Actually, in her new book, *Slow is Beautiful*, Cecile Andrews, America's sage of simplicity, is all those and more. With great personal stories, the courage of her convictions, uncommon insight and disarming wit, she challenges our "more and faster is better" society and shows how we can live better with less speed and less stuff. If this book weren't so clear and straightforwardly honest, it would be subversive, in the best sense of that word. The ideas it contains surely are. You'll be hard pressed to put it down once you start reading. But don't just read it; DO it!

— JOHN DE GRAAF, co-author of
*Affluenza: The All-Consuming Epidemic*

Don't be fooled! In Cecile Andrew's lively mind there's nothing sluggish about thinking slow. In her new book, *Slow is Beautiful*, Cecile delivers hard facts, timeless wisdom and puckish humor with a punch that is passionate, personal and political. This is a compelling work: well before the last page you'll love the message and the messenger.

— PETER C. WHYBROW MD, Director of the Semel Institute for Neuroscience and Human Behavior at UCLA, and author of *American Mania: When More is Not Enough*

Read this book. Then give it to your teenager, your dentist, your best friend and the clerk at the grocery store. With trademark lucidity and intelligence, Cecile Andrews illuminates a path out of denial and despair, into a human community of authenticity, joy, compassion and justice.

— JULIET SCHOR, author of *The Overspent American*


Despite what the title implies, *Slow is Beautiful* is a fast read! It will leave you plenty of time to go out and enjoy yourself as Cecile Andrews recommends, and indeed, insists on! (Although reading the book is pretty fun in itself.)

— FRANK LEVERING & WANDA URBANSKA, authors and producers of the "Simple Living with Wanda Urbanska" national public television series


This book made me laugh out loud! Being with Cecile is always a good thing, and her book feels like being with her. Cecile's funny and poignant stories, combined with her research and reflection, make the case that by reweaving our lives with what we all really want — community, conviviality, and simply having more fun! — we will simultaneously help create the kind of society we all really want — one characterized by greater equity, compassion, and sustainability.

— MICHAEL SCHUT, Editor of the award-winning *Simpler Living, Compassionate Life: A Christian Perspective*

# slow

## is beautiful

### new visions of community, leisure and
### joie de vivre

CECILE ANDREWS

NEW SOCIETY PUBLISHERS

**Cataloging in Publication Data:**
A catalog record for this publication is available from the National Library of Canada.

Cover design by Diane McIntosh.
Cover images: Getty Images, Photodisc Blue/Photodisc Green.

Poem "Shiftless" by Raymond Carver, excerpted on pp. 223-224, is from *Ultramarine,* copyright 1986 by Raymond Carver. Used by permission of Random House, Inc.

Printed in Canada.
First printing August 2006.
Paperback ISBN-13: 978-0-86571-554-7
Paperback ISBN-10: 0-86571-554-8

Inquiries regarding requests to reprint all or part of *Slow is Beautiful* should be addressed to New Society Publishers at the address below.

To order directly from the publishers, please call toll-free (North America) 1-800-567-6772, or order online at www.newsociety.com

Any other inquiries can be directed by mail to:
New Society Publishers
P.O. Box 189, Gabriola Island, BC V0R 1X0, Canada
1-800-567-6772

New Society Publishers' mission is to publish books that contribute in fundamental ways to building an ecologically sustainable and just society, and to do so with the least possible impact on the environment, in a manner that models this vision. We are committed to doing this not just through education, but through action. We are acting on our commitment to the world's remaining ancient forests by phasing out our paper supply from ancient forests worldwide. This book is one step toward ending global deforestation and climate change. It is printed on acid-free paper that is 100% old growth forest-free (100% post-consumer recycled), processed chlorine free, and printed with vegetable-based, low-VOC inks. For further information, or to browse our full list of books and purchase securely, visit our website at: www.newsociety.com

NEW SOCIETY PUBLISHERS                                    www.newsociety.com

*For Paul, my husband, and Maggie,*
*our bichon frise — they're slow*
*most of the time and beautiful always.*

# Table of Contents

ACKNOWLEDGMENTS . . . . . . . . . . . . . . . . . . . . . . . . . . . . . . . . . . . . . . . . . . . . . IX

CHAPTER 1
Toward a Philosophy of Slow . . . . . . . . . . . . . . . . . . . . . . . . . . . . . . . . . 1

CHAPTER 2
The Truth about Happiness . . . . . . . . . . . . . . . . . . . . . . . . . . . . . . . . . 13

CHAPTER 3
Reversing the Spell of Status . . . . . . . . . . . . . . . . . . . . . . . . . . . . . . . 43

CHAPTER 4
"Fast" and the Consumer Society . . . . . . . . . . . . . . . . . . . . . . . . . . . . 55

CHAPTER 5
Work Slowdown . . . . . . . . . . . . . . . . . . . . . . . . . . . . . . . . . . . . . . . . . . . 73

CHAPTER 6
The Subversiveness of Joie de Vivre . . . . . . . . . . . . . . . . . . . . . . . . . 91

CHAPTER 7
Visionary Leisure . . . . . . . . . . . . . . . . . . . . . . . . . . . . . . . . . . . . . . . . 139

CHAPTER 8
Slow Together: Exuberant Community . . . . . . . . . . . . . . . . . . . . . . 163

CHAPTER 9
Slow Is Beautiful ......................................... 197

Bibliography ............................................. 227

Endnotes ............................................... 231

Index .................................................. 241

About the Author ........................................ 245

# Acknowledgments

IREMEMBER EXACTLY when I decided to submit a book proposal to New Society Publishers. I was speaking at a conference they were sponsoring in Vancouver, BC, and editors Chris and Judith Plant were there with a book table. As I browsed their collection, I thought to myself, "I have half of these books in my own library! I want to work with these people!"

I had been buying New Society Publishers books for years, starting back when the only venue was a newsprint catalogue that came through the mail. All my life I've looked for kindred spirits, never expecting to find them in a publishing house!

If there is any belief system we must crack, it's the myth that making money is our chief goal in life, something that comes before all else — integrity, civic engagement, kindness, honesty, social responsibility. How nice to be working with a group like New Society Publishers who puts these qualities at the top of their list.

And I knew what I wanted to write about — how our experience of time affects the quality of our lives and the fate of the planet. I have been working with the Take Back Your Time Movement for several years. To my mind, this is the revolution of our age — one that ties in with every other movement, from the gap between the rich and the rest of us to the future of the human race.

The Time campaign underpins a larger philosophical framework — the Voluntary Simplicity Movement, a global undertaking that asks us to make conscious choices about how our behaviors affect the well-being of people and the planet. Many of us in the Simple Living Network (more kindred spirits) have worked together many years. In particular,   we've created a broad membership organization, Simple Living America.

I'm grateful to these two organizations, Take Back Your Time and Simple Living America, for their work and inspiration.

One day I reached a point when I was through writing this book. But there was still a lot of editing to be done! Luckily, the very best editor in the world lives with me. I gave the book to my husband Paul and said, "Do with it what you will!" He even added a few of his own little stories. Which was OK with me, because he's also the best writer I know.

We then turned the manuscript over to the capable hands of Judith Brand, whose solicitous editing caught numerous mistakes and added zip to the narrative. For the remarkable cover of *Slow Is Beautiful* I must thank Diane McIntosh, whose subtle and striking design captured the book's essence poetically. My gratitude for the soothing presentation of the book's pages goes to Teresa Lynne and Greg Green.

Ingrid Witvoet orchestrated the project through to the object you hold in your hands, and Sara Reeves ensured that word of publication got to all the right people. I hope the book rewards the faith of many others who contributed ideas and support. Thank you one and all!

CHAPTER I

# Toward a Philosophy of Slow

WE HAD JUST ARRIVED IN PALO ALTO, and we weren't prepared for what happened.

My husband and I were walking back to our car when we heard a loud, incessant honking. A middle-aged woman was trying to parallel park, and a young woman in a huge SUV had crowded up behind her, leaning on the horn and refusing to give her room to maneuver.

Suddenly the SUV driver squealed up next to the other car, rolled down her window and started screaming. Then she turned and reached over to grab something. My husband and I froze — we expected gunshots.

Instead, she threw something through her window — it looked like a handful of rocks. "Fucking bitch!" she screamed, jerked the car into gear and sped off.

My husband took down her license number and called 911 on his cellphone. The older woman, her voice trembling, thanked us. We told her we would serve as witnesses if need be.

That evening the Palo Alto police called us and reported that they had investigated the incident and given the SUV driver a warning.

The officer told us that the SUV driver said she had thrown chocolate-covered raisins at the woman.

How bizarre.

My husband and I found the incident surprisingly upsetting. Although no one was physically hurt and we had not been directly involved, we couldn't get it out of our minds. The driver's SUV towered over the older woman's four-door sedan and seemed closer to a lethal weapon than a car. How had it come to this? We had lived in Palo Alto 20 years earlier and had never experienced incidents like this!

We don't know much about the SUV driver. She undoubtedly saw herself as a rising star, a fast-tracker on a meteoric path to success. But when you're in too much of a hurry to let someone park in front of you, when laying on the horn seems a better strategy than simply backing up a few feet, and when anger consumes you to the degree that you pick up anything handy to throw at someone, you're probably a candidate for a "Slow" transfusion.

What really surprised me, though, was the response we got when we told people about the incident. Nearly everyone responded with a road rage story of their own. They told us of drivers gunning their engines menacingly, cars ramming other cars, SUVs driving over traffic circles, motorists wielding handguns. There was one pickup truck driver who ran down and killed a motorcyclist after an argument, and almost everyone knew about the maniac in San Jose who grabbed a woman's dog from her car and threw it into onrushing traffic, killing the dog. Everyone had a tale of terror.

What most intrigued me was a friend's reaction to the chocolate-raisin story. Instead of sympathizing with the older woman, as most people had, she felt sorry for the SUV driver. "What kind of a life is she living to do something like that?" she asked.

## Mining the experience for meaning

I've thought a lot about this story, because it's come to symbolize for me so many of our society's urgent problems. What stands out, of course, is what she was angry about. She was in a hurry. She didn't want anyone to slow her down or get in her way. Who hasn't felt close to rage when someone gets in their way? Why are we like this? UCLA psychiatrist Peter Whybrow, author of *American Mania*, says we are being pushed to our physical and psychological limits because we are under such acute time pressure. We're being driven out of our minds with the stress of speed. Everyone understands this on a basic level and complains about it. No one defends it as healthy or sustainable. But we seem to be helpless to address it.

Next, I doubt that this driver was just having a bad day; she was having a bad life. You don't get that enraged if you're just a little upset. Her anger signifies the growing unhappiness in our society. Happiness has been on the decline for the past 40 years, and depression has shot up. America has the highest rate of homicide in the industrialized world. Our time deprivation is making us unhappy, yet we don't know what to do about it. How did this happen? Apparently Americans are confused about the nature of happiness. What is it? How do we get it? We can't make progress on our problems unless we understand this basic issue.

*Apparently Americans are confused about the nature of happiness. What is it? How do we get it? We can't make progress on our problems unless we understand this basic issue.*

Next, think about what she was driving. If anything symbolizes our taunting of nature and our indifference to the environment, it's an SUV. These gas guzzlers not only pollute the air, contributing to a situation that sends us to war for oil, they are a big part of global warming, something that was brought to the public's attention in a horrific way in the fall of 2005 by Hurricane Katrina. One of our primary problems is our destruction of the environment. Did the SUV driver know this? Might she have felt subconsciously guilty about her choice of car?

Why do people drive SUVs? The only possible explanation is to keep up with the Joneses — the pursuit of status. In our American search for bigger and bigger, SUVs are a visible symbol of our pathology of status. In the last 40 years, as many other problems have exacerbated, something else has been happening — an increasing gap between the rich and the poor, withering away the middle class. In fact, the biggest indicator of the health of a nation, as measured in terms of longevity, is the distribution of wealth. The bigger the gap, the lower the life expectancy. This is not just because the poor people on the bottom are sicker and bring down the average. All of our lives are shortened as we frantically career through our existence. Status is like an invisible pox that we must understand and address.

Certainly, the locale of the SUV incident was a citadel of status pathology — Palo Alto, one of the richest places in the country. To me, Palo Alto exemplifies the wealth divide in our nation — because on the edge of Palo Alto is East Palo Alto, an area of bleak poverty. The average CEO in 2004 made 431 times the average worker, almost $12 million, and the average worker not even $30,000. Since the gap continues to widen so fast, I hesitate to even include numbers. In 2003 the ratio was 301 to 1, so by 2006 it should be at least 500 to 1. This wealth divide, as we'll see, is responsible for many of our societal traumas. We had lived in Palo Alto before, at a time when it was essentially a sleepy little college town. But then came Silicon Valley and the era of the dot-coms, and wealth erupted like lava in Palo Alto. Suddenly there were ritzy little chains driving out the independent stores, expensive cars crowding out parking and cell-phoned suits striding impatiently down University Street. The feel was entirely different.

The road rage incident was just a few blocks from Stanford University, one of the nation's leading institutions. Certainly Stanford has done its job turning out those pinstriped and soulless CEOs. Again, an example of societal contradiction — higher education should be one of the solutions to our ills. But more and more students use education simply as a ticket to a high-paying job. Think of who runs corporations. I doubt there are a handful of people who didn't graduate from college, particularly from high-status MBA programs like Stanford's. It is the highly educated who are damaging our country. They're the ones destroying the environment, paying people minimum wage, sending us to war. University presidents no longer stand as moral beacons or learned elders — they're hired to be glad-handing fundraisers.

Stanford also represents something further. I got my doctorate in education there. I credit those years with teaching me to think. One thing I learned, however, is that education serves the economic

society and not the other way around. We usually turn to education
to save our societies, but in America education is besmirched along
with the rest of the competitive culture.

As an example, educaton has not been able to halt the decline
of our professions. Being a professor or a doctor or a lawyer or a
teacher is just not what it used to be. Satisfaction in our work has
plummeted. It's not just the long hours, it's the unpleasantness of the
workplace and our declining control over our workload. Who knows
a really happy lawyer? What high-school teachers feel they are really
getting to do their job? Which health care workers feel they are actually healing people? So we must address our experience of work as
well as its increasing pressures.

Let's continue to analyze our chocolate-raisin incident. What
part of the country were we in? Silicon Valley, the citadel of technology. Technology has slammed us against the wall. It's one of the
reasons we have no time. It's one of the reasons we can't escape from
work. It's allowed us to go faster and faster, and it keeps us from ever
escaping — we're always connected.

But the core of the matter is the young woman's rudeness and
unkindness to another human being. Community and civility are on the
decline. Silicon Valley has the lowest "social capital" (time for other
people) in the country. People need to feel cared for and valued and
appreciated, but how many times have we had someone scream at us
like the driver did? As we will see, caring and feeling cared for are at the
heart of well-being.

Time scarcity, stress, unhappiness, hostility and decline of
social capital, destruction of the environment, status and the wealth
divide, technology; somehow these are related. Just as detectives in
mystery stories look for patterns to solve a murder, we need to connect
the dots of our cultural scurvy. That little road rage incident represents
homicide in so many ways — the death of our children's future, the
death of the American dream, in fact, the ultimate in dying that occurred
in New Orleans in September 2005. Whatever the outcome to
the death and destruction stemming from a right-wing Republican
administration's obloquy and neglect, the story of Hurricane Katrina

represents, as do all these other issues, one underlying theme: the decline of concern for the common good.

But I want to return to the car. The SUV signifies something else — a phrase that is just now breaking into people's consciousness — peak oil. We are about to begin the parabolic decline in worldwide oil supply. And of course oil is central to everything we do. Every consumer item involves oil in its manufacture or its shipment, let alone the gas we use to go to the malls. What will happen as oil declines? Certainly we see one example in George Bush's policies — war in the Middle East. Richard Heinberg, author of *Power Down*, outlines four possible scenarios: In "Last One Standing," we pursue a path of war and competition for the remaining oil. In "Waiting for a Magic Elixir," we hope some technological marvel will save us. These bogus paths are not acceptable, even though they are the policies we are currently pursuing. Heinberg instead promotes two others that we must pursue: "Power Down" and "Build Lifeboats." He describes these as the paths of cooperation, conservation and sharing, as well as community solidarity and preservation.

Our problems are severe to the point of irreversibility. Is there any hope? An important clue is embedded in the road-rage story. Let me tell you where we were parked and see if you can sense the significance of the location. It was a Whole Foods grocery store.

We were parked in front of something we wouldn't have foreseen 10 years ago. Now, I realize that Whole Foods is a very expensive place. And it's still a corporation. But it's supremely successful because it sells healthy, organic food! Who would have suspected?

The story of food is a hopeful one. For several years we've been destroying food — pumping it full of preservatives and hormones, pouring insecticides into the soil, spraying plants within an inch of their lives. We're processing food into something that tastes like cardboard — something that can last longer than cardboard! Who of our grandparents would have expected this to happen to the things we rely on for sustenance?

And how have we responded to the food chain's degradation? We gobble food on the run. We eat with one hand while driving. We take 10 minutes for dinner while watching television. Family members are so busy they rarely eat together. We diet constantly and deny ourselves food, but at the same time we've become obese. Our relationship to food is like the young woman's road rage: It's destroying the planet, and it's destroying us. We can see it, and yet we deny it.

But a reaction is underway. Several years ago many of us began turning to healthier food. We started natural-food cooperatives. (Ours is still going strong in Seattle, where I've been a member for 30 years.) People flock to farmers' markets or have organic food delivered to their doorsteps. We've turned to natural ways of healing involving nutrition.

And then, to cap it all off, we now have the Slow Food movement — an idea whose significance may save us from all the destruction we've created.

*The Slow Food movement, an Italian effort to preserve traditions of conviviality around food and wine, is much more significant than it might at first appear.*

The Slow Food movement, an Italian effort to preserve traditions of conviviality around food and wine, is much more significant than it might at first appear. It has become a maypole for resisting the destructive forces in modern life. It's the badge of a sea change circling the globe as a way to deal with both our personal and our cultural problems. As patently obvious and uncomplicated as it might seem, much of the solution to our culture's and our planet's ills lies in simply slowing ... things ... down.

When I first heard about the Slow Food movement, I was absolutely fascinated. When use of the word expanded to Slow Cities, I thought — what if this could be a metaphor for a lot of different, yet related, changes? If there's slow food and slow cities, why not slow education? Or slow neighborhoods? Slow health? Slow travel? I began to think about what "slow" could mean. As I talked about it to people, some would frown — "slow" sounded like dull and pokey to them. They needed the rush of speed and excitement! But as they thought about it further, they could sense that underlying so many of our problems is the velocity of our lives. Maybe there is something to simply slowing down. So when I looked back on the road-rage incident, the fact that it happened in front of Whole Foods seemed significant. Perhaps the seed of an answer was there.

The Slow Food movement emerged in Italy in the late 1980s in reaction to McDonald's moving into Rome. Its instigators knew immediately that introducing fast food to Italy could destroy its tourist base. Who would come to the Piazza San Pietro if it turned into some dull suburban strip mall — or even a sellout villa like Palo Alto? The Italians could see that fast food was really a symbol of a way of life that embodied blandness and sterility and the destruction of the well-being of people and the planet. Fast food was a bacterium chomping away the United States. What I found exciting was that the Slow Food movement wasn't just trying to change life on the personal level by encouraging people to take their time eating good food in good company. The movement understood that personal change can only go so far. Sooner or later, if corporate farming continues to have its way, there won't be any good — or healthy— food left! So the movement (see www.slowfood.com) has gone on to focus on the health of the environment and biodiversity of food. Further, it encourages small farmers, small restaurants and shopkeepers and helps them maintain their heritage.

"Slow," then, has come to stand for resistance to "Fast," and "Fast" embodies all the problems embedded in the road rage incident — time-poverty, stress, hostility, inequality, destruction of the environment and, indeed, destruction of our whole civilization as we run out of oil. In the Fast Life you rush through your day, spending most of your time working, shopping and watching TV. In the Slow Life you move at an unhurried, leisurely pace, savoring your day, spending time in reflection and contemplation, making sure you have time to spend with friends and family. The Fast Life is about money, achievements and status. The Slow Life is about joy, leisure and community. The concept of the Slow Life not only offers a way to improve our lives, it offers a method of dealing with myriad problems. Instead of fighting on each front, one by one — environment, justice, peace — the Slow Life addresses them all at once.

And so, I began to see a wonderful solution to all of our problems: the Slow Life. I liked it because it seemed subversive rather than confrontational; it had a sense of humor instead of being dour and gloomy. I also discovered Carl Honore's *In Praise of Slowness: How a Worldwide Movement Is Challenging the Cult of Speed* — a book that provides a compelling introduction to the way this movement is spreading around the world. Honore shows an entirely different way of living:

> In this book, Fast and Slow do more than just describe a rate of change. They are shorthand for ways of being, or philosophies of life. Fast is busy, controlling, aggressive, hurried, analytical, stressed, superficial, impatient, active, quantity-over-quality. Slow is the opposite: calm, careful, receptive, still, intuitive, unhurried, patient, reflective, quality-over-quantity. It is about making real and meaningful connections — with people, culture, work, food, everything.

John de Graaf edited *Take Back Your Time* (to which I contributed an essay) that outlines the problems and shows the way new laws can make changes. For true change we need new policies as well as a new belief system. In *Slow Is Beautiful*, I'll be building on these two books and showing how you can begin to change your life and to change society.

The last sentence is very important. I have always believed that any solution must be concerned with several levels of change: the personal, the institutional, and the policy level. Personal change alone isn't enough, but it's where the solution germinates. We won't have new laws unless the legislatures know there's a strong movement pushing for them. To build that movement we must first transform people's individual lives and provide ways to come together to work for greater change. In particular, I'll be addressing this last issue: We not only need to change people's personal lives and develop new policies, we must create a methodology of change! It's obvious we need some new strategies. We're way behind. I just read that 24 polar bears were found dead because they got trapped on ice floes as global warming broke apart an Arctic glacier. I can barely stand to hear such stories. We need to hear them, but we need something more than stories of doom to motivate us. Taking a cue from the Slow Food movement, any solutions to our problems must be concerned with pleasure as well as principle. The good life is ethics and enjoyment. We want not only to serve life, but to savor life. As it stands, we do not have time to do either.

*The Slow Life movement*

*offers a template for ways*

*to analyze and confront*

*the problems of our times.*

The Slow Life movement offers a template for ways to analyze and confront the problems of our times. It is a critic of corporate lust for money and power, but it relies on a method of change that focuses on pleasure and community by bringing people together to work for both enjoyment and social change.

## Putting the Puzzle Together

Where do we begin? First, we need to look closely at the causes of the problems. In subsequent chapters I'll explore the most recent research on happiness, status, the workplace, and the consumer society.

Additionally, we have to address people's withering sense of spirit. People are beaten down, overworked, stressed, and depressed. They are not people who have the energy or the vision to work for a new future. I'll explore what we need — the notion of *joie de vivre*: the state of feeling vital and alive. Of being caught up by exuberance, enthusiasm and excitement — high spirits and high energy. Of recapturing those youthful moments when life seemed wonderful and all you felt was yes, yes, yes!

Then I'll explore the idea of leisure. It's about so much more than one might expect. Yes, it involves time away from work, but it is also a philosophy of time. Leisure offers a contemplative approach to life that brings greater depth and greater wisdom. Reading about debates over leisure through the ages, I've been enthralled and inspired.

And then I'll talk about the idea of community, the core of happiness. Community is a face-to-face caring — a just, egalitarian connection with others. It's a state in which we feel accepted for our true selves and connected to others.

All of these are linked, of course. To have more community, we need more leisure; to make the changes to have more leisure, we need the energy of joie de vivre. But we won't have joie without community. It's a circular association. In fact, the circle is a very nice symbol of what we're talking about because it counterpoints our usual symbol of life in corporate consumer society — the ladder.

Finally, I'll show how these elements are at the heart of the Slow Life and how thinking about the Slow Life brings us a new vision of the good life. The Slow Life is when we reclaim our time for the things that matter. It's an unhurried pace in which we learn to savor life. It's a belief system that says that the well-being of people and the planet must come before profit. It's a subversive counterculture meant to undermine the corporate consumer society. Finally, it involves a visionary method of social change and education.

That's when the phrase "slow is beautiful" — a play off E.F. Schumacher's classic 1973 handbook, *Small Is Beautiful* — occurred to me. To make the Slow Life resonate, we need a new vision connecting slowness with beauty and wonder and all the good things in life. Change doesn't come unless people are first inspired. The consumer society stands for competition — destruction and division. That's what the word consume means — to devour, as in "the house was devoured by fire." I've long thought that to countermand the consumer society we needed a culture of connectedness — where we're connected with our true selves (integrity), each other (community), and life (nature and the universe). Having thought this for a long time, I was happy to discover that one of my favorite writers, Philip Slater (*Wealth Addiction* and *The Pursuit of Loneliness*), called for a Culture of Connection in an article for *Utne* magazine's April-May 2003 issue.

Slater talks about how the radical Right supports a culture of division, a preoccupation with control over nature and over other people. It tries to control people's feelings (through advertising, television and religion) and their personal freedoms (opposition to pregnancy termination and freedom of sexual orientation). The extreme Right wants to control what teachers teach, what newspapers print and what we see on television. It has an either-or view of the world and supports hierarchies with control from the top. It sees all of life as a war, from the war on drugs to war against Christmas to conflict with other countries.

Slater feels that people on the Left have been sucked into this divisive approach and have fallen prey to tactics of control themselves. In particular, we on the Left have taken a reactive role, putting all of our energies into "fighting" back when the Right does something. Often we have ourselves become militant, attacking people who don't agree with us and adopting an elitism that dismisses others' opinions.

Instead, he says, we should be creating a Culture of Connection in which we focus on togetherness and communication, the removal of walls. We are already doing this with efforts like growing organic food, working on peace issues and the Julia Butterfly Hill approach of spending two years in an old-growth redwood and building an organization, Circle of Life, on the basis of her work. (A very slow form of protest!) These are new, exciting strategies capturing peoples' attention and imagination.

A host of efforts exists to help build this Culture of Connection — such as car-sharing, cohousing, ecovillages, farmers' markets. They all come together in the Slow Life. Normally we associate change with moving fast. In this case, change evolves through moving Slow.

Can you imagine how that SUV driver in Palo Alto would have acted ... if only she'd been living the Slow Life?

# CHAPTER 2

# The Truth About Happiness

HAPPINESS IS DECLINING in the most powerful country in the world. As Robert E. Lane, Yale professor emeritus, states in his book, *The Loss of Happiness in Market Democracies*:

> Amidst the satisfaction people feel with their material progress, there is a spirit of unhappiness and depression haunting advanced market democracies throughout the world, a spirit that mocks the idea that markets maximize well-being and the eighteenth-century promise of a right to the pursuit of happiness under benign governments of people's own choosing. The haunting spirit is manifold: a postwar decline in the United States in people who report themselves as happy, a rising tide in all advanced societies of clinical depression and dysphoria ... increasing distrust of each other and of political and other institutions, declining belief that the lot of the average man is getting better ... a tragic erosion of family solidarity and community integration together with an apparent decline in warm, intimate relations among friends.

Richard Layard, a British economist and member of the House of Lords, echoes these words in a book called *Happiness: Lessons from a New Science*, writing that a nation's policies should be guided by happiness, not Gross Domestic Product (GDP). He says we should return to the classic Jeremy Bentham idea of the greatest happiness for the greatest number.

Peter Whybrow, head of the Semel Institute for Neuroscience and Human Behavior at UCLA, says that the character of today's culture is one of mania — we're going faster and faster, reaching and grasping for happiness in futility until we crash into the next manic cycle, that of depression.

Obviously, the subject of happiness is a topic of interest to more and more scholars. But what interests me is that when I start talking about happiness to progressive, liberal audiences, some of them start getting upset, arguing that happiness is a shallow thing to be concerned about and that our goal should be social justice. Of course, it goes without saying that we care about social justice. But what is the ultimate goal of justice? For people to suffer less and be happy! Happiness always assumes social justice.

I would think this is obvious, but I've found I need to defend the idea right from the start by doing a song and dance about the importance of happiness. Robert Lane does a nice job of explaining why happiness is important, so I always use the list he pulls from his survey of happiness literature. Happy people are more creative and productive in their thinking. They're nicer; they consume less. They're healthier and harbor less prejudice. By contrast, Lane says, depressed people make poor parents, cause coworkers to enjoy their jobs less, take more sick leave and suffer life-shortening health problems. "If going from the money standard to the companionship standard reduces these human and financial costs, we would all be better off," Lane writes.

Lane presents a pretty good argument, but I'm still bothered that we need an argument in the first place. After all, isn't our country based on life, liberty and the *pursuit* of happiness? And didn't our founders consider this to be *self-evident*? Why is it hard for so many of us, particularly on the progressive end of the political spectrum, to understand that happiness should be our goal? Actually, I understand why people object. It's because the idea of happiness has been distorted and linked to the pursuit of wealth and material things. As I'll continue to point out, all of our important life-sustaining concepts have been distorted and diminished. (And, as I'll also continue to argue, we need a national conversation on these issues.)

It's imperative that we understand happiness because the pursuit of happiness is being used to seduce people into the corporate consumer lifestyle that is destroying our planet and putting us at war. Understanding happiness is important because if we are going to be able to get people to change, we must show them alternative ways of living that truly make them happy and do not destroy life. Our tactics of change themselves must make people happier! Most of our methods (lecturing, writing books, creating citizen initiatives, working to pass a law) simply bore people. Our protests, marches and boycotts scare or alienate others. We must develop methods of change that in and of themselves make people happier.

*It's imperative that we understand happiness because the pursuit of happiness is being used to seduce people into the corporate consumer lifestyle that is destroying our planet and putting us at war.*

Psychologists are beginning to understand the importance of happiness, and in the last few years, research has exploded. I'm still somewhat skeptical of the research because self-reports of happiness, which most of the studies rely on, can be misleading. If all you've ever felt is a lukewarm sort of comfort and never any ecstatic exuberance, you will define happiness as lukewarm comfort (thinking that's as good as it gets!). But most researchers, while acknowledging that self-reporting has its limitations (what else can they say?), conclude that it seems to be a fairly reliable way to measure happiness. I'm not totally convinced — and some researchers *have* gone beyond self-reporting to look at measurable factors such as health consequences and neurological activity.

Further, it seems strange to me that we need to resort to research to try to understand happiness, when wise people have drawn the same conclusions about it throughout the ages. It may be that today, science more than wisdom is what gets people to listen.

## Money and Happiness

The biggest factor researchers agree on is that after a certain point more money does not bring more happiness. If you're poor, more money makes you happier. After that? Nothing. In fact, in some cases happiness declines as affluence goes up. (Because as you have more and more money, you have less time for the things that matter. Making, managing, and spending money take a lot of time! As my husband's father likes to say, the more things you own, the more things own you.)

This is an incredibly significant finding because it goes counter to all of our beliefs. Everything we do is aimed at making more money. All of our dreams of success focus on money, money and more money. We grow up with Horatio Alger stories of people going from rags to riches. We watch professional athletes and CEOs and poker stars pull down the big bucks and think they have it made. Apparently the mythology is potent; about 35 percent of people in this country believe that they will one day be among the top 1 percent of income earners! (Obviously it's one of the reasons that people haven't risen up to oppose the multiple tax cuts given to the rich and privileged during the Bush administration.)

If there is one fact that everyone should know, it is this one. We must see through the myth that if you're rich you'll be happier — because this myth is the basis of unhappiness and ill health, as well as corruption and injustice and war. Clutching at profit is the reason companies pay people low wages, make products that ruin people's health, cheat employees out of their retirements and investments, destroy the environment, and go to war to try to control oil.

Yet even though the evidence is clear, it's amazing that at some level we all still believe that getting rich will make us happy! Prime case in point: Everyone wants to win the lotto. Yet research on actual winners shows that after the first few months of excitement, people go back to normal. By the end of the first year, that spike of pleasure is not only gone, people may be less happy than before. A *New York*

*Times* front-page article in December 2005 describes how the winners of a $34 million lottery purchased expensive cars and a huge estate but were dead (from alcoholism and suspected drug overdose) within three years. Most of us, though (myself included), feel that *we* would be an exception — if *we* won, we would indeed be happier, because we, unlike those other poor saps, would know how to use the money.

So what *does* make us happy? Again, there's complete agreement. It's warm, caring relationships with other people. Happiness has been on the decline because we live in a cold, cutthroat, uncaring culture. Most of us have rarely experienced being truly, truly cared for. Obviously, caring relationships are important for all kinds of reasons. Let's look at the needs that Abraham Maslow outlined in 1943: food, water and sleep; we need to feel safe, and then we need to feel loved and accepted by others; then we move to esteem needs of respect from others and self-respect. Finally, he suggests the need to be self-actualized — to express our true selves — and to experience self-transcendence — connection with something beyond one's self. All of these needs are met through relationships. We need other people if we are to feel safe, loved and accepted; we need others' respect and esteem; we only become self-actualized by what we are able to offer humanity as a whole. It is people who give us a sense of security, and it is caring for others that gives us a sense of meaning.

Finally, happiness is increased when we have complexity, or richness, in our lives — not the complexity of being overwhelmed, but the richness of being enthralled and absorbed. Mihaly Csikszentmihalyi has worked with this in his exploration of flow, a highly desirable feeling of being totally absorbed in something to the point that you lose awareness of yourself and the passage of time. This kind of experience brings more satisfaction than passive entertainment like television, where the brain flatlines after only a few minutes of watching. Further, complexity involves the avoidance of putting all your eggs in one basket: if all you do is work, when you lose your job you will be devastated. But if family, friends, community, and creativity have received a lot of your attention, you will have a support network to buoy you up.

The other big question is, then, Why do we pursue things like money if they don't make us happy? A couple of reasons: In part, striving for money and status made sense in our evolutionary past. When you don't have much wealth, you need to pursue it, and for most of our history, the vast majority of people have lived closer to a survival level. In the past, having high status in small groups gave you a leg up on having more offspring, an evolutionary instinct.

Another good example is a point that Peter Whybrow makes: We evolved to live in a feast-or-famine mode. We only had meat once in awhile, and for the rest of the time our provisions were limited. We did not evolve to have food at our disposal all the time, as we do now. But we haven't moved past the temptation! So what we have is a set of inclinations and instincts that don't work in our modern society.

Further, several researchers have found that having more autonomy and control in our lives elevates our well-being. On the surface, one would conclude that more money gives you more autonomy and control, and in some ways it does. But ultimately, people who give all their attention to money (and having lots of money can demand that) have no attention left for anything else. The desire for money resembles eating disorders. After a certain point, something in our systems goes haywire, and we can't control our actions and behave rationally.

And of course, the biggest reason we think money and material things will make us happy is that advertisers tell us over and over it will — and link greed for things to our basic desire for caring.

We must break free from living on automatic pilot and resist our tendency to live life in default mode. We need to learn to make conscious choices. We need to build reason and reflection into our lives. We need to educate people about the facts of happiness and build habits and institutions that encourage us to work toward true well-being.

Let's look at these issues in more depth by exploring some of the research — in particular David G. Myers's, *The Pursuit of Happiness: Spiritual Hunger in an Age of Plenty*, Tim Kasser's

*Psychology and Consumer Culture: The Struggle for a Good Life in a Materialistic World*, Robert Lane's *The Loss of Happiness in Market Democracies*, Peter Whybrow's *American Mania: When More Is Not Enough*, Martin Seligman's *Authentic Happiness: Using the New Positive Psychology to Realize Your Potential for Lasting Fulfillment* and Richard Layard's *Happiness: Lessons from a New Science*.

## David G. Myers

Psychologist David Myers has been working on this issue for some time. He finds, as do all the other researchers, that in countries like Bangladesh where people are very, very poor, having money does make you happier. But in countries where almost everyone can afford life's necessities, increasing affluence matters very little.

Myers gives a little background. In 1940 two out of five homes didn't have a shower or a tub and a third had no toilet. Homes were typically heated by a wood stove or coal furnace. In 1957 Americans' average income, expressed in Year 2000 dollars, was $8,700; today it's $20,000. We're literally more than twice as rich, we have twice as many cars, our homes are twice as big. In 1957 few of us had dishwashers or air conditioning or other conveniences. Certainly there were no cell phones, computers or answering machines.

And are we twice as happy? No. In fact, we aren't even *as happy*. The number of Americans who say they are "very happy" has gone down from 35 percent in 1957 to 32 percent. At the same time, the divorce rate has doubled, teen suicide has tripled and the violent crime rate has almost quadrupled. More people are depressed.

Myers calls this the American paradox:

> More than ever, we have big houses and broken homes, high incomes and low morale, secured rights and diminished civility. We excel at making a living but often fail at making a life. We celebrate our prosperity but yearn for purpose. We cherish our freedoms but long for connection. In an age of plenty, we feel spiritual hunger.

## Tim Kasser

Kasser is doing some of the most exciting research, helping us to understand in greater depth why more money doesn't make us happier. He acknowledges we know that *having* more wealth does not bring more happiness after a certain point, but then he takes it a step further: Merely *desiring* more money makes us unhappy. People whose goal in life is fame, status or wealth have a lower sense of well-being. They have more depression and anxiety. That is because once basic needs are met and they feel secure, they naturally graduate to human needs of self-worth, self-actualization and relationships. Yet if they keep pursuing materialistic goals, they have no time or energy for intrinsic needs. In fact, pursuing one goal undermines the other because when we focus mainly on money and fame, we can become pretty selfish, narcissistic people — traits guaranteed to drive relationships away!

In talking about happiness, Kasser uses the phrase "social well-being." He says that our well-being comes from meeting our psychological needs of safety, security and sustenance; competence, efficacy and self-esteem; connectedness, autonomy and authenticity. To measure well-being, he asked people about authenticity and self-actualization, vitality ("overflowing with that wonderful feeling of being alive"), autonomy, competence and relatedness. He also asked about depression, anxiety and physical symptoms like headache, stomach and other bodily ills — factors that erode well-being.

Kasser distinguishes between intrinsic and extrinsic values. Intrinsic values are those oriented toward personal growth, relationships and community involvement; extrinsic values focus on financial success, image and popularity. People with intrinsic values score higher on measures of social well-being; people with extrinsic values score lower. He also defines extrinsic values as *materialism*, which he measures as concern about money, status and popularity. Materialists have low scores for self-actualization and vitality and high scores for depression and anxiety.

People who value fame also tend to value money; they also are usually narcissistic (vain, expecting special treatment and admiration,

manipulative and hostile). Narcissists tend to be possessive, non-gen-
erous and envious of others. They score low on relatedness to other
people, a primary source of well-being.

## ENVIRONMENTAL LINKS

An *intrinsic* values orientation also predicts better ecological stew-
ardship, Kasser says. The link between social well-being and
ecologically responsible behavior was explained by people who have
intrinsic values as being more mindful. (One of Kasser's co-
researchers, Richard Ryan, found that happiness is related to
mindfulness — making conscious choices rather than behaving in an
automatic manner.) So a sustainable way of life enhances both personal and collective well-being, which Kasser refers to as a life of
voluntary simplicity.

## TIME LINKS

People who work fewer hours were also found to be better ecological
citizens. (In fact, Juliet Schor concludes that the only way we can
encourage people to be better ecological citizens is to reduce working hours. Just exhorting people to change doesn't work. But if they
trade money for time, they will consume less — not only because
they have less money, but because they will be
indulging in activities that bring them more sat-
isfaction than shopping. They literally will not            *People who work fewer*
have the time to spend hours in the mall.)
     Not surprisingly, work hours have a neg-                *hours were also found to be*
ative correlation to life satisfaction, and the            *better ecological citizens.*
happiest nations are those with relatively low
work hours. (Happiness also has to do with the distribution of wealth,
which we'll discuss later.) Time affluence, then, is positively associated with social well-being when compared to material affluence.

## EXPLANATIONS

People who watch a lot of TV and people who have materialistic parents are more likely to be materialistic and insecure and driven by

unmet needs of safety and security. This pushes them to the malls, further decreasing their satisfaction and setting up a vicious cycle.

Materialism in children is often related to how their parents treated them, in particular, when the parents don't listen or don't acknowledge children's feelings. These parents are often possessive of their kids, believing that they can't take care of themselves. They often use harsh, punitive measures while failing to provide structure.

Insecure kids are especially susceptible to consumer messages that exploit insecurities, messages that encourage them to look for approval from others. High self-esteem comes from growing up with warm, supportive parents and having the chance to use one's competencies and abilities to attain one's goals. Low self-esteem comes when people are neglected and don't get the caring they need.

Family is one source of insecurity, but culture is another. Insecurity and fear encourage materialism, and people in our culture suffer from many insecurities and fears. They might be afraid they will lose their jobs, that they will get sick without health insurance, that they could become homeless or be victims of violent crimes. At some level, we all worry that when we're old we'll be ugly, rejected and alone. And of course, terrorism (and our dysfunctional response to it) has exacerbated our fears. The Katrina disaster shows us just how unprepared our government is to take care of us in an emergency. All of these fears are realistic — not just some sort of individual neurosis. It is not surprising that since we are a very materialistic culture, we are not a very happy one.

Kasser further finds that people with high wealth almost always want more, even though they show no increase in happiness when they get it. It certainly looks like addictive behavior — continuing to pursue something that not only brings you no happiness, but takes your time away from things that do. I think that people who are very rich are insecure because they focus all their energy on making money, and money cannot give them back any fulfilling human qualities. Money cannot boost their self-esteem and competence, so they feel an internal vacuum that makes them even more needy. It sets up another vicious cycle.

Kasser says that many of us suffer from contingent self-esteem — that is, our self-esteem depends on meeting external standards (getting good grades or having good jobs). Contingent self-esteem has a lot in common with material values because it plummets if you don't get what you aim for. Then people develop narcissism as a defense against low self-esteem, making them less able to form satisfactory and rewarding relationships.

So for those who have materialistic goals, unhappiness comes either from not getting what they want or from getting what they want and discovering that it's empty. Often materialists' goals are false or inflated: They think rich people are smart and happy, and they see themselves as falling short. Of course media is a primary cause of these false goals, and materialistic people watch a lot of TV. "The consequences of believing that the wealthy have wonderful lives and of frequently viewing idealized ads are that people become frustrated with their current state and thus less happy," Kasser writes. Television tends to make us dissatisfied with our lives, which leads to materialism, which leads to unhappiness.

Materialistic values are directly opposed to benevolence (welfare of those with whom we're not in frequent personal contact) and universalism (welfare of all of life), Kasser adds. Materialists conclude that caring about others does not bring success or profit. People who spend a lot of time thinking about consuming and buying are likely to treat others as objects — which philosopher Martin Buber referred to as an "I/It" relationship with life. When we commodify others we ignore their feelings and see them only in terms of how useful they can be to us. "In such relationships, other people become reduced to objects, little different from products that may be purchased, used and discarded as necessary," Kasser writes.

So empathy and generosity decline. Materialists are less likely to give to charity. Instead of friendships, they have contacts. They tend to score high on measures of Machiavellianism — choosing responses such as: "Never tell anyone the real reason you did something unless it is useful to you." They tend to believe that people are lazy, cynical and deceptive; they are self-centered and distrust others.

They feel that anyone who completely trusts anyone else is asking for trouble, and they don't mind lying for their own benefit. People who score very high in Machiavellianism are interpersonally cold, have relationship problems and are narcissistic. They are very high in materialistic values.

Kasser concludes:

> We have thus far seen three ways in which materialistic val-
> ues detract from our well-being: they maintain deep-rooted
> feelings of insecurity, they lead us to run on never-ending
> treadmills trying to prove our competence, and they interfere
> with our relationships. There remains to be explored one
> other way in which materialistic values work against our need
> for satisfaction and psychological health: they diminish our
> personal freedom. Said differently, a strong focus on the pur-
> suit of wealth, fame and image undermines the satisfaction of
> needs for authenticity and autonomy.

This is counter to our belief system that we find freedom in our vast array of commodities — that we are free to express ourselves through our purchases. Of course, advertising sells you "pre-packaged individualities." It doesn't encourage you to be authentic and autonomous — to choose to live as your true self and not worry about meeting others' expectations.

Non-materialists want to choose their own goals and are con-cerned with freedom and creativity. Materialists choose their goals based on status. (You become a doctor because of the status, not because you love helping others.) "Materialism derives from a moti-vational system focused on rewards and praise," Kasser writes. "Autonomy and self-expression derive from a motivational system concerned with expression of interest, enjoyment, and challenge, and of doing things for their own sake."

People with high materialistic scores report they pursue their goals because they believe they ought to, because they would feel ashamed, guilty or anxious if they didn't, because someone else wants them to, because the situation compels it, or because they will get rewards or avoid punishment. "Such motivations reflect pressure and coercion, and thus work against satisfaction of needs for autonomy and authenticity," Kasser says.

Strong materialism scores didn't even give people freedom in shopping or making money — they said they did these things in order to have more than others or to prove they weren't stupid. They weren't motivated by their own desires, but to prove themselves to others. We can see this in compulsive shoppers — they actually get little joy from it. Rather, they derive a sense of power from the credit card or deference from store clerks. (Compulsive shoppers have low self-esteem and higher rates of depression, anxiety disorders and substance abuse disorders.)

## MARRIAGE

Things seem to get even worse if you're married to a materialist, Kasser says. You won't feel that they love you as much as you would like them to; you'll feel they don't understand you. When you fight, they will be aggressive, manipulative and distrustful. You might come to feel that your spouse is using you to bolster his or her self-esteem.

## COMMUNITY

Materialistic values lead to antisocial or self-centered decisions; people will be more concerned about getting ahead than cooperating. They will treat others as objects to be manipulated and used; they will be less concerned with making the world a better place and rarely concerned about equality, justice and civil society.

A wonderful example of one of these congenial fellows is Lee Iacocca — the man who cut merit pay for Chrysler employees but took a $20 million bonus for himself. His comment when challenged: "That's the American way. If little kids don't aspire to make money like I did, what the hell good is this country?"

"When materialistic values dominate our society, we move farther and farther from what makes us civilized," Kasser says. "We treat each other in less-humane ways. We allow the pursuit of money to take precedence over equality, the human spirit, and respectful treatment of each other. We permit materialistic values to undermine much of what could be the very best about our communities."

Tim Kasser has done wonderful work on the issues of happiness, showing us that materialism leads not only to unhappiness for the individual, but to a decline in concern for the common good. Fellow researcher Richard Ryan summarizes what we are doing as we feed a culture of materialism:

> Most of the world's population is now growing up in winner-take-all economies, where the main goal of individuals is to get whatever they can for themselves: to each according to his greed. Within this economic landscape, selfishness and materialism are no longer being seen as moral problems, but as cardinal goals of life.... Vast numbers of us have been seduced into believing that having more wealth and material possessions is essential to the good life. We have swallowed the idea that, to be well, one first has to be well off. And many of us, consciously or unconsciously, have learned to evaluate our own well-being and accomplishment not by looking inward at our spirit or integrity, but by looking outward at what we have and what we can buy. Similarly, we have adopted a world view in which the worth and success of others is judged not by their apparent wisdom, kindness, or community contributions, but in terms of whether they possess the right clothes, the right cars, and more generally, the right "stuff."

## Robert Lane

While people like Tim Kasser are performing their own studies, others synthesize the research on happiness. One of the most eloquent of these is Robert Lane, professor emeritus of Yale University. He brings a huge amount of material together to buttress his central theme that happiness depends on warm social relationships. He writes with typical incisive eloquence:

> My hypothesis is that there is a kind of famine of warm interpersonal relations, of easy-to-reach neighbors, of encircling,

inclusive memberships, and of solidary family life. There is much evidence that for people lacking in social support of this kind, unemployment has more serious effects, illnesses are more deadly, disappointment with one's children is harder to bear, bouts of depression last longer, and frustration and failed expectations of all kinds are more traumatic. Thus, the malnutrition model explains why the search for increases in objective hardships will fail, for the causes lie not in the rise of objective traumas but in the increased vulnerability of the public. A weak version of the metaphoric flu will then do the damage of a more virulent strain because people without social support are less resistant.

Lane asks why we do not choose behaviors that lead to greater well-being. He blames it on an *economistic* culture, misleading belief systems and the tendency of humans to choose short-run benefits that lead to long-term costs. He feels that at a certain point in our history our focus on money and getting ahead did make us happier, but no more. We're stuck in a rut and are failing to evaluate what's really happening. As he says, "The death of a culture is not usually encountered by cataclysmic events, not by a bang or a whimper, but by failure to adapt, a monotonous repetition of what had been done before."

Lane tries to define happiness, noting that psychologists often use different factors in measuring happiness. Happiness seems to involve looking forward to each day, having a sense of meaning, feeling hopeful about the future, feeling in control of the events in your life, having high self-esteem, a sense of worth, and low anxiety. He feels that self-reports of happiness correspond pretty well to others' reports, but that depression is easier to measure because it exhibits specific symptoms such as decreased appetite, insomnia, loss of interest in sex, loss of energy, feelings of worthlessness, diminished ability to concentrate, and thoughts of death or suicide. People who are depressed experience hopelessness, helplessness and worthlessness. The stresses of loneliness, isolation and lower status cause a significant decrease in well-being. In particular, lower status is caused by unemployment and authoritarian treatment. A sense of being treated unfairly reduces well-being and often occurs in highly competitive settings. Competition goes up as people have more money, and the rewards for winning are greater. And, certainly, competition undermines relationships.

What contributes to happiness, in Lane's eyes? Social skills, self-esteem, a sense of personal control, and optimism. Why do people continue to believe that more money will make them happier? Because they are told that it will — told over and over, in the news, in advertising, in our educational system.

*We tend to analyze a relationship in terms of What's in it for me? This provokes a decline in warmth and in what I would call conviviality.*

How do we know that companionship brings more happiness than income does? Polls and research have uncovered a variety of links. The number of friends you have turns out to be a better predictor for well-being than anything else — even including income, attractiveness, intelligence, or education; qualities that most of us strive for. People say that what they really want is intimacy. They want people they can confide in. Certainly enjoyment of work is greatly influenced by the enjoyment of your coworkers.

In our highly stressed society, companions become even more important because having friends reduces stress. Affection lets you feel cared for and loved, esteemed and valued. Research has found that being cared for not only reduces the stress you feel, but is better for your health. Further, your self-esteem often rests on your relationships with others. Having friends gives you the feeling that you have more control over your life because you can turn to them for help, advice, information, and contacts. In spite of this, about 26 percent of Americans report that they are lonely, and it seems to me that our lives are so inured to loneliness that we don't really even notice it. You would have to be really, really lonely to be able to admit it to yourself — I suspect the level of actual loneliness is much higher.

Even though people report that their friends and family bring them the most happiness, when asked what they need in life, they say more money. Clearly we have not examined our belief systems around money.

Lane echoes Robert Putnam's work showing that affiliation time has diminished in the last several years; and further, the nature of our interactions has changed. We seem to increasingly "scorn spontaneous affection." (Certainly I've found that as our status goes up, we become more reserved, and since people ape those with higher status, the problem spreads to the whole society.) Lane also feels that we don't have enough "face-to-face" time, so relationships are not as satisfying. (You don't laugh over e-mail, you need to be with others in order to laugh.) In the past, in small towns or small business, we found ourselves in the middle of relationships without really trying — now we often have to consciously work to create relationships. Finally as our gap between the rich and the poor continues to grow, and as corporations become more corrupt, trust among people is declining. With competitiveness increasing in general, it's hard to keep it out of personal relationships. So not only do we have fewer relationships, those we have are plagued by distrust and competitiveness.

Of course this leads to decreased intimacy, and lack of intimacy is the strongest predictor of loneliness. Lane thinks of intimacy as warmth, a quality associated with generosity, humor, sociability and an easy-going nature. Lack of intimacy is experienced as coldness, hostility and self-centeredness — "impersonality, treatment of each other as numbers, as machines, on the surface, without self-disclosure."

In our culture we think about reciprocity between people — you do a favor and expect one back. In collectivist societies, A does a favor for B, B for C, and it eventually comes back to A. Our relationships tend to be based on the ability to withhold favors, goods or flattery. We tend to analyze a relationship in terms of What's in it for me? This provokes a decline in warmth and in what I would call conviviality.

Of course stress is bad for happiness, and most of our stress comes from the workplace. Being unemployed is the nadir: It causes depression and drinking, and attempts at suicide are eight times more common.

Much to my surprise, inflation does not seem to affect happiness or depression rates. Yet as a culture we hear much more kvetching over inflation than over laying people off. Every day we read of corporations announcing layoffs as if it were just something to be expected. No one seems to show any shock or concern. But let the inflation rate start to head up, and there's Sturm und Drang in the financial pages. Of course, we must remember that insecure workers are good for profits because they don't demand pay raises or make any other kind of fuss.

In the last 40 years there has also been a decline in job satisfaction — particularly in a sense of fairness as well as in confidence that what you do can make a difference to the well-being of society. The most significant factor in well-being at work, the congeniality and companionship of coworkers, also has plummeted.

Lane is distraught about the decline of our relationships and thinks it should be our priority in trying to bring about social change.

## Martin Seligman

Martin Seligman seems to have dedicated himself to getting psychologists to pay attention to happiness. He works with the idea of "positive psychology," finding in his research that optimists succeed better than pessimists in school and sports, suffer less depression, achieve more of their goals, deal with stress better and live longer. He says that there are three levels of happiness: the pleasant life, the engaged life, and the meaningful life. He thinks that too often we focus only on the pleasant life. The other two levels involve what he refers to as "using your core strengths."

Core strengths are the values found in every religion and advocated by the wise and just. They include the eternal values of wisdom, courage, love, justice, temperance, spirituality, and transcendence. Your greatest happiness comes from expressing these strengths in your own authentic manner. The positive emotions we feel when we use these strengths bring us happiness and longer life. Seligman says that to be happy we need to experience the following values:

- Positive emotions about the past: pride and satisfaction
- Positive emotions about the future: hope and optimism

- Pleasure: ecstasy, joy, and mirth
- Gratification: flow, immersion, and absorption in work, play, or love
- Meaning: attachment to something larger.

We develop these by using our strengths. Wisdom and Knowledge strengths include:

- Creativity: thinking of new ways to do things, as well as artistic expression
- Curiosity: taking an interest in all sorts of things and exploring new things
- Open-mindedness: being willing to listen to new ideas and change one's mind
- Love of learning: creating one's own life-long learning projects
- Perspective: being able to look at things in new ways.

Courage strengths include:

- Bravery: speaking up for what you believe is right; acting on your convictions
- Industry/Perseverance: persisting in spite of obstacles
- Authenticity: presenting oneself in a genuine, real manner, without pretense; speaking the truth
- Zest: approaching life with excitement and energy; feeling alive.

Love strengths include:

- Intimacy: close relationships with others; being close to others
- Kindness: doing nice things for others, taking care of them
- Social Intelligence: being aware of others' feelings; understanding how to act in different social situations; understanding how others feel and what motivates them.

Justice–civic strengths that underlie healthy community life include:

- Teamwork: working well as a member of a group

- Fairness: treating all people the same; giving everyone a fair chance
- Leadership: encouraging and organizing group activities and helping them happen.

Temperance strengths include:

- Forgiveness: giving people a second chance; not seeking revenge
- Modesty/Humility: not seeking the spotlight; not feeling you are more special than others
- Prudence: taking care about your choices; not taking undue risks
- Self-Control/Self regulation: being disciplined; controlling your appetites and emotions.

Transcendence strengths that forge connections to the larger universe and provide meaning include:

- Awe, appreciation of beauty and the mystery of the world: noticing beauty and excellence in all parts of life from nature to art to science to everyday experience
- Gratitude: being thankful for the things in your life and expressing that thankfulness
- Hope: deciding to work for a better future and feeling committed to the idea that it is possible
- Playfulness: laughing and smiling and seeing the light side of life
- Spirituality: developing your beliefs about the meaning of life and where you fit within the larger universe; having beliefs that give you comfort and offer you guidance.

I have some concerns over Seligman's self-promotion, but his work seems to have spurred considerable new research. *Time* magazine's January 17, 2005 issue featured a whole section on happiness research, including a broad discussion on health and physical well-being, that covered the following key points:

- Richard Davidson, a professor of psychology at the University of Wisconsin, studied Buddhist monks and found that a happy brain affects health by actually increasing antibodies by 50 percent

- Research has found that happiness reduces heart disease, pulmonary disease, diabetes and upper-respiratory infections
- A Dutch study of older people found that cheerfulness reduced a person's risk of death 50 percent over the nine-year research period
- Some researchers measured brain activity and found that when you feel good, there is more activity in the left prefrontal cortex.

Now, it's hard to know if the cortex is reflecting the happiness or creating it; apparently it's both. Accordingly some people are just born more positive (as any parent who has more than one kid knows!), but at the same time you can act in ways to increase your happiness.

The research on marriage shows that married people are happier than single people, but it may not be cause and effect. It may be that happier people are more likely to get married.

The research on having pets is more clear-cut: A pet can lower blood pressure and aid recovery from a heart attack. Pets reduce loneliness and depression and make people more cheerful. I'm sure other pet owners will respond with affirmation, as I have, to these studies! Pet owners have reason to be sensitive: If there's anything I experience negative feedback on, it's loving my bichon. Again, it's liberals who often seem to feel that my loving my dog means loving people less. Actually, I think it works the other way. Loving is a natural ability that needs social reinforcement. A society such as ours de-emphasizes caring, and thus we experience less of it. So I relish telling my stories about my little bichon frise, Maggie, visiting the University of Washington campus. The students always seem to be plodding along, staring at the ground looking very, very low. They're probably exhausted. But when they

*A pet can lower blood pressure and aid recovery from a heart attack. Pets reduce loneliness and depression and make people more cheerful.*

see my dog, they smile. The comment I hear over and over is, "That's the happiest dog I've ever seen!" Certainly Maggie is also one of the laziest, slowest dogs I've ever seen — living proof that the Slow Life is good even for dogs. But you don't have to be a researcher to know that pets lower stress. When I pick up my little dog, I feel like my insides are melting.

One of my favorite observations about happiness comes from Barry Schwartz, author of *The Paradox of Choice: Why More Is Less*. He says that people who are *satisficers* are much happier than maximizers (perfectionists). Perfectionists always want the very best, and whenever they make a choice, they keep thinking that there might have been something better out there, and so they keep searching and are rarely satisfied with their final choice. (If only they could have searched just a little longer!)

Satisficers, on the other hand, can't face doing all that deciding on the best thing, so they never even think about having the best. As a result, they tend to appreciate more what they have. Further, they're just not as judgmental of themselves. I often find myself saying, "Oh that's good enough!" This obviously contributes to greater self-acceptance! (I recommend people use that phrase many times throughout the day.)

This is hard for perfectionists to hear, I know. And we can't blame people for being perfectionists because it's usually part of their nature. But I've always been grateful I wasn't one. It's difficult for them because they pay attention to *all the details*. Of course, those of us who prefer to ignore the pesky little details are always lucky to have perfectionists in our lives. I know this because my husband is one. He can't bear a typo or small grammatical mistake, so I appreciate having him proofread my work.

At the same time, he can be pretty hard to live with. He tends to walk into a room and look around to see what's moved, missing or broken. We used to have a lot of fights because he would say something like, "Why is the burner on?" when it was obvious I had forgotten and left it on. I found a good answer to his non-question, though: "I'm heating the kitchen, dear..."

My husband's perfectionism ultimately hurts him the most because it means that his workload is much higher. Why should I do something if I know he's going to check it anyway! So he does the infrastructural chores like keeping track of our finances, and I do the fun "happiness maintenance," like keeping in touch with our friends, planning dinner parties and working in the garden. Basically, I'm the one who makes sure we enjoy ourselves.

Ultimately, "good enough" people always enjoy themselves more and guess what — even perfectionists benefit from enjoyment.

So, if you're a perfectionist, let me give you a few tips. (The rest of you can go back to reading your novel.)

Consider dinner. Who needs a lot of variety or new dishes? You only need three or four meals you can make. Sometimes our time is just too precious to spend cooking. (Unless you actually *like* to cook. I wish someone in my family did.)

Or how about housekeeping? In my workshops I used to discuss shortcuts we could take. One of my favorites was not washing our sheets every week the way our mothers did. I quit using that example, though, when someone came up to me in a restaurant and asked if I was the person who "never washed her sheets."

I like counters and tabletops to be somewhat clear, but I see no need for having my drawers neat, with everything nicely folded. In fact, I often think it's better to leave your socks and underwear in the laundry hamper in a closet and just forage for them every day.

My goal in grooming is to "pass." I've always done the minimum, but it's getting a little riskier with age. I don't want to look like a bag lady — sometimes I come perilously close when I go out in my sweat clothes. I always assume that I won't see anyone I know (yeah, like that works!). I've gotten by (I hope) with wearing no makeup and having a wash-and-wear haircut. I just don't want to spend time fiddling over my appearance!

The things you eliminate are up to you, but you might want to repeat the phrase "good enough" as much as you can. I don't know if it could qualify as a mantra, but it's an expression I use a lot.

## Peter Whybrow

In the eyes of Peter Whybrow of the Semel Institute, Americans are suffering from a profound disorder. We have been pushed to our psychological and physical limits, and we're starting to break down. His main theme is that human beings evolved to live in another kind of world, and that we have not adapted to the new world. We have "created an accelerated, competitive lifestyle that steals away sleep and kindles anxiety, threatening those intimate social webs that sustain family and community. For many Americans the hallowed search for happiness has been hijacked by a discomforting and frenzied activity." To him, the way we live looks like the clinical definition of mania: "a dysfunctional state of mind that begins with a joyous sense of excitement and high productivity but escalates into reckless pursuit, irritability and confusion, before cycling down into depression."

Human beings, Whybrow says, are by nature curiosity-driven, reward-seeking and harm-avoiding creatures. For most of our history, we've been in situations of danger and privation, and we are not suited to a state of perpetual abundance. Our bodies do not expect to have so much food all the time, so we have become obese. Further, Americans are at particular risk because so many of us are immigrants or descendants of immigrants. Immigrants, Whybrow points out, are wired differently. They tend to be more competitive, restless, curious and willing to take a risk. We're in a culture that exacerbates our native traits, making us run faster and faster, making us sick. We are living in a state of chronic stress: surfeit of material goods, abundance of fast food, fragmented sleep, travel, relentless competitive demand, and an unstable marketplace. Whybrow notes the piquant irony of our self-destruction:

> Prolonged exposure to such conditions tends to confuse our ancient protective mechanisms, exhausting the body's stress-arousal systems and lowering resistance to disease .... And yet despite these warning signs we press on. Drawn forward by debt, desire, or both, Americans are emerging as the first

addicts of the technological age, driven still by some ancient
instinct for self-preservation that in our time of affluence is
misplaced. Ironically, we are better tuned physiologically to
face the privations and dangers inherent in an unexpected
terrorist attack than we are to endure the relentless proposi-
tions and stressful abundance of our consumer society.

Whybrow offers the same analysis as others on happiness. The
passwords are community and caring. But somehow we have the
wrong impression of the world. Seventy-eight percent of Americans
think that they can become rich if they work hard enough. But average
personal savings dropped to minus 6 percent in 2001 — something
that hasn't happened since the Depression when 25 percent of people
were unemployed.

Whybrow argues that selfishness is innate, and when reinforced by culture it becomes greed — for more money, food or power.
The urge toward empathy, he says, is a function of the more recently
evolved part of the brain, and is not as strong. It needs to be nurtured
by families and community.

Selfishness is born not just in advertising and competition in
schools — it's the general lust for wealth. Between 1977 and 1999
income decreased for the majority of Americans. During that same
time period, the average pay of a corporate CEO rose 500 percent,
from $1.8 million to $10.6 million. The richest 1 percent has more
money than all other Americans. And all the evidence indicates that
both health and happiness suffer when the wealth of a nation is
poorly distributed.

## Richard Layard

The British economist Richard Layard goes one step further and ties
happiness to policy issues. He feels that government, instead of focusing on GDP, should be concerned about what actually makes people
happy (Jeremy Bentham's greatest happiness for the greatest number).
Government needs to relearn caring for the common good. It should
start by discouraging the pursuit of status. That means eliminating

things like performance-related pay and motivating people through rank. Emphasizing rank means that *most* people will feel like failures because there's only one person at the top and he or she is always vulnerable to losing the spot! One way to undermine status differences is to reinstate progressive taxation — taxes that discourage people from working for more and more money.

It's easier for government to prevent misery than to create happiness because misery is easier to measure. So Layard argues that government should focus on helping the poor and mentally ill. One of the best ways it can help people is to give families more time by creating more family-friendly policies.

As for education, Layard asks us to teach the principles of empathy and service and to provide and study role models.

Although I agree we must try to make changes through education, we can't forget that policies of education are determined by society as a whole. My argument is that we must go beyond the formal institutions of higher learning to focus on community education, as Scandinavian countries have done with admirable success.

## Daniel Nettle

There is science behind your smile, argues Daniel Nettle, who also confirms that status and stuff won't make us happy. He makes a point I think others overlooked — the inadequacy of self-reporting. Most people will say they are fairly happy, even though levels of depression and anxiety contradict them. One reason is that society has defined happiness as having a good job and being married. If they're working and wed, people assume they're happy. It's like the early research on women and marriage. Women assumed that if they were married they must be happy because that was the goal for women. It was difficult for them to understand why they felt so depressed and anxious — until they could acknowledge that marriage was not necessarily making them happy.

Further, to admit you're not happy is to admit you're a failure — again, something too painful for us to do. Researchers found that people rated themselves happier in polls conducted in person rather than via a written survey. When the interviewer was of the opposite sex, they claimed to be even happier!

Nettle describes three levels of happiness. Level one involves momentary feelings of joy and pleasure. Level two concerns your evaluation of your life, and this is where people tend to give themselves high ratings. Level three is about fulfilling one's potential (not an emotional state).

Nettle concludes that happiness comes from the pursuit of something challenging — and its accomplishment. Participation in community, being involved in something greater than yourself that brings meaning and connection. Living in an equal society and participating in activities that allow you to feel equal and valued. Having complexity — several sources of fulfillment. Engaging in some sort of contemplative activity.

He elaborates on the final precept — contemplative activity — by arguing that we need to understand that many of the things we do were necessary for our evolution and simply don't work any more in the pursuit of happiness! He says we must use our reflective, reasoning processes — honed by evolution — to choose paths that further evolution. We must explore how community, caring, acceptance, and appreciation make us truly happier. We must explore why we don't pursue happiness, when the research is so clear.

> People who work part-time, control their own lives, join community organizations, or get involved in active leisure are happier than those who do not. Yet the vast majority of people do not make these choices. Instead, their positional psychology drives them to work harder and harder to amass a greatly increased range of material goods.

It is clear to me that one of the Slow Life's purposes is to help create such a reflective, contemplative mechanism or tool for change. (Much more on this later.) What is important here is that there are three levels, and we must work through all of them. Americans are taught to ignore the third level, but too many of us dismiss the first level. Activists often become self-righteous or judgmental and can't join in the pleasures of everyday life. Nettle's summary clarifies my initial question. What if there is a level of happiness that has become so beyond our reach that we can't even imagine it, leaving us satisfied with an inferior sort of happiness? I would add a fourth level to Nettle's list, a level of happiness that is almost transcendent — one that involves taking a huge risk, with a community of people, for something you believe in.

I was moved to add this to the list after receiving an e-mail from Arthur Waskow, a rabbi and head of The Shalom Center. Waskow is a longtime activist and a name I remember from the '60s. His e-mail gives me hope that not only can we imagine a new kind of happiness, we will begin to see its link to integrity and the common good. Part of it describes his experiences at a demonstration against the Iraq War in which he and others were arrested:

> Friends,
>
> Prisoner # 151 reporting out of the 370 arrested in the White House protest Monday by the US Park Police. According to the US Park Police who arrested us, the LARGEST number EVER arrested by the Park Police. More than 3 x what they had expected. Cornel West among those arrested — I had a warm and interesting conversation with him as we marched toward 1600 Pennsylvania Avenue — and Cindy Sheehan — and Marie Dennis of the Maryknolls — and many other clergy and religious leaders, Unitarians, Quakers, Protestants, Buddhists, Catholics.
>
> Since the police were not ready for so many of us, we were in custody from about 1 pm (still on the streets) till about 4 pm (then they handcuffed us, arms behind backs, and stored us on buses the Park Police had to requisition from DC Metro; then ultimately we were driven to the lock-up in far Anacostia. Releases, beginning about 11 pm, went on far far into the night.
>
> The whole weekend was extraordinary for us all. And for me, though I have lived an intense life, this weekend capped the

most intense two weeks I have ever shaped a life in ....

The march on Saturday afternoon — both deeply serious and deeply humorous, wonderfully varied and good-humored ...

Then the Tent REVIVAL MEETING — a multireligious version of the classic evangelical Protestant revivals — was WONDERFUL. The different traditions and teachings meshed brilliantly, and people were indeed moved by the Spirit. I was asked to give the "invocation" — so I invoked the One God Who unfolds and is unfolded by all our traditions and who is present in all the life-forms of this planet. The God Who erupts like a volcano, like a lightning-flash of truth, when we dare to demand that a king, a ruler, meet with us face-to-face.

There were singers galore — including gospel singers, a Buddhist monk who sang "Go Down Moses" in such a way as to channel Harriet Tubman, the Elat Chayyim Jewish renewal staff who had sung at our Shabbat service, and many more; an amazing sermon by Rita Nakashima Brock — a scholar who brilliantly brought the crowd into roars of passion with her litany: "Mr. President, if you learned in Sunday school as I did that God is love — WHERE IS THE LOVE in your war? WHERE IS THE LOVE in your hostility to gay marriage? WHERE IS THE LOVE in your contempt for the poor?" —

...Today, just for a moment, dayenu! — To celebrate a spiritual victory. That joy is enough for us.

Today.

## Bruce O'Hara

Finally, a few thoughts on happiness from Bruce O'Hara, an activist in the Take Back Your Time movement and author of *Enough Already: Breaking Free in the Second Half of Life.* He found that when people were asked what made them happy, they would list consumer items. When asked what gave them contentment, peace of mind or satisfaction, they listed the joys of loving relationships with friends and family, serving a larger purpose, the excitement of learning and personal growth. Obviously consumer forces have co-opted the word "happiness" — we need to take it back.

O'Hara refers not just to research but to ancient philosophers. I particularly like his reference to Epicurus, who lived from 341 to 270 BC. Epicurus said that to be happy, people needed three things: friends, freedom, and an analyzed life. By freedom he meant leisure — the time to pursue what you want to do. The analyzed life is one where you understand what brings true, enduring happiness. Wealth, power, and status bring only transient happiness. The pleasures Epicurus identified as eternal were love, friendship, and service. "For Epicurus, the way to maximize happiness was to minimize the energy you put into transient ego 'highs' so as to leave more time and energy available for the durable pleasures of the heart."

# CHAPTER 3

# Reversing the Spell of Status

*The fact is, while most people think of ordinariness as a fault or limita-*
*tion, Gandhi had discovered in it the very meaning of life — and of*
*history. For him, it was not the famous or the rich or the powerful who*
*would change the course of history. If the future is to differ from the past,*
*he taught, if we are to leave a peaceful and healthy earth for our children,*
*it will be the ordinary man and woman who do it: not by becoming*
*extraordinary, but by discovering that our greatest strength lies not in how*
*much we differ from each other but in how much — how very much — we*
*are the same.*        —Eknath Easwaran, *The Compassionate Universe*

WHAT IS THE MOST PERNICIOUS force undermining our well-being?
What keeps us from following researched findings on happiness
and directing our efforts at behaviors that guarantee happiness?

It's our longing for status.

Most of us don't run across many really new ideas. Usually we're
vaguely familiar with a concept even if we haven't studied it thoroughly. We are not surprised, after a certain point, that money doesn't
make us happier. And I'm sure it's no surprise that our society is very
stressful — nor that stress harms our health and our relationships.
Further, it seems common sense that positive people are healthier.

Nothing is really new or striking about any of these ideas. But one idea out there is really just astounding — an idea I've only become familiar with in the past few years. It's about the health of a nation.

Imagine if someone asked you where the United States ranks in terms of health. Most of us would put America close to the top. After all, we are the richest nation, we have the greatest laboratories and technological accomplishments and we spend more on health than any other nation. Certainly the US has conquered most diseases plaguing humanity.

But our assumptions are wrong. There was a time, in the '50s, when we were at the top. No more. Not only are we not the healthiest, out of 25 industrialized Western nations we are at the bottom. What went wrong?

The research is clear: the biggest predictor for the health of a nation (measured in the customary way, longevity) is wealth inequality — the gap between the rich and the poor, the size of the middle class. Study after study has confirmed it.

In the 1950s we had a strong middle class and a small gap between rich and poor. (People whose incomes exceeded $200,000 were taxed at a 91 percent rate! Can you imagine! Now *that* was a progressive income tax.) Now out of the same 25 nations mentioned above, we're last in equitable distribution of wealth: bigger gap, lesser well-being.

For confirmation we can turn to Japan. In 1960 Japanese ranked 23rd in longevity; now they are the world leader. Researchers looked at several different explanations for the reversal. Was it diet? The Japanese diet didn't change much in those years, yet life expectancy soared seven and a half years for men and eight for women.

Healthier habits? Japanese men smoke at twice the rate of American men. Yet deaths attributable to smoking run at only half the American rate. And smokers in Japan live longer than smokers in the US.

Is it Japanese medicine? They have discovered no super cures. Only one Japanese medical scientist has ever won a Nobel Prize. Medical science has not improved faster than anywhere else.

The Japanese have a life expectancy of 80 years — three and a half years longer than in the US. In epidemiological terms, this is an enormous gap. If Americans stopped dying from heart disease tomorrow, life expectancy in the US would jump only to levels the Japanese have already achieved. (And heart disease is our number one health problem.)

Another shocker: When Japanese move to US, they lose their statistical advantage.

There's only one noticeable change in the Japan of today: markedly narrower gaps of income and wealth between the affluent class and the average worker.

How can this be? Does inequality really cause disease? In his exciting book, *Greed and Good*, Sam Pizzigati writes:

> How foolish this question sounds to American ears. We who have been raised on the germ theory of disease can readily understand how deadly to our health a virus can be. But inequality is no virus, no saturated fat, no carcinogen. How can inequality "cause" disease? The honest answer: We don't yet know for sure, just as, generations ago, we didn't know exactly why foul water makes people sick. Still, researchers and analysts do have some ideas on how inequality is doing us in.

It is important to realize that the ills of inequality affect everyone. Remember that most people assume that average lifespan is statistically lowered by the poor. It's because the poor are not getting good health care, we assume, and because they are more likely to smoke and eat junk food. It's also true that the rich live longer than the poor. But the longest-living people in an unequal society do not live as long as they would in an equal society. If you're middle-class and you live in an equal society, you will live longer than the middle class in an unequal society.

Researchers continue to speculate about the causes, but many have pinpointed what they call social cohesion. That's the way Pizzigati explains it: As societies grow less equal, there's less trust, greater conflict, more crime, less "social capital", and more racism. Certainly this correlates with what we've just learned about happiness: happier people are healthier. And social cohesion — strong, positive, warm relationships — drives happiness.

On the flip side, highly unequal societies produce more individuals suffering from stress associated with low status and weak social ties (such as limited links with others, including kin and friends). While stresses normally lead to hormonal responses helping individuals survive, the chronic stress of inequality takes a withering cumulative toll. Social stresses lead to bodily changes that reduce immunity, raise the risk of heart disease and other illnesses, and lead to dangerous behaviors, such as heavy drinking. All of this boosts the toll of disease and death.

*Social stresses lead to bodily changes that reduce immunity, raise the risk of heart disease and other illnesses, and lead to dangerous behaviors, such as heavy drinking. All of this boosts the toll of disease and death.*

A government study released in December 2005, raised alarms over Americans' life expectancy. Half of Americans from 55 to 64, including the oldest baby boomers, suffer from high blood pressure, and 40 percent are too fat. While Americans' overall life expectancy increased slightly, from 77.3 in 2002 to 77.6 in 2003, the US trailed Japan (81.9), Monaco, Switzerland, Australia and other countries by three to four years — a substantial margin in this benchmark. Study researchers warned that life expectancy in America might actually begin to fall for the first time since 1900.

The British researcher Sir Michael Marmot says it in a different way: In an unequal society you have less control over your life and less opportunity for participation. In an unequal society, more wealth gives the people at the top more power — political as well as economic. They can manipulate prices and wages, putting people in positions in which they have no way to resist or speak up. When you live in a country where most of the profit goes to the people at the top and they lay off employees with impunity, the vast majority of people have little control over their lives. When the people at the top have control over politicians because they contribute to their campaigns, the populist majority has little say in decisions.

By contrast, Pizzigati shows that, in a society lacking a huge gap, social cohesion helps people feel that they are respected, valued and safe. It is something that no doctor can prescribe, and it only comes about in cultures in which people really care for one another.

It is absent from unequal societies such as ours where the goal is profit, and where people will do anything to get profit, including mistreat others. Enron employees who lost their pensions didn't feel respected, valued or safe. Vioxx heart-attack victims don't feel respected, valued or safe. Hurricane refugees in New Orleans — and everyone trying to rebuild the crippled city — didn't feel respected, valued or safe. Behind the callousness in each of these situations was wealth and power. And as we saw in Kasser's research earlier, people who have a lot of money always want more, because inordinate wealth tends to make one materialistic, and materialism parents greed.

It's like the lotto. When there's a huge prize, everyone is more excited and buys a ticket — even though they know they have decidedly less chance of winning. Big money incites a sort of craziness. When the stakes are high, everyone wants to be a winner. So, when there's a big economic gap in the country, people scramble even harder for profit. They abandon fairness, decency and democracy. No one really protests when thousands of people lose their jobs while CEOs make millions — they identify with the CEO, not the rank and file. As we saw earlier, being unemployed is one of the most psychologically damaging experiences people can experience, and yet we lay people off without a qualm. Reading about it in the paper is a regular occurrence. We become numb. Ho hum .....

Let's go back to what Marmot says, though. He sees the problem in terms of the actual slights you feel from those above you. There's always an arrogance about people with higher status. They assume they're smarter and more capable than you, so their time is more valuable than yours. Studies on language behavior have consistently shown that those with more power are listened to more. The people with less power get interrupted, ignored and have to stand around looking impressed and laughing at their superior's jokes. It's all very stressful.

Pizzigati, taking the damage of inequality further, demonstrates how even big corporations contribute. Business seminar after seminar tells supervisors to treat their employees with more respect, and that one way to do this is to flatten the hierarchy. But Pizzigati argues that the people at the top prefer several layers of management because it allows them to have higher salaries. He shows how people at the top sometimes spend more time taking over companies than they do actually managing their companies — because after a merger, the people at the top always get a big salary boost.

So what can we do? In the '60s we discovered that there were still a lot of poor people, many of them black. Not only did we have a civil rights movement, we also had the War on Poverty. Today almost all the programs started then are gone (and the Republicans keep decimating Head Start as well.) What Pizzigati says is that just helping the poor doesn't work, because sooner or later people with money start resenting being taxed for social programs. What has to happen, he says, is to emulate European countries. They pay more taxes, but everyone feels taxes' benefits. In most nations everyone works fewer hours (than the US), gets health care, parental leave, and free or inexpensive college educations. And the tax system preserves a more equal society, resulting in greater longevity for everyone.

So we must find a way to equalize income in this country (Pizzigati suggests a top/bottom ratio of 10 to 1). First, we have to help people see the enormity of the problem. In 2002 America's top 20 percent in income held over 50 percent of the nation's annual personal income, the highest discrepancy ever. Among the top 1 percent, the average income was $10 million. *New York Times* columnist and economist Paul Krugman pointed out that from late 2001 through 2005 average hourly earnings of non-supervisory workers actually fell.

Next, we have to help people understand the consequences of inequality. We have to demythologize the American Dream whereby more than a third of the public thinks it has a shot at the top 1 percent income level. People need to know that when affluence goes up, community goes down, and that as we have seen from the research on happiness, relationships with others is the biggest predictor of happiness. Philosophers and prophets have always argued that too much inequality "tears at the ties that bind the human community." Plutarch says, "An imbalance between rich and poor is the oldest and

most fatal ailment of all republics." Confucius says, "Excess and deficiency are equally at fault." Adds Toynbee: "They all said with one
voice that if we made material wealth our para-
mount aim, this would lead to disaster." An
English cleric, Charles Colton, observed in
1822: "Our incomes are like our shoes, if too
small, they gall and pinch us, but if too large,
they cause us to stumble and trip." And the
redoubtable Louis Brandeis, Supreme Court
justice, intones: "We can either have democracy
in this country or we can have great wealth con-
centrated in the hands of a few, but we can't
have both."

*People need to know that when affluence goes up, community goes down, and that as we have seen from the research on happiness, relationships with others is the biggest predictor of happiness.*

So what can we do? First it's a matter of
changing a belief system. To begin with, the average person must see how little chance there is
that poor people will get rich. When Arthur
Ashe won Wimbledon and the US. Open and created a generation
of aspiring black tennis players, his first message in talks at schools
and universities was to have fun with sports but stick with a good
education because so few black athletes made it as professionals. We
still have the rags to riches idea in this country because it gets inter-
mittent reinforcement, the most powerful kind. So many poor people
believe that someday they will make it big, or at least that they will
win the lottery. But they won't. We have very few who move up from
poverty: According to a *Wall Street Journal* article in May 2005:

> As the gap between rich and poor has widened since 1970,
> the odds that a child born in poverty will climb to wealth —
> or a rich child will fall into the middle class — remain stuck.
> Despite the spread of affirmative action, the expansion of
> community colleges, and the other social change designed to
> give people of all classes a shot at success, Americans are no
> more or less likely to rise above, or fall below, their parents'
> economic class than they were 35 years ago.

Data from a government survey of Social Security records for thousands of men born between 1963 and 1968 showed only 14 percent born to fathers on the bottom 10 percent of the wage ladder made it to the top 30 percent.

Next, as I emphasized in the previous section, we still believe that more money will make us happier. People have to come to understand how that's false.

Further, people need to know that other countries do things differently. They need to hear how people live in Europe. They need to know that it was different in our past. They need to hear the stories of the populist era when people changed things. They need to be inspired by hearing words from a populist congressman from Alabama who said:

> Plutocracy should be called the great national crime. The spirit of avarice is devouring the great heart of this nation. The greed for gain gets such possession of men's souls that they become demons. They rush into the maelstrom of money-getting, and soon lose all fear of God and love for their fellow men, and before they realize it, they have become slaves to a passion which is as cruel as fate and remorseless and unrelenting as death.

But how do we change things? Looking at history we can see that change involves strikes and protests and boycotts. Most of all, it involves huge masses of people in a movement. I'll continue to come back to the issue of creating a movement, but the first step is always trying to change people's belief systems. There will be no progress if people believe that big gaps in income are acceptable.

I had a first-hand experience, one day, of the need for change.

I had been asked to speak about voluntary simplicity to women inmates in a halfway house — their first step into society after serving time in prison. Since talking about cutting back on one's consumerism seemed ludicrous under the circumstances, I decided to talk about the gap between the rich and the poor, thinking I would find an interested audience among low-income women. The group was divided between black and white, and as the evening progressed, I could see that the white women were not pleased with what I was saying. One woman accused me of attacking people just because they were rich! The black women completely understood, though. They could see injustice much more clearly. The white women, it seemed, still harbored hopes that they could strike it rich in the Horatio Alger vein.

Hopefully some day we will again come to a time when vast numbers of people believe that inequality is wrong, as we did during the American Revolution. Until then, we need to try to figure out how to reach people.

Certainly there are several paths. For instance, I think it's pertinent to ask why activists, so many of whom are privileged, want more equality rather than more money. I found some interesting answers in Alain de Botton's book, *Status Anxiety*. There are some of us who are privileged *and* believe in an equal society. We would rather give up some of our privileges for the common good. How did we come to believe this? Why don't we just want to climb the twin peaks of status and wealth? Certainly many of us reject wealth because of our Judeo-Christian background. But not all of us — research finds that those countries like the US, which have a high percentage of people who say they are religious, also have much higher rates of divorce, homicide and teen suicide. So being religious does not guarantee that one is more moral, as you might expect.

But here is where our academic system has had some effect. Education did not prevent the gap from widening, but it has inspired many of us to work for a more equal society. It was our education in the humanities, an education that introduced us to the great ideas throughout history, that affected us. What I found so exciting were de Botton's comments about how 19th-century Victorian literature fostered these ideas. Victorian novels certainly were a big influence on me — I took all the classes I could get as an undergraduate English major and spent all my extra time reading them. I learned how Jane Austen in *Pride and Prejudice* and *Sense and Sensibility* ridicules the rich and shallow and shows that true character is often found in the poor person. De Botton says,

> Standing witness to hidden lives, novels may act as conceptual counterweights to dominant hierarchical realities. They

can reveal that the maid now busying herself with lunch is a creature of rare sensitivity and moral greatness, while the baron who laughs raucously and owns a silver mine has a heart both withered and acrid.

This was a central theme of one of my all-time favorite books — George Eliot's *Middlemarch*. The main character, Dorothea, after a disastrous but respectable first marriage, ends up marrying a man with no social standing. Eliot says:

> Her finely-touched spirit had its fine issues, even though they were not widely visible. Her full nature spent itself in channels which had no great name on the earth. But the effect of her being on those around her was incalculably diffusive: for the growing good of the world is partly dependent on unhistoric acts; and that things are not so ill with you and me as they might have been, is half owing to the number who lived faithfully a hidden life and rest in unvisited tombs.

What a beautiful thought! When I read this, I cried, because it made me think of my mother, someone who never desired status and only spent her life caring for and loving others. De Botton goes on to say that these lines define one of the goals of a novel: to help us understand and appreciate "the value of every hidden life that rests in an unvisited tomb. George Eliot, herself, said: 'If art does not enlarge men's sympathies, it does nothing morally.'"

But the depiction of status is present in other forms of literature besides Victorian novels — including comedies that poke fun at the rich and powerful, de Botton adds:

> Jokes become attempts to cajole others into reforming their character and habits. Jokes are a way of sketching a political ideal, of creating a more equitable and saner world .... As Samuel Johnson saw it, satire is only another method, and a particularly effectual one, of "censuring wickedness or folly." In the words of John Dryden, "The true end of satire is the amendment of vices."

## Bohemia

So a literary education can help us begin to think about the issue of status. But the study of history can do the same, particularly if we read about countercultural movements — movements that, throughout history, always criticized status differences and lauded equality. One such era was the Bohemian movement, whose role was to resist and outrage the bourgeoisie.

Beginning in the 19th century, a new group of people in western Europe and the US rejected conventional mores. They dressed simply and lived in cheaper parts of town. They spent a lot of time reading, seemed not to care about money, and their allegiances were to art and emotion rather than to business and material success. They often had unconventional sex lives. They were not considered respectable by the bourgeoisie, which suited them just fine!

"Hatred of the bourgeois is the beginning of wisdom," writes Gustave Flaubert. Flaubert accuses the bourgeoisie of prudery and materialism, of immersing themselves in trivia. As Stendhal says, "The conversation of the true bourgeois about men and life, which is no more than a collection of ugly details, brings on a profound attack of spleen when I am obliged to listen to it for any length of time."

But the biggest difference between the Bohemians and the bourgeoisie was how they felt about status. The Bohemians shunned economic status in favor of great ideas and art. They wanted to write, paint, play music, travel, and just hang out with friends. They said they would rather starve than waste time on day jobs they despised, so they existed without much money. Big boats, big buggies and big houses were indications of superficiality. To be a true Bohemian, you needed conversational agility or writing flair.

As de Botton concludes,

> Whatever the excesses of the outer wings of bohemia, the movement's enduring contribution has been to pose a series of well-considered challenges to bourgeois ideology. The bourgeoisie has stood accused of failing to understand the role that wealth should play in a good life; of being too hasty to condemn worldly failure and too slavish in venerating signs

of outward success; of placing too much faith in sham notions
of propriety; of dogmatically confusing professional qualifi-
cations with talent; of neglecting the value of art, sensitivity,
playfulness and creativity; and of being over-concerned with
order, rules, bureaucracy and timekeeping.

What this discussion of Bohemians says to me is how important it is to show people that there are different paths — that the way
we do things in conventional society is not the only way!

The striving for status eats us up. We must try to protect
ourselves from it on the one hand and to undermine its cultural sway on the other. Obviously,
we must work to change the gap between the
rich and the poor, but that is going to take a
long time.

*The striving for status eats*

*us up. We must try to protect*

*ourselves from it on the one*

*hand and to undermine its*

*cultural sway on the other.*

In the meantime, we must help people
see social climbing as the empty, cruel process it
is. We must help people liberate themselves by
continuing to support acts that unmask status,
by encouraging people to read history and literature and to think for themselves.

You wouldn't expect to find much Bohemian influence in
today's ad-driven media, which exists as a propaganda arm of the
wealthy and powerful. But a recent episode of CBS's *60 Minutes* featured a sly poke at the nouveau bourgeoisie. Morley Safer did a
segment on "mansionization" — the practice of tearing down perfectly liveable homes and building huge, garish and tasteless
structures that dominate a neighborhood and disrupt community. As
one mansion matron prattled on about her gym-sized kitchen and
how she loves to cook, the segment cut abruptly to commercial. It
was as though Safer was saying, "Yada yada yada, we've had enough
of her!"

Who knows if the ending was intentional or accidental?
Either way, it was a glimmer of bohemianism in a nightmarishly
bourgeois world.

CHAPTER 4

# *"Fast" and the Consumer Society*

THE TRUE SOURCES OF OUR CULTURE'S PROBLEMS are becoming apparent. Happiness is declining because of our belief system about money — the myth that if we're rich we'll be happy — and the empty pursuit of status. Many of us, particularly those of us in the Simplicity movement, have challenged these tenets. But even personal change is difficult. You would think that once you discover a false idea it would be simple enough to change the belief. But it's not.

First, there is so much momentum behind these beliefs. It seems like it should be self-evident that more money doesn't necessarily make you happier — that you could look at your own life and see it. But in a weird twist of human nature, when we are unhappy or unfulfilled, we often cling to money even more. As Kasser shows, materialism sucks you into a debilitating vortex: pursuing money makes you materialistic; materialism reduces your well-being, so you grasp even harder for power and money, putting you more deeply into the unsatisfying clutches of materialism. It looks like getting more money makes you want more money. Is it like being addicted to cocaine? You can see it ruining your life, but you are enslaved by it. Or perhaps it emulates an eating disorder — after a certain point, you can't control your own eating behavior, and you need outside

55

help. Or maybe it's like my dog. She does something in one particular way, and that's the way it always has to be done. While walking her, you stop and rest at a park bench one day, and from then on, every time you pass that bench she has to stop and rest.

The impulse for money, possessions and status does appear to be something deep within our psyche — something left over from the time in human history when we were barely surviving and we learned that more is better. We just don't seem to be able to move on.

Maybe the real point is that it's in the interests of those in power to keep us believing in the centrality of money, because if we were free from that belief, we would be free of their power. Most of the people at the top, those whose focus is accumulating even more, long ago sold their souls for the drugs of money and power. And just as drug addicts commit crimes to support their habit, so do these power junkies at Enron and Worldcom and Tyco and Qwest and on and on commit crimes for their habit — anything to keep and increase their profits. They've lost the ability to control their appetites for more.

To change, we first have to be aware of the forces keeping this belief system in place — the forces embodied in the consumer society. Let's look at the word "consumer." How could we accept being called consumers? What does it mean to consume something? Think about it: Consuming is a very destructive concept! It means to devour or to destroy. A building is consumed by fire. A man is consumed by jealousy. You're hardly ever consumed by something good! You're devoured by something alien to you; an evil genie takes over and you lose control. When fire consumes something, nothing is left! So what's it mean to accept being called consumers?

Being a consumer means that you turn to something outside yourself to fill up emptiness. To consume is to take something in, to ingest. You don't turn to something within yourself, you don't turn to friends or family, you don't turn to community. You turn to a thing — a dead, lifeless piece of merchandise. To condition you to do this, the consumer society makes you feel deprived and incomplete; first, it works at lowering most people's wages, making them feel anxious about their future. Even if you're earning less money, the consumer society tricks you into lusting after that new car so that you think it will make you happy. Advertising broadcasts this message over and over: You are inadequate. You are lacking. Buy this; it will make you whole. But when you follow the Svengalis of Madison Avenue, you never learn to believe in yourself, putting you at the mercy of the brainwashers. No wonder people become such easy targets for "free" credit cards that then start piling up debt in fees and interest.

*With fitting irony, the badge of "consumer" is really the most accurate title we could have, because we truly are a consumer society — we are destroying things and devouring life.*

   With fitting irony, the badge of "consumer" is really the most accurate title we could have, because we truly are a consumer society — we are destroying things and devouring life. We're destroying nature, we're destroying people's financial health, we're destroying their happiness. The South African poet Breyten Breytenbach says that "Americans have mastered the art of living with the unacceptable." And so much of life in a consumer society is unacceptable. Let's look more closely at its characteristics.

## Control

The forces of glut have taken over our lives and subverted our ability to exert control over ourselves — the most invidious being the way the Right Wing, backed by powerful consumer interests, has stolen our vote. Not just by election fraud but by media distortion, false advertising, and outright lies.

   Much of this covert control is done in subtle ways — especially through advertising. Most of us understand how advertising tries to control, and many of us think we're free of its power. But you're never free of the social mores in your culture. I think of how feminism worked to free women from enslavement to their appearance. We chose to be more natural — not shaving our legs, not wearing much makeup, not wearing high heels. But today, cosmetic surgery is rising (among men as well), and processed hair, high heels and constricting bras all are back. We all experience the pressures — for instance, my dilemma is about whether to "color" my hair. (No one says "dye" any more — too low class.) I don't want to color it; I think it's a form of inauthenticity. Yet when everyone else does it, it's very hard to resist. It begins to look like you're just not observing the basics of grooming and cleanliness. Cultural mores are subtle but powerful influences.

Hair coloring may be something small, but so many trends affect us. For instance, political pundits are forever telling Democrats they must appeal to the center, when what politicians really need to do is speak the truth! Many years ago I discovered a book that has gained vital pertinence in recent years. It's about the German public when the Nazis and the Third Reich took over, titled *They Thought They Were Free: The Germans, 1933–1945*, by Milton Mayer:

> What happened here was the gradual habituation of the people, little by little, to being governed by surprise; to receiving decisions deliberated in secret; to believing that the situation was so complicated that the government had to act on information which the people could not understand, or so dangerous that, even if the people could understand it, it could not be released because of national security .... One had no time to think. There was so much going on.

Note the reference to time. They had no time to reflect and act on what was happening, and so gradually they lost their freedom and democracy. We cannot afford to think that the Slow Life is irrelevant to our democracy — it's at the very heart.

## Commandeering our time and resources

A central theme of this book is that we need more time. We work too many hours. We spend much of our lives doing things controlled by the consumer society: working, watching television, shopping. There are so many ways the consumer society eats up (devours/consumes) our time! Advertising, shopping, spam e-mail, commuting, and, always, the long work hours. Somehow we've made everything — even shopping — difficult and inconvenient. Try learning a new hobby, going back to school, meeting new friends, volunteering, getting involved in your neighborhood. We don't have a clue how to do these things! In the old days of small towns and a more leisurely pace, they were taken for granted. Now we must consciously seek them out. The government puts little time into making necessary resources available.

We need to become de-consumers. Granted, it will involve conscious effort. Getting involved in community or hobbies takes a lot of time. But there's an interesting new item to be added to the list — something that has just emerged in the last few years — affecting the core issue of time for relationships. It's online dating. I have several friends who are attractive and successful and single and who have no way to meet potential dates. No time, no places, and no activities. So they've tried online dating — and they all complain how long it takes to meet someone interesting via the Internet! First, you have to create your own description of yourself, get a decent picture, figure out which service to use (there are lots of them). You have to sort through false descriptions and fake pictures, which losers put in hoping they can make up for it in person. Then, after spending hours writing your ad, you have to read all the responses and try to decipher which ones to follow up on. Then you meet the person and the games begin, with each trying to project an attractive image and not be the one rejected. There have been Internet dating successes, yes, but that's primarily because so few alternatives exist. No one considers online dating an effective way to get to know someone. As the comedian Chris Rock says, you're not meeting the real person, you're meeting their representative!

Lack of time pervades even the romantic side of our lives. But lack of time is really only a cover for deeper issues. Behind the commandeering of our time is commandeering of our resources: in a word — greed. Almost every problem we have comes back to people grabbing for more — more than they need, more than others have, and more than the planet can sustain. We may be focusing on time, but the underlying issue is greed — taking more than your share and stealing from others.

## Commodification of life

Another way to approach greed is to think of it as the commodification of life. Just as we have come to put our hopes for happiness in commodities, so have we come to turn life itself into a commodity. We have come to believe that all of nature is or should be at our personal "disposal." We can do what we want with nature, with other people and even with our own health and welfare. It's all there for our exploitation.

Social observers have long recognized the dangers of following the exploitation path. American commentator Erich Fromm calls it the choice between "to have or to be." Jewish theologian Martin Buber sees it as the choice between living a life of I/It or I/Thou. Lives that turn everything into an "it," an object to be used, become empty and devoid of meaning. Lives that try to "have" everything rather than just "be" can never be fulfilled. Happiness research says that deep personal relationships are central to well-being. When people are just out to use each other, there can be no true caring.

*Every time we do something because it will help us get ahead, we lose touch with that inner guidance — the little voice inside — that tells us what path to follow. Sooner or later we can't hear our inner voice at all.*

Whenever we pretend to like someone because it advances our career, we have commodified and cheapened our lives. Whenever we do something we secretly hate just because it will look good on our résumé, we've commodified ourselves. We've turned our lives into objects! That makes life itself a thing — a dead and lifeless thing! It never really works. You can't keep faking enthusiasm, the little guy inside starts protesting. I've discovered that whenever I do something that I don't want to do, but think to myself, Oh, this will help my career, I almost always end up hating it, feeling soiled and dropping it. As Thoreau says: "Do nothing merely out of good resolutions. Discipline yourself only to yield to love; suffer yourself to be attracted." Every time we do something because it will help us get ahead, we lose touch with that inner guidance — the little voice inside — that tells us what path to follow. Sooner or later we can't hear our inner voice at all. (Wouldn't you quit speaking too if no one listened?)

## Commercialization of life

Why have we commodified life? Because we measure everything in terms of money. As a *New Yorker* cartoon put it, "Money is life's report card." Everything is for sale. Corporations run schools, hospitals, daycare centers and prisons — not for the betterment of society but simply for profit! I find this incredible! With everything measured in terms of the bottom line, of course people compromise on their ethics and integrity. We don't have another way to measure things. If people die, if a species is destroyed, if employees lose their retirement, it doesn't matter. Profit rules! The corporation just does a cost-benefit analysis and figures out how much the lawsuits will cost them.

The list could go on and on. Take Tom Mboya, a born leader in Kenya backed by Washington to defend US commercial interests in Africa. After he was shot in 1969, an emergency rescue squad hooked him up to a resuscitative device from the US called the Res-Q-Aire. What the emergency technicians didn't know is that the device had been recalled for being totally ineffective.

The incident was emblematic of US business's practice of selling tons of medical devices, bad drugs, carcinogens, toxic agents, poisoned foods and other products banned or ousted from American markets. In 1972, 400 Iraqis died and 5,000 were hospitalized after consuming wheat and barley coated with an organic mercury fungicide, whose use had been banned in the US. Egyptian farmers and more than 1,000 water buffalos died after being exposed to leptophos, a chemical pesticide never approved for domestic use by the Environmental Protection Agency but exported to at least 30 countries. Cancer will strike children from around the world who wore clothes treated with a carcinogenic fire retardant called Tris, forced off the U.S. market after public outcry and a Congressional investigation. A synthetic male hormone, found to stunt the growth of US children, is nonetheless used in Brazil as an appetite stimulant for children. Baby pacifiers and teething rings have been exported to other countries after US bans.

Some other specific corporations and their crimes include Bayer and its anti-cholesterol drug Baycol; Clear Channel's imposition of right-wing programming; Diebold's flawed, reprogrammable voting machines and hacker-susceptible software; Halliburton's overcharges in Iraq; Inamed's defective breast implants; Merrill Lynch's corrupt executives and on and on.

It's a discouraging litany of lies, greed and institutionalized hooliganism. But the area that upsets me most is the commercialization of education, especially from Kindergarten to grade 12. Seattle residents have been fighting the commercialization of our schools for years and have won many battles, thanks to organizations such as the Citizens' Campaign for Commercial-Free Schools. We've fought advertisers in every way possible because they are looking for every nook and cranny of marketing space they can find, including direct sales of soft drinks, which give companies exclusive contracts; direct advertising through billboards, book covers, sports equipment, uniforms, and events; indirect advertising through educational material; direct advertising through the station Channel One, a TV program that gives 12-minute newscasts that include 2 minutes of advertising. The companies say they are just trying to help support education through advertising, but often their lobbyists have worked to reduce funding for schools. When they speak among themselves (they've learned to keep their mouths shut these days) they speak of branding children. They continue to give schools promotional samples, to sponsor contests in which students claim prizes from franchises, to offer free training for teachers, and to make presentations at conferences as though they were a service provider for educational programming.

It's often been hard to rouse the public over this issue because we're always suckers when we think we're getting something for free. But recent alarm over obesity in children might get some attention. Think about what is advertised to children — it's not encyclopedias!

It's not just that products are being sold in a setting that should be devoted to the search for truth and exempt from manipulation (when was the last time we expected truth in an ad?). It's that a philosophy of consumerism is drummed into kids' heads. Children learn very young that you solve problems by buying things, and you are acceptable only when you reflect the ads' images. Advertising teaches envy, materialism and competitiveness — all values that, as we saw, undermine real happiness.

It's not just grade schools that attract corporations; it's also colleges and universities. One particularly telling account, in *University Inc.: The Corporate Corruption of Higher Education* by Jennifer Washburn, shows how universities are becoming more and more commercialized:

- Academic administrators refer to students as consumers (and students certainly see themselves that way, demanding their money's worth in the form of high grades).

- Colleges talk about branding and marketing just as traditional corporations do.

- Academic departments have financial partnerships with private corporations, giving them profits that come from inventions made by faculty who are often supported by public money. (Even private universities get government grants and their students, public funds.)

- Colleges are outsourcing services like bookstores and food services to corporations.

- And of course, universities sell themselves in terms of the kinds of jobs their students will get.

One of the biggest problems comes when corporations start interfering with academic life. For instance, when a company funds a research project, it will try to control the findings. When researchers have found something wrong with a product, the corporation often tries to change the report, bury the findings with delay tactics, undermine the professor's tenure, or discredit either the researcher or the research.

Increasingly, university research agendas are dictated by products companies want (particularly drug companies), things corporations can profit from, not necessarily something that would serve the common good. This isn't easy for individual professors to resist, particularly if they are in the sciences, because government funding is drying up. Researchers on issues like cancer spend more and more time that could be devoted to valuable research in the tedious pursuit of grants. As Paul Krugman writes in the December 2005 *New York Times*: "The past quarter-century has seen the emergence of a vast medical-industrial complex in which doctors, hospitals and research institutions have deep financial links with drug companies and equipment makers. Conflicts of interest aren't the exception — they're the norm."

Corporate influence affects not just labs and research projects but the whole university campus, because the most valued professors are in sectors that bring in money from alums or corporations or government — fields like business, medicine and science. The valued professors become not those devoted to teaching, but those who bring in the most money. This means, of course, that medical schools, business schools and computer science programs have a lot more power than the English department or the school of education. Departments that don't generate money may be abandoned. Huge undergraduate classes have graduate students teaching them, and even graduate students reject teaching because their future jobs depend on résumés packed with research and publications!

Commercialism is demeaning to professors who have integrity. I can't imagine what they must think about some of the buildings — such as the Ken Lay Center for the Study of Markets in Transition at Rice University (yes, the same Ken Lay who destroyed Enron). Imagine holding the K-Mart Chair of Marketing at Wayne State University! Or being the BankAmerica Dean of the Haas School of Business. I remember once, when I gave a guest lecture at the University of Washington, noticing that even the classroom displayed a plaque crediting a company. (I remember thinking how cheap Nordstrom must be, because my room's sound system was so poor!)

We expect universities to give us disinterested, objective, honest information — to pursue the truth. But a lot of research is not independent. What is most troubling is how some institutions have sullied their reputations by allowing corporations to force scientists to compromise. For instance, drug companies have paid professors to put their names on studies written by the drug companies, even though the professors had nothing to do with the study. Corporate sponsors often have control over the design of the study, the data and which results get reported. Often the lead researcher owns equity in the company, so he or she has direct financial interest in the results. During the 1990s the tobacco industry paid academic scientists to write letters to journals and newspapers downplaying the health risks of cigarettes. Enron paid academics to write reports advocating Enron's model of deregulation of electricity — and later, after the collapse of the market, got them to claim that Enron had not tried to manipulate prices. Shamefully, Harvard Business School issued glowing reports about Enron.

We have crushingly serious problems like global warming, peak oil, genetically engineered crops, and human cloning. If scientists have investments in companies sponsoring the research, we can predict what will happen: Government reports based on expert panels with direct financial ties to manufacturers. In a pernicious daisy chain of payola and bribery, more than half the experts hired to advise regulatory agencies on drug safety reportedly have financial links to companies targeted for regulation. When journals ask experts to review studies, they often don't know that the reviewers have financial interests in the products being studied.

My husband has been a journalist all his life and early in his career participated in drawing up an ethics code for his newsroom, restricting gifts and favors for reporters. As a technology writer, he carefully avoided investing in technology companies. Unfortunately, not all journalists or newspapers exercise such discretion, and the news profession's credibility has suffered along with academia. Hardly any occupation, it seems, is immune to the blandishments of corporate influence.

Derek Bok's message is a little softer in *Universities in the Marketplace: The Commercialization of Higher Education* — as one would expect from a past president of Harvard. But he, too, is concerned about the integrity of universities as they form partnerships with corporations for research. For instance, he cites evidence showing studies funded by drug companies are more likely than independent research to have positive findings. He's also concerned about the increasing involvement of drug companies in continuing education programs for physicians. Doctors need continuing education to retain their licenses, and Bok says that a third of the cost of the education is paid for by corporations.

Bok concludes that the commercialization of college athletics invites corruption and destroys academic integrity. Certainly commercialization exists in all parts of our lives, but I think having blatant commercialization in our schools, our health care system and our sports programs touches every single one of us. It makes us think that this is "normal," that this is the way life is supposed to be. So we begin to "master the art of living with the unacceptable." Take just one little item, a clothes logo. It may be small, but it is basically saying, I'm here to further the interests of multinational corporations. Bring 'em on!

Some of you might be asking, How does this relate to the speed of our culture? How is this part of the Fast Life? We have to understand how the consumer society as a whole erodes our ability to slow down and enjoy life and make a difference. We must look at it in its entirety, because it is all of one piece.

## Competition

One of the most egregious causes of our increased speed is competition. What compels us to turn life into a commodity? Competition. On your mark! Get set! Go! They're some of the earliest words we hear. Everything in our lives is a competition. I always remember taking my children to an Easter egg hunt when they were very little. The kids were lined up, and the eggs were spread out in front of them. A toy gun blasted the start. It wasn't an Easter egg hunt, it was an Easter egg race! For me this little memory has come to epitomize so much of what's going wrong in this country. Competition increases society's speed, undermines relationships and traps people into leading second-hand, inauthentic lives.

It's obvious that competition causes our lives to go faster, but why the inauthentic? Because when you compete, you let others set your goals and standards. You are always trying to be what others want you to be. That's what it means to win. Winning means that your true self is ignored and repressed, and you're living someone else's goals.

But maybe the most serious consequence of competition is how it undermines warm, human relationships. Everyone is your enemy in this race to be a winner. When I was a senior in high school, something happened that affected my outlook on life. Several of us were in the finals for the competition to be a commencement speaker, and members of the senior class had to vote for three people. One of my best friends and I were both in the running, so when I voted I put down both of our names. I accidentally saw her ballot, and I saw that she had left my name off! I felt very bad! Why did she do that? Apparently she felt that leaving my name off would give her more votes. The senior class chose neither of us. I wound up being chosen by teachers because, of course, I had always been pretty much a teacher's-pet type. My friend didn't get to speak at all.

*We have to understand*

*how the consumer society*

*as a whole erodes our ability*

*to slow down and enjoy*

*life and make a difference.*

*We must look at it in*

*its entirety, because*

*it is all of one piece.*

That was a clear example of the evils of competitiveness — betray your friends if it will help you get ahead. Psychoanalyst Karen Horney, in *The Neurotic Personality of Our Time*, writes about the fact that extreme competitiveness in our work lives spreads into personal relationships:

> Modern culture is economically based on the principle of individual competition. The isolated individual has to fight with other individuals of the same group, has to surpass them and, frequently, thrust them aside. The advantage of one is frequently the disadvantage of the other. The psychic result of this situation is a diffuse hostile tension between individuals... It must be emphasized, however, that competitiveness,

and the potential hostility that accompanies it, pervades all human relationships. It pervades the relationships between men and men, between women and women, and whether the point of competition be popularity, competence, attractiveness, or any social value, it greatly impairs the possibilities of reliable friendship.

Finally, our competitiveness undermines democracy because we are instructed to believe only in the people at the top. We are taught over and over that the winners in the contest are superior to us. If others get good grades, test well and get into good colleges, we've learned to defer to them as being smarter. And so we give deference to anyone who is considered an expert, and we quit thinking for ourselves. Further, we ourselves develop a false sense of superiority if we're the ones who have the stamp of academic success. Too often I hear liberals say, "People are so stupid!" Not at all! It's just that people have been given no opportunity or encouragement to think for themselves!

Alfie Kohn, an ardent fighter in the campaign to unmask competitiveness, shows that competition is not innate to human nature, and it rarely produces the results that we would like in terms of pleasure, achievement or productivity. Rewards don't make you more interested in what you're doing. Rewards make you more interested in getting rewards. Further, Kohn finds that competition has a negative affect on psychological health, relationships, motivation, and achievement. It just doesn't work!

## Corporatism

More and more of life is controlled by giant companies that are usually immoral, irresponsible, and impersonal, and whose practices diminish the dignity of the human race.

I worked for a community college for many years until I couldn't stand it anymore. I loved the idea of a community college, but over the years I saw it going corporate. In their drive to be No. 1, colleges turn more and more to businesses for money. And in the process they begin to ape corporate ways. It happens in little ways, as in the often-cited frog story: Apparently if you try to cook a frog by throwing it into boiling water, the frog will jump out. But if the water is just lukewarm at first, the frog will swim around not noticing the water getting hotter and hotter until finally it's cooked! (This little homily, which gets a lot of play in anecdotes and news stories today, seems to symbolize life in the US.)

I saw it happening in my school. The president had to spend more time with companies, courting them for funding. That meant he had to start acting more like corporate executives — dressing in dull, conservative suits, concealing any trace of personality. And then the president started expecting it of the staff. We had to start "dressing for success," carrying slim little briefcases, and modulating our voices. No more casual, informal, laid-back educators concerned with truth and beauty — we had to look like the corporate managers. Not long before my exit (which you will read about) the corporate image started gagging me. I discovered that I could no longer wear coats and ties, so I switched to sweaters. I couldn't stand wearing nylons any more, so I started wearing black tights. After awhile I couldn't stand carrying that little briefcase and instead used a backpack. (It was a black leather backpack, so I was able to "pass.")

As things began to change, the school started to feel less and less comfortable. Coworkers began distrusting one another as we all became infected with the desire to look and act corporate. No more animated conversations in the hallways — we kept our voices down and walked quickly past each other, showing how busy we were. No more hanging around in the halls chatting. Laughter was suspect. Smiles became tight and insincere.

Corporations don't allow workers to feel free to be themselves. There is no freedom of expression, no chance to really be honest. You don't reveal aspects of your personal life because you might look like a failure and you need to look like a winner all the time. Your marriage could be falling apart or your kids driving you crazy, but when someone says, "Hi, how are you?" you respond that you are just fine. And then you move on.

The worst part is the pretense. It's not only pretending that your life is perfect, it's pretending that you respect or admire your boss. It's pretending to yourself that your job is contributing to the common good — or even that you like your job. A lot of people get sick from too much pretending, and then they start to change. No wonder *Dilbert*, the cartoon that relies on true-life stories of corporate pretension and foppery, became the number one comic strip in America. It strikes home in so many ways.

Corporate size and commitment to profit means there is little sense of caring, equality, democracy, social responsibility, or just plain conviviality and enjoyment. The Corruption of the American Dream has been caused by a growing, shocking, huge gap between the rich and the poor. All of the above factors — from commandeering our time and resources to competition to commercialism — have contributed to this gap and the shrinking of the middle class, so it is the culmination of all that is dangerous in the consumer society.

But this gap has put our culture into extreme danger that Americans seem unable to grasp. Above all, as we examine the Slow Life, we're celebrating experiences that are threatened with extinction, such as community, leisure, and joie de vivre. Why? Because as the gap widens, our insecurity about our jobs and our money increases. Corporations increasingly drive up their share price by laying people off or moving to another country. When jobs are in danger, no one speaks up at work. We have little freedom in the workplace. Further, as people worry about their jobs, they work longer and longer hours. Partly there is more to do — layoffs mean that one person must do the work formerly done by two or three people. But it's not only the extra work, employees also engage in "image management" of their own, putting in "face" time so they appear to be dedicated, indispensable workers.

As we work faster and longer, our social cohesion declines, our happiness declines, our health declines. Our job takes over everything. There is no time to organize to change things, even to get together with our neighbors to talk about what is happening. We need a new vision of society. Instead of a society that devours and destroys — the consumer society — we need a culture that cares and creates, a culture of connectedness.

## Social inventions

One source of hope comes from new ways of doing things that consumerism and corporatization have seized from our control. In San Francisco, Mary walks from her apartment down the street to pick up the Prius she uses in a car-share program, an idea spreading to many metropolitan communities throughout North America. Instead of buying a second car, she and her husband pay a monthly (it can alternatively be hourly) fee, which covers gas, insurance, maintenance, and other costs for the shared vehicle. Not having to buy and pay for a second car has saved them a lot of money. Sharing the car with others has saved the planet another sliver of grief.

In Seattle, Tom opens his front door and picks up a box of organic vegetables left on his porch earlier in the morning. Tom is involved in community-supported agriculture, a program in which he pays a basic fee to a local organic farmer who then delivers produce weekly. The small farm is able to have financial security, and Tom not only saves money but loses weight and lives healthier by eating better. And by reducing transportation, handling, and maintenance costs for the produce, the program saves the planet another sliver of grief.

In Ithaca, New York, Fred buys vegetables from a local store that accepts his time dollars — something also called local currency. It's a system in which people essentially are bartering, but they don't have to do it directly one-on-one. Someone performs a service and gets paid in terms of a currency that represents, say, 10 hours of work valued at 10 dollars an hour. (Everyone's time is valued at the same amount, eliminating any income gap.) There are many local currency systems around the country, but Ithaca Hours is one of the oldest and most successful. The approach keeps money in the community, supports local businesses and gives people on the lower end of the socioeconomic spectrum a chance to purchase things they otherwise could not afford.

Mary, Tom and Fred are participating in social inventions, new ways that help people live more simply, more sustainably, more slowly, and more cooperatively. Social inventions help people work with others in a fashion that encourages community and caring. They have the additional asset of taking back goods and services from the consumerist establishment.

*When people participate in a car-share program, a community supported agriculture program, or a local currency, they experience a new view of reality, a new belief system that says that human relationships are more important than money.*

Social inventions challenge the way we view money in this culture. They help people see that the key to happiness is supportive relationships, meaningful work, a sense of purpose and self-realization. When people participate in a car-share program, a community supported agriculture program, or a local currency, they experience a new view of reality, a new belief system that says that human relationships are more important than money. They also call on essential, neglected, purposely discouraged (by a consumer society) human characteristics: creativity and ingenuity. America was founded on, and became great via, ingenuity and innovation. But in a culture where you buy almost everything you need — from products to medicine to prepared foods to entertainment — we are losing our flair for the creative.

Sooner or later our culture will come to a point when we are all forced to change and live together in a more caring way. It might be an environmental disaster. It might be an economic meltdown. And we know that we're facing the situation of peak oil. Everything in our society uses oil — growing things (fertilizers), making things (machinery), transporting things (ships, trucks and planes), and selling things (we drive to the malls). When the crisis comes, experience with social inventions will give us the implements to not only survive, but thrive.

# CHAPTER 5

# Work Slowdown

CLEARLY THE CONSUMER SOCIETY IS UNSUSTAINABLE. It is destroying people and the planet. But what propels its mad engine? The workplace — the source of more and more of our problems.

Several years ago, with fear and trepidation, I decided to leave the conventional workplace. I resigned my position as a community college administrator after a very painful, but increasingly common, experience. I've never once regretted it.

It started one day at lunch. I was eating at my desk (as too many people do), and the president of my college opened the door and walked in. He was a man I often felt embarrassed for. He was so false in his hearty gregariousness, always trying to be the "hail fellow well met." He didn't seem to notice how people drew back when he approached with that perpetually outstretched hand and unctuous, sycophantic look on his face. Above all else, my president wanted to get ahead, and as I was to discover that day in my office, I had done something to put him in disfavor with his boss.

"Did you say something negative about the new chancellor to a faculty member?" he asked.

"Yes, I did," I replied. I wasn't going to lie.

"Well, if you do it again, I will fire you."

I was stunned — but more indignant than wounded. "You can't do that," I replied, "This is a democracy! You can't fire me for saying something!"

I had been a community college administrator for many years — always with high evaluations. But the evaluations were irrelevant, really, because college administrators were never fired unless they'd done something really awful like embezzle funds or sexually harass a student. Even then, they were encouraged to leave, not threatened with being fired.

Moreover, I was hardly alone in criticizing the chancellor. Everyone did it. We saw the position as a form of make-work. Most community colleges are independent, having a president and reporting only to a state board for community colleges. But in Seattle there were three campuses reporting to a district office. The district administrators (often people that were "promoted" because they did nothing on their campuses) spent their time trying to make themselves look good by dreaming up projects that the "real" administrators on the campuses could do. And so, through the years, the individual campuses complained and whined about the district office, hoping it would go away. Usually, our particular ire was aimed at the top person, a position that seemed even more useless than the other administrators. The chancellor in office at the time of my story was particularly unpopular.

It's important to say that sometimes we had good chancellors who saw their role as being supporters of the campuses and creating visions of what the community college might be. And that was important. The community college movement was something I had always valued — it was a second chance for people who had not achieved in their high school education. Even if they had dropped out or done poorly, they could try again. The teachers and support staff were a dedicated and caring group. They saw themselves as making a difference in people's lives, not just grinding out graduates for the corporations. So having a leader who kept alive our original vision was important.

But this particular chancellor had a ruthless edge. The board that hired him probably thought he could raise money — something that seems to have become the chief criteria for hiring heads of educational institutions. He liked to brag about how he had suppressed student rebellions in the 1960s by calling in the police. He was out of place in a liberal community like Seattle.

He was also a hypocrite. He liked to refer to us as "one big family," but if anyone spoke up, they were punished. (Perhaps that was his vision of a family!) There was not a sincere bone in his body.

What had led my president to chastise me about criticizing the chancellor was something minor. I was the director of continuing education for the school — the arm of the school that created non-credit programs for the community. My policy for my classes was that if someone was disappointed with a class, they got a refund. But forgetting to come to a class did not merit a refund. After all, I paid the teachers out of the class tuitions.

A woman who had forgotten to attend her class came to our counter one day and demanded her money back. Of course the student worker politely told her what the policy was. She was furious. But, instead of demanding to see me, she had recently heard about a new chancellor being hired, so she decided to go straight to the top!

So a few days later, I received a call from the vice chancellor, saying that the new chancellor wanted me to give back the money. I at first argued that it was unfair to make exceptions, then provided the refund. But I grumbled about it to whoever would listen, including faculty members.

Tenured faculty were the only ones who could really speak freely to the chancellor. One of the leaders of the faculty, a man to whom I had recounted my story, decided to make a complaint to the chancellor, telling him that the faculty did not like how he had treated me.

The chancellor went ballistic! My president soon heard about it, and what a spineless little weasel he turned out to be. I heard through several of my friends that during one of the president's cabinet meetings he had announced that some administrator had criticized the chancellor, and he didn't want it to happen again. (Apparently each of them thought he was talking about them! As I said, we all criticized the chancellor.)

I tried to stick it out. First I demanded that my division chair arrange a sabbatical for me. If I didn't get the sabbatical, I threatened to take the whole incident to the local newspaper. After the sabbatical, though, I realized that the joy had gone out of my work. So I resigned. Now, many years later, I kind of wish I had gone to the paper. What I could see, though, was that my colleagues were very frightened that I would continue to make a fuss and that I would get all of them in trouble. We were all fairly close and worked well together, and so I didn't really want to put them under such stress.

In fact, they were already under too much stress. Over the years I had watched people become more and more reluctant to speak up over any injustice. At one meeting, the president asked if anyone had a topic to discuss. I raised my hand and asked him what we could do about the problem of overwork. Over the years, I explained, there had been more and more cutbacks in funding, yet we were all expected to do more projects. People were grumbling that they were expected to do more with fewer resources, and they were upset by the fact that those at the top kept thinking up new projects to impress the legislators and corporations. "Maybe we should be taking on fewer, rather than more, projects," I suggested.

I waited for others to raise their hands and join in the discussion. But there was only silence. Finally one other person spoke up. But everyone else, people who had complained bitterly to me about how much work they had, sat passively.

So I knew if I'd gone to the paper, I would have made others very uncomfortable. I assumed that most of them could not afford to quit and didn't want to risk their jobs. My husband and I had long lived below our means, so I knew that if I wanted to quit, I could. Actually, as I realized later, it was much more complicated than that. No matter what their financial situation, people tend to be threatened by the possibility of losing their job. Too much of their identity, security and self-image is bound up in their job.

Even I would never have dreamed of quitting my job had I not been involved in the voluntary simplicity movement. I had met lots of people who decided that they no longer wanted to work and had found ways to survive. And through my involvement in the simplicity movement, my life's goals had changed. Career success, in the conventional mode, didn't appeal to me much any more.

What allowed me to leave was my sense of calling, which superseded my workplace goals. I saw myself as an educator, not as an administrator, and I knew I could continue to devote myself to education even if I wasn't a wage earner at an institution. And what I've come to learn is that I could, indeed, be more of an educator working outside the system.

I see clearly, now, that the threat of losing their job was more than just a financial issue to my coworkers. It was a threat to their whole sense of identity and recognition in the community. Even I remember thinking as I was considering resigning, Who will I be? I won't be the director of anything! What will I put on my business card? What will I say when people ask me what I do?

And since then I've come to see more clearly the poverty and pain of our day-to-day work experience. People are constantly anxious — worried about getting all their work done, worried they will get laid off, worried they will be reprimanded by their boss. In the past few years, our work hours and work stress have been documented repeatedly. We work more hours than anyone in the industrialized world; America's work hours have continued to pile on in the last several years. More and more people have been laid off, and those left behind have sucked up extra workloads. As work speeds up, it becomes more cutthroat and nasty, with people talking behind others' backs and lying about and covering up their mistakes. Workers are forced to dissemble and kowtow, to pretend they like and respect their boss when they know he or she is a charlatan, to pretend their work is important when they know it isn't, pretend they have everything under control when it is in chaos. They leave work feeling soiled, that they have betrayed themselves.

All of this I have come to realize not just from my own experience, but from talking with others. I hardly know anyone who likes their work! They may like what their work could and should be, but they don't actually get to do it! Nurses and doctors don't have time to spend with their patients. Teachers must teach to the test. High-tech workers never know when their company will disappear. Lawyers represent companies, not real people — companies often acting illegally or irresponsibly. Professors face more and more pressure to publish something, no matter how inane and irrelevant.

*I hardly know anyone who likes their work! They may like what their work could and should be, but they don't actually get to do it!*

Recently there have been news stories about "successful" women — young women lawyers and MBAs from high-powered universities like Stanford and Harvard who have dropped out to raise their children instead of trying to do it all. It's indeed difficult to work and have children, but that's not the primary reason they're dropping out. It's because the workplace is just plain unpleasant. In moments of candor any of these women will admit it.

The workplace has become inimical to our well-being and happiness. But what we don't know, and what I didn't really know until I began to read and think about this subject more deeply, is the extent to which we have become "willing slaves," British writer Madeline Bunting's description. Somehow we have gradually acquiesced to the work ethic dominating our lives. Somehow we have come to feel that success in our careers is what's most important in life. And, on a deeper level, that "success" — which often is simply looking like an important person — is what matters most.

We all want to be somebody. We are terrified of being nobodies. And until we get over it, we won't be able to change things. One book that articulates this point extremely well is *A Spirituality of Resistance* by Roger Gottlieb. He compares our behavior in the workplace to what happened in Nazi Germany. Few of the Nazis set out to destroy the Jews. There were some fanatical Jew haters, of course, but so many just went along with their bosses. They took pride in doing a job well, even when it was running a concentration camp — at least they were doing something well, whether it was getting the trains to run on time or just making their bosses' lives easier. We must never forget the words that were over Auschwitz, Gottlieb notes: *Arbeit Macht Frei* — Work Makes One Free.

Gottlieb says that when work becomes too central to our lives, when we feel lost without it, we are likely to compromise when our jobs are threatened. We find ourselves going along with things we don't believe in. He describes the career of a young man in Germany in the 1930s — a young man whose father died young, who always tried to get his stepfather's approval, who went through various jobs and then got hired as a policeman. His stepfather seemed to approve. He began to rise in the ranks. He felt respectable and respected. But then in 1938, Germany took over Austria, the SS gained control of the Austrian police and the young man was assigned to a Nazi Euthanasia Institute to provide "order" in the killing of ill and retarded "patients." He did a good job and was given a promotion to the death camps. He ran first Sobibor and then Treblinka. Under his reign 8,000 Jews were slaughtered.

On trial later, he said he hated what was happening, but he couldn't leave. He had his place; he was making his mark. Some Nazi middle managers wrote about their pride in improving the efficiency of the gas chambers and accelerating the rate of extermination. Another bureaucrat in charge of Treblinka was proud of himself because he had not pilfered from the money and jewels confiscated from the Jews, as other bureaucrats did. The bureaucrat's son said of him that the black SS uniform made him feel like a "somebody."

And, says Gottleib, so it is for us in the environmental crisis: "Our drive to have the kind of work that makes us feel important is very dangerous." He compares our experiences to the Holocaust because it is the "signal event of our time. Like a signpost in the gloom, it can help us find our way toward the light; but only if we read it with the greatest of care."

The Nazi analogy is abused and overdone in today's contentious world. But Gottlieb's insights justify his invocation. He asks us:

When our communities face pesticide-spraying airplanes, dioxin-spewing industrial chimneys, chemical food contaminants, and leaking landfills, do we remember the Zyklon B flowing in the gas chambers? .... When we listen to our children cough, and wonder why so many have asthma, and continue a way of life that creates the air pollution that weakens their lungs, do we remember how well-meaning, passive bystanders helped make the Holocaust possible? .... When we hear of some corporation lying to the public to protect some toxic chemical, or paying off a legislator to get some environmental regulations weakened, do we remember how the Nazi elite got rich off Jewish slave labor?

And the crimes of the corporations keep on coming — Merck manufacturing Vioxx, Bayer's toxic anti-cholesterol drug, Halliburton, Enron, Tyco, Merrill Lynch — to say nothing of companies not committing "crimes" per se but continuing to devastate the environment. Wal-Mart pays people poverty-level wages and then puts such pressure on individual store managers that they sneak in and reduce workers' timesheets.

There are decent people working for these places who feel they have no other choice but to go on with their jobs.

The fault is our pursuit of status. Gottlieb says that we all grow up wanting to be a "somebody," believing the only way we can do it is to succeed in our work. We're not given any alternatives. And now we've transferred our desperation to our children, pressuring them more and more along a Harvard-aimed fast track to success (to the point of competing to get them into the best Manhattan kindergarten).

Even as we're pressured to be somebody, we're given fewer and fewer options to do so. Fewer people want to go into public life. Artists don't feel they can survive at all. More and more rank and file are beaten down by corporations, heartless places that compound people's need to be recognized. We've moved away from the community experience that a village or even neighborhood can provide, and at the same time have failed to find ways to build community in our lives outside of work. We see the homeless and may think, There but for the grace of God .... But the most secure among us still feel the chill of a society that will allow people to lie alone and abandoned on a city street.

And so we work to bury any feeling of being betrayed by our culture and link our identities to our job. So many forces conspire in the same direction. For instance, I became a feminist in the early days, even before *Ms.* magazine published its first edition, and I worked as the head of a women's center for many years. Yet I think feminism did a disservice to our society when it became a movement dedicated to breaking the glass ceiling, manipulating women into putting their whole identities into empty careerism — careerism without conscience or caring.

Further, as we have acquiesced to the notion that to be patriotic means to consume (get out to the malls, as George W. Bush exhorted Americans after 9/11), we have reached a point where our savings rate hovers at zero. Many people indeed have no financial choice about obeying in the workplace. So where does that put us? We are indentured servants, compliant serfs. We can't speak up at work lest we lose our jobs.

Gottlieb feels we're driven by a fear of failure, a fear of being average, of being a nobody. We have no real sense of self outside of work. And so we identify with dominant — and destructive — institutions in order to feel that we are significant, that we matter, that we belong somewhere. Gottlieb compares us to Adolf Eichmann, who said that the highest goal of his life was to serve his superiors. This satisfied his desire to prove himself, no matter how he did it. It was more than just following orders — it was an effort to get recognition from one's work. Following authorities made Germans feel like good workers and gave them a sense of importance and validation. Yes, some followed orders for fear of getting shot or jailed, but historians have found also that some did refuse to cooperate and were not seriously punished. "Membership in the dominant institutions gave meaning, value, and a sense of personal security to people who had no other sources of purpose or importance in their lives," Gottlieb writes.

One reason we have become willing slaves is that we give people so few alternatives for developing a sense of self. Gottlieb writes:

We face ruptured communities, urbanization, impersonal mass
media that replace traditional culture, geographical mobility,
the decline of religion, and the spread of a frantic commodification that puts everything up for sale. In such a society, we
cannot take for granted that we belong, that we have a place.
Selfhood, at once so needed and so without constraints, cannot be assumed. Rather, it must be achieved .... Work
becomes like a second home, our profession like a lover, our
institutional setting like the little village we never had.

People want to be recognized for their real selves. It's a core
human need. It is one of the reasons a gay person will come out, even
though it may mean severe consequences. We want to be seen for
who we are. Without that, we can never be sure others really care for
us. They may only care for the image we present, and not for the real
person. Yes, when we express our true selves, we may lose some status. But we know that there will be somebody who cares for us —
and it will be honest, true caring.

One way to fight the workplace's suasion is to give people
opportunities to feel cared for outside of the office. People must have
a variety of involvements that contribute to their well-being, particularly to their sense of identity and sense of worth. That's one big
reason why we must reduce our workloads. When we put in such
long hours, we can't become involved in anything else. We can't pursue our college passion for writing poetry or painting. We can't throw
ourselves into playing tennis. We can't get to know our neighbors.
We can't develop a rich inner life. All we have is our work. When we
have kids, we try to maintain some balance. But if we don't have kids,
or they've grown up, we find no reason except work to exist. And
then, if something happens at work, our whole identity and sense of
worth is destroyed. We have nothing else to fall back on.

We become willing slaves. We cannot feel truly free, no matter how much *Arbeit Macht Frei.*

Ultimately we must change the workplace, but we won't be
able to do that until we are not bound to it both economically and

psychologically. People who are happy at their work feel challenged but in control. They have bosses who express appreciation, and they enjoy their coworkers. They find meaning in what they do. Yet Gallup found in 2004 that only 29 percent feel *engaged* — the word Gallup uses for happiness — in their work. More than half, 55 percent, were not engaged, and 16 percent were actively disengaged. Most people still assume that job satisfaction is tied to pay or benefits. But beyond a certain point it becomes measured in positive relationships with coworkers and a supportive boss.

Central to workplace change is shorter hours. John de Graaf, founder of the Take Back Your Time Movement, points out that Americans are working 20 percent longer today than in 1970 while work-time has declined in other industrial countries. The Center for a New American Dream found 93 percent of Americans agreeing that people are "too focused on working and making money and not enough on family and community." Half said that having more time with friends and family would make them more satisfied with their lives. Our vacations are disappearing — a recent Harris survey found that 37 percent of women earning less than $40,000 a year (and 28 percent of all working women) receive no paid vacation at all. On average, Americans work nearly nine weeks (350 hours) more each year than western Europeans.

And America seems to stand alone in the world: A Harvard School of Public Health study of 168 nations shows that "the United States lags dramatically behind all high-income countries, as well as many middle- and low-income countries, when it comes to public policies designed to guarantee adequate working conditions for families." According to the study,

- 163 of 168 countries guarantee paid leave for mothers in connection with childbirth. 45 countries offer such leave to fathers. The US does neither.

- 139 countries guarantee paid sick leave. The US does not.

- 96 countries guarantee paid annual (vacation) leave. The US does not.

- 84 countries have laws that fix a maximum limit on the workweek. The US does not.
- 37 countries guarantee parents paid time off when children are sick. The US does not.

A study by the National Association of Working Women shows what happens to workers without paid sick days. They often lose their jobs when they have to stay home with a sick or injured child. Half of all American workers and three in four low-wage workers have no paid sick leave; only one in six part-timers has any paid sick leave.

But those are just raw statistics. In his book *American Mania*, Peter Whybrow brings the data alive through the story of a young woman who was at the top of her game — a corporate lawyer. She prided herself on being able to handle anything, but during one tough stretch flying between California and Paris on a weekly basis she found herself in the hospital. It was cold, dark and dank in Paris, and on the way home from a meeting she came down with stomach pains bad enough to send her to the hospital. They checked her over and found nothing wrong except nervous exhaustion. So the hospital sent her home. But it wasn't over for the young woman. She found herself waking at night with her heart pounding, and she began to experience night terrors, feeling that she couldn't breathe and that she was going to die. She was having panic attacks.

Whybrow related the young woman's story to one of his colleagues at UCLA, a Dr. Bystritsky, professor of psychiatry and an expert on panic attacks. Bystritsky estimates that today 33 percent of the population suffers anxiety disorders, up from 19 percent 10 years ago. He says attacks are increasing in the US because of time pressures, sleep deprivation and extreme competitiveness. The young woman's work life bore this out — it involved vicious rivalry, greed, lack of loyalty and a treadmill kind of existence. Relationships were superficial. But she liked the money, the excitement and the status.

According to Whybrow,

> In America's demand-based and time-driven commercial world, competition is replacing collaboration and social concern .... It is a shift that offers significant commercial advantage, as is apparent in America's global dominance. But it also has the drawback of fostering personal greed ... and of generating stress and anxiety by eroding the bonds of mutual support and social sentiment ... that are essential to human happiness.

What I found particularly interesting was that the young woman said she began to feel she was a fake. Not a fake lawyer but a fake person. I found her comment compelling because it's something I've heard from women over the years. And it's not just a case of modesty, but a real feeling that one has abandoned one's real self. It's a theme I found echoed in Douglas Labier's *Modern Madness: The Hidden Link Between Work and Emotional Conflict*. Labier is a psychologist who deals with what he calls the "working wounded." They are people who are suffering from the same symptoms as the young woman above. They are hard-pushing, ambitious, successful people in the eyes of the world. Yet they feel depressed, despairing, anxious, and joyless. They speak of feeling empty and detached; they lack passion and are out of control. They often have dreams in which they're trapped in a plane or train, where they're terrified of a crash. Labier argues that the hard-driving competitive atmosphere described by Whybrow forces people to develop certain personality traits and to abandon others. Certainly gentleness, compassion and a sharp sense of the absurd are not highly valued traits in the corporate boardrooms. To succeed in such settings, people need to develop a shell, to harden their hearts, to learn self-promotion and the fine art of undermining others. The result is often a feeling of self-loathing that Labier calls "self-betrayal." People feel that they are forced to pretend to be someone they're not; they're forced to posture, to abandon any ideals they may have had. They're forced into the position of "I'll get mine no matter what I have to do."

It's interesting thinking over my career. The aspersions I've faced have been along the lines of bleeding-heart liberal and do-gooder.

Certainly I was always viewed with suspicion as being too radical. And I was working at a supposedly progressive community college in one of the nation's most liberal cities! I remember a conversation at lunch one time in which the college president and district chancellor were discussing how the faculty needed to learn to dress better!

We've talked about how research shows that after a certain point work is not about more money — it's about a sense of meaning, good relationships with coworkers, a supportive boss. But at the core of our economic system lies the belief that profits justify any behavior. And so we have corruption, destruction of the environment, increasingly low pay (with incredibly high salaries at the top). The prevailing wisdom is that the vision is set at the top. Yet as I write, we have George W. Bush masquerading as our president, ruling an inept, corrupt government, exemplified by his appointment for the Federal Emergency Management Agency — heckuva job, Brownie — and the ruination of New Orleans after Hurricane Katrina. News reports continue to document how administrative posts responsible for vital, internationally sensitive matters such as pandemics and bioterrorism are filled by political hacks, sycophants and cronies who have no expertise or experience. Morale for government employees must be at an incredible low. The leadership "vision" for most major corporations consists of cutbacks and layoffs while CEOs make millions.

Thinking over these issues takes me back to my first year out of college when I taught high school English for a year. I remember when the class read Melville's *Bartleby the Scrivener: A Story of Wall Street*. What a strange, stirring short story. The class was fascinated, and we had long discussions about how Bartleby was treated and what would have happened in modern America.

Bartleby was a "law-copyist" who worked for a lawyer. He was honest and steadfast and the lawyer trusted him totally. One day the lawyer asked Bartleby to help him check something, and Bartleby replied, "I would prefer not to." He began to repeat "I would prefer not to" whenever he was requested to do something, even as he continued his copying.

Finally, Bartleby decided not to do any work at all, declaring once again, "I would prefer not to." The lawyer couldn't figure out how to deal with the situation. He felt sympathy and compassion for Bartleby, but how could he accept an employee not doing anything? He finally decided to put up with Bartleby — that it was just his fate to have Bartleby always with him (literally so, since Bartleby never really left the premises). As a reader you feel glad for Bartleby.

But then Bartleby's presence began to embarrass the lawyer, and he worried about losing clients. So he decided that the only thing to do was to himself leave — to move out of his quarters and find another office. He told Bartleby he must go, but of course Bartleby would not leave. The lawyer moved everything, leaving Bartleby standing alone. Someone else rented the space, and after a lot of confrontations called the police. Bartleby was taken to the Tombs, the prison.

The lawyer heard about Bartleby and went to visit. Bartleby was very upset with him.

"I know you," he said, without looking round, "and I want nothing to say to you." A few days passed and the lawyer returned to the prison. He found Bartleby in a yard all alone, curled up and lying on the ground, his eyes open. He was dead.

But that's not the end. Melville adds on a curious fact. He says that the lawyer continued to inquire about Bartleby and heard a rumor that Bartleby had worked for the postal system — in the dead letter office. Melville concludes with the words: "Ah Bartleby! Ah humanity!"

Now, I cannot remember what I learned about this short story in my college English class. I'm sure there are many complex inter-pretations. But what strikes me is that there seems to be no good answer to how to treat Bartleby. Certainly no one today would have been so patient with him. He would have been fired and removed within a couple of days after refusing to do what his employer wanted him to do. He would be one of the homeless we see lying on the streets. We all think that, of course, Bartleby was being unreasonable. We can't say in our workplace, "I would prefer not to."

Yet we also feel very sympathetic toward Bartleby and sense that he really does have a right to say no. What was Melville saying? The story was published in 1853 when slavery was a contentious issue of the day. Was Melville seeing the worker's position as one of slavery? This was also the beginning of the Industrial Revolution where people moved from country farms to city factories. Was Melville looking into the future to see that the only possible conclusion from this situation was that people would become "willing slaves?"

*We may technically have freedom of speech, but who dares use it? We ostensibly have freedom of the press, but does it really exist in an age when major television networks and newspapers are owned by just three giant corporations?*

Was Melville saying that having employers and employees just will never work, even if the employer is a well-intentioned person? Was Melville saying that when you are an employee, you lose your freedom and that there is just no way things will work out right under true capitalism?

And the dead letter office! What does that mean? Dead letters are those that have never reached their destination. It is a vision of a breakdown of connection between people. The letters might have contained a "pardon for those who died despairing; hope for those who died unhoping; good tidings for those who died stifled by unrelieved calamities." People reaching out to others but failing to connect with them. Was this the vision that Melville saw in the new work-centric society?

It sounds strange to say, but as I sit here what comes to my mind is the devastation of Katrina — the help that never reached these people. People who were left to die because in our selfish country the people who rule care only for profit and power. One can imagine a lot of dead letters in New Orleans.

I think Melville was saying that our system is flawed, and our country ultimately would not make it. That the workplace just wouldn't work. When our country began, we had not yet started down the path of cold, cruel capitalism. But we are here to witness what Melville suspected.

The outspoken attorney Gerry Spence calls us the "new American slaves" in his book, *Give Me Liberty*. We may technically have freedom of speech, but who dares use it? We ostensibly have freedom of the press, but does it really exist in an age when major television networks and newspapers are owned by just three giant corporations? We may believe we have freedom of religion, but does it matter if church is boring and irrelevant to so many?

Given any real choice over accepting ersatz ideals and fake freedoms, we would prefer not to. But with the prospect of winding up like Bartleby, we do anyway.

# CHAPTER 6

# The Subversiveness of Joie de Vivre

*Yes, we're bored .... we're all bored now. But did it ever occur to you, Wally, that the process that creates this boredom we all see now may very well be the result of a self-perpetuating, unconscious form of brainwashing created by a worldwide totalitarian government based on money, and that all of this is much more dangerous than one thinks, and that it's not just a question of individual survival, but that someone who's bored is asleep, and somebody who's asleep will not say no? ...*

    *I think New York is the model for the new concentration camp, where the camp has been built by the inmates themselves, and the inmates are the guards, and so they exist in a state of schizophrenia where they are both guards and prisoners, and as a result they no longer have the capacity to leave the prison they've made or even see it as a prison.*

    — André Gregory in *My Dinner with André* (by Wally Shawn)

    *We teach children how to measure, how to weigh. We fail to teach them how to revere, how to sense wonder and awe. The sense of the sublime, the sign of the inward greatness of the human soul and something which is potentially given to all men, is now a rare gift.*

    — Abraham Joshua Heschel

*Anything worth doing is worth doing poorly.*

— G.K. Chesterton

*All the earth is gay;*
*Land and sea*
*Give themselves up to jollity,*

*In a thousand valleys far and wide,*
*Fresh flowers; while the sun shines warm,*
*    And the Babe leaps up on his Mother's arm:—*
*    I hear, I hear, with joy I hear!*
*Whither is fled the visionary gleam?*
*Where is it now; the glory and the dream?*

— Wordsworth, "Intimations of Immortality"

ONE COOL, CLEAR NIGHT a few years ago my husband and I set our alarm for 2 a.m. and drove across the Golden Gate Bridge into the hills above the San Francisco Bay. We drove farther and farther into the darkness until the lights of the city were just a faint gleam and we'd reached a promontory overlooking the ocean. Keeping our flashlights low, we walked through the dark to a meadow where we spread out our sleeping bag, lay down on our backs, and for two hours watched the shooting stars of a meteor shower not expected again till the year 2099. All around us people were stretched out — we couldn't see them, but we could hear them quietly talking and laughing. When one particularly bright meteor would zoom across the sky, leaving a brilliant trail of cosmic dust, we would all gasp together. When it was over and we drove back across the bridge, I felt an incredible sense of excitement and aliveness.

The next morning, I felt clearly that I needed more of this! I needed more excitement and aliveness! I wanted my life to be more like that night of shooting stars. But at the same time, Wordsworth's words came to me, "Whither is fled the visionary gleam? Where is it now; the glory and the dream?" I knew that my life could be deeper and more transcendent. In so many ways it seemed diminished and trivialized — from spending time deleting emails to waiting in line to return a defective phone; from reading the manual for a new piece of software to trying to solve a case of identity theft. (Identity theft! How can someone steal your identity! Is who you are a sum of your credit cards and bank statements?)

Most of us feel this way. Our lives could be so much more than they are. Robert Lane expresses it in the title of his book, *The Loss of Happiness in Market Democracies*. I know we can't have a perpetual feeling of ecstasy, but joy should be the undercurrent of our lives. Why isn't more of my life filled with awe and wonder? So many negative things are going on, starting with shame over the United States as a force for destruction in the world. It's hard to find the excitement and expansiveness of that night of shooting stars.

Sometimes I worry I'm like the man in Thomas Cahill's *How the Irish Saved Civilization*. Cahill describes a man who lived in the final years of Roman Empire. He was a very successful man — a high government official, wealthy, connected to important people, known for his poetry. But in truth, he was a dull, sterile, bland, shallow person. His poetry was trite and conventional, revealing a stunted inner life. How could he be anything else in the debauchery and dissipation of the declining years of the Roman Empire?

My first thought, of course, was, Is this what we've all become? Have we all become sterile and shallow as a result of being surrounded by so much lifelessness? Is it possible to live with excitement and joy in a United States that is plundering the world in its lust for profit and control? Is this what the best and the brightest of us has become? Are we all just shadows of what we could be? And the distressing thing is that I doubt if that man ever really grasped how sterile his life was. If bland and conventional is all you've ever known, how could you realize that you were missing something! But maybe he was like Ivan Illich in Tolstoy's short story — the man who lies dying and hears what others really think of him — discovering that people felt little affection and no respect. (And miraculously has a last-minute transformation as he dies. Perhaps there's hope.)

I don't want a bland, sterile life, even if I'm "successful" by society's standards. (And I have come to believe that if we are successful, we're more prone to being bland and sterile.) What do I want? There's a movie that sums it up the best — *Zorba the Greek*. We're the character Alan Bates plays — the repressed, clueless young man. Hopefully we'll all get to turn to someone like Zorba and say, "Teach me to dance." I want the equivalent of that afternoon after everything collapses — dancing above the sunny Aegean Sea. (I want the balalaika music as well!) I want to experience more often the sense of aliveness and exuberance that I have felt periodically but never often enough throughout my life.

※

*I know there are so many problems, but we can't give up our joyfulness. We can redeem our experiences from their sterility and blandness!*

Talking about this, though, is difficult. There are so many silly books that advocate a shallow cheeriness and don't address, or even recognize, all the problems in the world. In a way it's hard to feel that we, as privileged Americans, have any right to happiness when we're at the source of so many of the problems that threaten the world. How can we focus on crises and at the same time feel joyful? Do we need a split-screen in our minds, keeping open both sides at all times, experiencing simultaneously the suffering and the joy?

Many of us on the Left realize the enormity of the challenges we face, and I think we may have given up on feeling joyful. We continually obsess on what's wrong. But are we defeating our chance to really change things if we're so negative? Because joy is an experience of energy, and without energy, maybe we can't change things. We have to have both concern and exuberance.

For instance, every Tuesday morning since before the Iraq War, our local peace and justice group has had an anti-war vigil. I don't go every time, in part because at first the people were so unresponsive. Just getting them to smile or laugh was a chore, and I'd think, "Who will ever want to join us if we're so unfriendly!" But after all this time, people have gotten to know each other, and they laugh and talk more. It makes such a difference. People are so much more likely to come back! I know there are so many problems, but we can't give up our joyfulness. We can redeem our experiences from their sterility and blandness!

And so, I keep searching for ideas or experiences that will give me those feelings of joy. I found something recently that expressed it well for me. Evelyn Underhill, known for her book *Practical Mysticism*, published in 1915, has a parable "Eyes and No Eyes" about two people who experience life differently:

> 'No-Eyes' has fixed his attention on the fact that he is obliged to take a walk. For him the chief factor of existence is his own movement along the road; a movement which he intends to accomplish as efficiently and comfortably as he can. He asks not to know what may be on either side of the hedges. He ignores the caress of the wind until it threatens to remove his hat. He trudges along, steadily, diligently; avoiding the muddy pools, but oblivious of the light which they reflect. 'Eyes' takes the walk too: and for him it is a perpetual revelation of beauty and wonder. The sunlight inebriates him, the winds delight him, the very effort of the journey is a joy. Magic presences throng the roadside, or cry salutations to him from the hidden fields. The rich world through which he moves lies in the foreground of his consciousness; and it gives up new secrets to him at every step. 'No-Eyes,' when told of his adventures, usually refuses to believe that both have gone by the same road. He fancies that his companion has been floating about in the air, or beset by agreeable hallucinations. We shall never persuade him to the contrary unless we persuade him to look for himself.

Now, it's easy to see that Eyes is more fully alive. And it seems easy to answer the question as to which one will value his life more; which one will fight harder to preserve his life. But how many of us are trying to live like Eyes?

Of course, Underhill's sentiment has been expressed by so many artists! There is one in particular who has been with me for most of my life, and his vision of the good life has always guided me. I discovered him when I was 16, sitting in Miss Newell's English class. It was there I experienced the words that have kept me alive,

have kept me (I hope) from becoming No Eyes. Henry David
Thoreau writes:

> I went to the woods because I wished to live deliberately; to
> front only the essential facts of life and see if I could not learn
> what it had to teach, and not, when I came to die, discover
> that I had not lived ....

Those are the words that have stayed with me over the years
— and not when I came to die, discover that I had not lived. And so
my question has always been, what do I do so that when I die, I will
feel I have lived life to its full? What do I do so that I can experience
life the way 'Eyes' experienced life? How do I avoid becoming that
Roman citizen who is bland and trite and doesn't even know it?

One phrase captures what I'm looking for: joie de vivre, French
for "joy of living." For my generation it was a common phrase
through the 1960s and 1970s, then it kind of fell from the lexicon.
As I've talked to people about my book, I've been surprised how
many people haven't heard of the term. Could this mean that the
actual concept of joy is disappearing? If we have no words for something, can we feel it? As we've seen, the evidence about happiness
indicates that we no longer feel joyful very often.

At the core of joie de vivre are enthusiasm, exuberance, excitement, energy, and spontaneity. I doubt that there are many people
who don't want more joie — how could they not? — but they don't
act like they want it. They don't do things that bring joy. It's as if
they've been hypnotized by some evil genie (Wall Street, maybe?)
who tells them that what they want is money and fame and stuff.

Money (after a certain point) doesn't bring us happiness.
Community does.

One might respond, "I'm with people all day, and it's not much
fun! I can hardly wait to escape at the end of the day." True, the consumer society does that to us. At night we just want to go off by
ourselves! It's because we're not enjoying each other at work — we're
not laughing and relaxing. Why? For one thing, as I outlined, the
workplace has become a cutthroat place. Additionally, even though

psychology research shows that people who are materialistic are less happy, we don't have a belief system that challenges materialism.

At one time religious life challenged materialism, and for some it still does. But religion has been co-opted by the fundamentalist Right, who have become guardians of a selfish status quo. Born-again Christians keep the right wing in power — a sect that is showing itself not only to be dishonest and corrupt in its thirst for money and power, but also cold and uncaring to people around the world. It has ruined Christianity for me, and that's such a shame, because the real Jesus was nothing like this gang of mercenaries. And so I've continued to look for a belief system that challenges our consumer society. A belief system that embraces and embodies Thoreau's incredible words, "Surely joy is the condition of life."

Not many years ago I attended a workshop and discovered a belief system that has, for me, come to be the foundation of a new view of life rejecting consumer society. Brian Swimme and Thomas Berry, a mathematician and an eco-theologian, are authors of a profound work, *The Universe Story: From the Primordial Flaring Forth to the Ecozoic Era — A Celebration of the Unfolding of the Cosmos*, published by HarperCollins San Francisco in 1992. For me, it lays the groundwork for what I think of as the *metaphysics of joy*.

## A metaphysics of joie de vivre

It's a creation story that makes sense to me — one that neither rejects science nor abandons humanity's enduring wisdom. As Berry and Swimme describe it, scientists can now measure radiation from the birth of our universe 15 billion years ago — commonly called the big bang. (Who picked such a silly name for this significant event? Berry and Swimme call it the Flaring Forth!)

I had studied this concept in high school — I remember my physics teacher, Mr. Teal, assigning a book on the big bang theory. So Berry and Swimme's basic facts weren't new to me. What *was* new to me was the vision of the role of human beings. Swimme and Berry say that we are expressions of that first Flaring Forth! We are all expressions of that first fiery explosion! And of course, how could we not be?

Somehow, without really thinking about it, my feeling was that human beings were somehow outside of the universe, independent of it. But we did not come from someplace else. We are part of the ongoing evolution of the universe that began with that first momentous explosion, we as well as the animals and plants that surround us! As Swimme puts it, "Thirteen billion years ago, the universe began as hydrogen. Left entirely to itself, the hydrogen became rosebushes, giraffes and humans."

Berry and Swimme go on to suggest that human beings' lives are not only an expression of the flaring forth, they are part of its evolution. We're not nothing. What we do matters! We're integral! Our human consciousness is part of the evolution of the universe. Of course! This makes so much sense to me. It is a scientific, yet also a significant metaphysical, concept. When you think of that force of energy, you can use the word "universe" or the word "God" to mean the same. It's easy to think of God as energy being expressed in the form of nature, art, science, and humanity. But labels are always limiting; so because "God" is so often taken to mean an old man sitting on a throne in a place called heaven, I rarely use the term. Instead I search for words like "universal force" or "cosmic energy" that everyone can understand — whether traditionally religious or not.

What this theory says to me is summarized in this paragraph:

> Awareness of an all-pervading mysterious energy articulated in the infinite variety of natural phenomena seems to be the primordial experience of human consciousness, awakening to an awesome universe filled with mysterious power. Not only is energy our primary experience; energy, and its multiple modes of expression, is also the primary concern of modern physics, its ultimate term of reference in describing the most fundamental reality of the universe.

So this seems to be what I'm seeking: to be in touch with this "all-pervading mysterious energy" at the core of our lives. It is something that I experience as joyful energy. Joie de vivre is, for me, a way of experiencing that energy — an energy that seems to have diminished for most of us in recent years.

I find echoes of this idea in others' work. Psychologist
Csikszentmihalyi says:

> Whether we like it or not, our lives will leave a mark on the
> universe. Each person's birth makes ripples that expand in
> the social environment: parents, siblings, relatives and friends
> are affected by it, as we grow up our actions leave a myriad of
> consequences, some intended, most not .... One cannot lead
> a life that is truly excellent without feeling that one belongs
> to something greater and more permanent than oneself.

We feel this energy the most through connection with all of
life. Csikszentmihalyi shows how science supports the sense of a
connected life:

> We are discovering how all forms of life depend on each
> other and on the environment. How precisely each action
> produces an equal reaction .... We learn that the conse-
> quences of actions may not be immediately visible, but may
> have effects in distant connections, because everything that
> exists is part of an interconnected system. Much of this has
> been already said, in one way or another, in the religions of
> the Plains Indian tribes, the Buddhists, the Zoroastrians, and
> innumerable other beliefs based on a careful observation of
> life. What contemporary science adds is a systematic expres-
> sion of these facts in a language that has authority in our
> times .... Those who identify with evolution blend their con-
> sciousness with it, like a tiny creek joining an immense river,
> whose currents become as one .... Hell in this scenario is sim-
> ply the separation of the individual from the flow of life.

Erich Fromm put it another way in his 1955 book, *The Sane
Society*: "The aim of life is the unfolding of man's creative powers."
This is what we're participating in when we see that we are part of
the unfolding of the universe.

## Psychic numbing

Yet we're not feeling this grand source of energy! We're not participating in this connected universe. We are experiencing a "psychic
numbing," a phrase coined by the psychiatrist Robert Lifton. Psychic
numbing is the human loathing of the atomic bombs we dropped in
Japan, and later our cultural response to the concept of a nuclear
holocaust. The threat is so massive that we can only respond by shutting
down. Thomas Berry calls it *spiritual autism*. I find it significant that
this term was born in response to our bombing Japan, because in so
many ways that was the moment we sacrificed our American idealism.
Our president in the '50s, Dwight Eisenhower, warned us to beware
the "military-industrialist" complex — a warning we failed to heed.

Certainly psychic numbing describes how we feel much of the
time. I think of it every time I see people walk by a poor person selling the Seattle street paper, *Real Change*. I
simply cannot understand how people can
ignore someone who is poor and probably
homeless when the paper costs a mere dollar!
And they are probably on their way to the mall
to buy something costing a hundred times that.
How can they walk on by! (I inadvertently first
wrote "walk on buy," an appropriate Freudian
slip.) If they thought about it, people might
realize that too often their trip to the mall is an
act of psychic numbing, an attempt to stifle the
feelings of guilt they experience because they
have passed by that homeless man. Give the
man a dollar and they might open their heart a
little! In fact, I think as Americans our psychic
numbing is a result of the fact that we do indeed
feel guilty because we *know* we have so much more than the rest of
the world. We *know* we're damaging the planet for our own gratification. How could we not be profoundly depressed over the state of
our soul? Lifton says that the numbing can protect us from going
mad when the grief and the threat to our sanity are too great. But

*I think as Americans our psychic numbing is a result of the fact that we do indeed feel guilty because we know we have so much more than the rest of the world. We know we're damaging the planet for our own gratification.*

there are side effects: Our overall ability to feel also shuts down —
including the ability to feel joy.

I'm not saying anything original. Lifton's idea has long been
an accepted psychological premise. But I haven't heard people talking about it lately. It's as if we've forgotten the threat of "psychic
numbing," that we have accepted our state of deadness, that we don't
care. We're not fighting back any more. Our silly and shallow actions
— like watching inane reality TV shows or playing endless video
games or spending time wandering the malls — are pathetic efforts
to feel alive. But of course it's a counterfeit aliveness, and it doesn't
even come close to Underhill's Eyes.

I have a quotation from Albert Schweitzer that I often use in
my presentations. The room always goes suddenly silent:

> You know of the disease in Central Africa called sleeping
> sickness .... There also exists a sleeping sickness of the soul.
> Its most dangerous aspect is that one is unaware of its com-
> ing. That is why you have to be careful. As soon as you notice
> the slightest sign of indifference, the moment you become
> aware of the loss of a certain seriousness, of longing, of
> enthusiasm and zest, take it as a warning.

Perhaps some might think I've veered off into la-la land, quot-
ing an aging Catholic priest (Berry) and a mathematician who
describes himself as a cosmologist (Swimme). But we each need to
answer certain questions for ourselves about our origins and our purpose in life. We need to answer those timeless questions, Who am I?
Why do we exist? And I can accept the ideas of Berry and Swimme
because they reject neither science nor humanity's timeless wisdom.
Haven't all of us experienced this transcendent energy at least some
time in our lives? It's experienced in so many ways — through nature,
community, the arts. In fact, even thinking of the original "flaring"
brings me some of the excitement I felt that night above the San
Francisco Bay, watching the shooting stars. The image of shooting
stars is such a wonderful metaphor for the emotional state we all are
looking for: an intense energy bursting forth from us. Maybe this is

why we love having fireworks at celebrations — it brings back that
original, first flaring forth of energy.

## Exuberance

*Nothing great was ever achieved without enthusiasm. The way of life is
wonderful; it is by abandonment.*                          — Ralph Waldo Emerson

The word that best captures the concept I'm talking about is
the word "exuberance," and I was excited to discover a book,
*Exuberance: The Passion for Life*, by Kay Redfield Jamison, professor
of psychiatry at the Johns Hopkins University School of Medicine
and a MacArthur Fellow. Exuberance is a human trait, one that
Jamison found to be absolutely essential for humankind. Exuberance
motivates people to take risks, to seek adventure, to try new things.
Exuberant leaders inspire and excite people to get involved.

What is it? Even the definition inspires: Exuberance is a
human emotion supremely expressive of joy. It's an ebullient, effer-
vescent emotion that is unrestrained and irrepressible. Pasteur said
that the Greeks gave us one of the most wonderful words — enthusiasm, from *en theos*, "a god within": "Happy is he who bears a god
within, and who obeys it." Exuberance is an irrepressible life force,
the emotion that comes to us when we stretch out on a clear night to
watch the shooting stars or when we think about the original flaring
forth of the universe.

"A passion for life is life's ultimate affirmation," says Jamison
as she ends her book. She shows that exuberance — enthusiasm, joy
and energy — has been key to the evolution of our species and, in
particular, the development of the United States. Her ending is bit-
tersweet, as she recounts the 9/11 tragedy and seems to wonder if
we'll be able to recover the exuberance that was once integral to the
American character: "To lose our joy is to lose our ability to fight
back and advance."

The core of the American character *does* seem to be optimism
and enthusiasm. Asked about their favorite emotion, Americans are
far more likely than other nationalities to cite enthusiasm. The same

holds true for optimism. One poll found that 65 percent of Americans, more than respondents from other countries, were likely to disagree with the statement, "Success in life is pretty much determined by forces outside our control." Albert Einstein said that America is more capable of enthusiasm than any other country.

Jamison asks:

> What happens, though, when the wine of the gods disappears, or if nothing matters enough to stake one's life and dreams on? What happens when enthusiasts become jaded? A passion for life is essential to the renewal of life. If passion is lost, the future itself is diminished.

The United States has become a negative force in the world. One statistic stands out: The US comprises only 4 percent of the population but uses 25 percent of the world's resources, contributing 25 percent of greenhouse gases to global warming. We can invade and occupy any country and do what we want, leaving death and destruction behind. We're made for money.

Yet we started out with such good intentions. We've done good things. We're confirming the old adage that power corrupts. Can anything save us? Jamison does a wonderful job showing how important enthusiasm is to our national character, but what does it really mean in our own lives? Exuberance combines the extremes of two continuums — pleasantness and vitality. Most of us exist somewhere in between. Exuberance is high pleasantness and high energy, and it seems to push people to move forward and explore and change — both now and through our long evolutionary history.

One pertinent point to bear in mind — much of our emotional identity is genetic. Many of us have taken the Myers Briggs personality inventory to find out if we're extroverts or introverts and discovered that these traits seem to be hard-wired. They're just part of our nature.

But it's not all genetics. We can learn to think, feel and act differently. Research on identical twins has found that their genetic structure accounts for only half of their personalities. So that means we have 50 percent wiggle room. And it's a significant 50 percent, because as Jamison says, "The energy, enthusiasm, and optimism of those who are exuberant tend to make them more socially outgoing, as well, and more likely to take risks." Joy fortifies ties between people.

So maybe one of the most important things we can do is help people experience this emotion of exuberance. This is an anchoring theme of this book, and of the Slow Life. We must first recognize that exuberance is an essential emotion we need to reclaim — both for our personal happiness and for the future of the US, which really means the future of the world. And then we must find ways to help people experience it. First, we must acknowledge that our native exuberance has become more like Whybrow's mania — a feverish vortex of consumer-fueled hyperkineticism, and that we're now in the downward cycle of depression and destruction. Only by getting involved in social change can we experience the emotion of exuberance, because it's not something that visits the bland and the sterile. It comes to us when we find a way to stand up against the forces of power and profit, and do it in a life-affirming way. Get involved in social change, but do it in a way that sparks celebration, caring, and joy: joie de vivre.

*Maybe one of the most important things we can do is help people experience this emotion of exuberance. This is an anchoring theme of this book, and of the Slow Life.*

## Choice

There are many belief systems, but in a way they boil down to just a few. I've rejected the religious doctrine of my childhood; I've rejected the materialist view of a dead universe of my college years. In the last several years, I've consciously chosen the belief system that makes sense to me and that supports not only science but psychological research about happiness — that happiness and joy are our goals in life and that we feel them when we join in making a difference. Some choose to pursue success that leads to status and wealth. Some choose fundamentalist religions that undermine freedom and feed hatred of those different from them. Both of those paths are destructive to people and the planet. But I choose a life of exuberance that is committed to social change. It's a choice we must make.

Aldous Huxley expressed it in poetry:

The choice is always ours. Then let me choose
The longest art, the hard Promethean way
Cherishingly to tend and feed and fan
That inward fire, whose small precarious flame,
Kindled or quenched, creates
The noble or the ignoble men we are,
The worlds we live in and the very fates,
Our bright or muddy star.

Living with exuberance is a decision to truly enjoy life rather than accepting the consumer society's pressure to spend our lives getting and spending and laying waste our powers. Striving for status and scrambling for success don't make us happy! We must find ways to experience the joy that seems to lie at the heart of the universe, joy that should be at the center of our lives. Joy that does not ignore the dangers we're facing but recognizes them as products of a counterfeit joy produced by forces of the consumer society.

This metaphysics of joie de vivre, a belief that at the core of life is an expanding energy and creativity, engenders its own ethic, according to Albert Einstein:

The fairest thing we can experience is the mysterious. It is the fundamental emotion which stands at the cradle of true art and true science. He who knows it not and can no longer wonder, no longer feel amazement, is as good as dead, a snuffed-out candle.

This is an affirmation of life. It's a belief that humans are an incredible species, that we are the expression of the first burst of energy, that we are part of a universe that continues to evolve and that we are part of that evolution. There is an inner fire in us and it's important that we keep it alive, that we express it and act on it by resisting all the deadening and destructive effects of the consumer society. To think about what this means makes me feel tremendously excited and hopeful.

## Authenticity

*There are two ways to live your life. One is as though nothing is a miracle. The other is as though everything is a miracle.* — Albert Einstein

If we are to experience joie de vivre, the first step is authenticity. What else could it be? We feel shallow and half alive because we're shackled by second-hand emotions and a phony persona. We feel what others expect us to — our emotions are implanted in our brain by demagogues and advertisers. At the start of a recent Christmas shopping season I felt embarrassed for people who were willing to debase themselves to get cheap goods. Who camped out overnight to be first in line at discount stores and got in fights over $30 DVD players and $400 laptops. I know many of these people have low incomes, but the shame of the matter is that they are convinced they need such schlock. This isn't their fault — their emotions have been colonized by the consumer society! How can you feel joy if your emotional life consists of lusting after sale merchandise! The words of Heschel help us understand this: "The beginning of our happiness lies in the understanding that life without wonder is not worth living. What we lack is not a will to believe but a will to wonder."

Authenticity is hard to talk about because it's been done, redone, and done again by all the self-help literature. Who has put it any more profoundly than, "To thine own self be true!" (And, although we're not focusing on community right now, it's interesting to remember Shakespeare's next line: "And it must follow, as the night the day, Thou canst not then be false to any man." Authenticity is necessary for community.)

Many years ago, in the mid '60s, I read a book that really affected me, maybe the first "self-help" book I ever read, *Adjusted American: Normal Neurosis in the Individual and Society* by Snell and Gail Putney. It discussed the fact that Americans so want to feel accepted by others that they adopt an image — one that seems acceptable to other people. But they discover that they're not feeling any better — they keep thinking that people might discover the real person behind the image. So their sense of acceptance isn't real. It never really works. They only have one choice, authenticity.

One reason that "authenticity" has come to seem trite and overused is because it so directly threatens the consumer society. When a word has been trivialized in our culture, it probably means that the term not only is extremely important, it challenges the dominant order. The dominant forces of society know that if you are true to the real self, they have no control over you. So they try to fool you by luring you with shiny things that aren't real. And it's easy to be fooled: money, prestige, glamour, fame. But we all have to commit ourselves to being the boy who said the emperor has no clothes. If there are times we can't bring ourselves to tell the emperor, at least we can keep telling it to ourselves.

Anne Morrow Lindbergh put it well in her book *Gift from the Sea*. When we think about simplicity, we usually think only of cutting back on "things." She shows, though, that it's much broader than that:

> I begin to shed my Martha-like anxiety about any *things*. Washable slipcovers, faded and old — I hardly see them; I don't worry about the impression they make on other people. I am shedding pride. As little furniture as possible; I shall not need much. I shall ask into my shell only those friends with whom I can be completely honest. I find I am shedding hypocrisy in human relationships. What a rest that will be! The most exhausting thing in life, I have discovered, is being insincere. That is why so much of social life is exhausting; one is wearing a mask. I have shed my mask.

Frederick Franck, in his book *Art As a Way*, discusses Rembrandt's genius as his vision of "the revelation of the mystery of existence, of the specifically Human existence in this mortal flesh. This is the vision that came to him and marks his ripeness." Franck says that Rembrandt died destitute because he could no longer "go on flattering and pleasing the little egos of these grand bourgeois, until all popularity, money, fame were lost. He had emptied himself of his narcissism and paid the price."

Committing to living authentically, you try to tell the truth — about everything. You don't put all of your energy into an image that says I'm successful! You don't try to look perfect or be perfect. If you don't like a popular movie, you find a way to say that you didn't like it. Not with superiority or disdain for others' views, of course. You just tell the truth — "I can see why you liked that movie, but it didn't excite me much." Even though you know that intellectuals or literati will disdain you for liking John Grisham, it's important to say that you like John Grisham and note that his constant theme is to challenge the greed of our society.

Every time you withhold your own opinion and say something you don't really think, you're not being authentic.

Every time you are impressed with someone simply because they are well-known, you're not being authentic.

Every time you pretend you've read a book when you haven't, you're not being authentic.

Every time someone asks you how you are and you automatically respond "Fine," you're probably not being authentic.

Being authentic, we'll still be polite and treat people with respect and dignity. But we won't feign affection or pretend that we're impressed when we're not. We might laugh a little out of politeness at a joke that's not funny, but not at a rude comment or unacceptable joke.

We won't pour out our life story when someone asks us how we are, but we don't have to pretend that our life is perfect and everything is wonderful.

We don't have to put people down, but we can be honest about how we feel about people. I hate the artificial niceness that so many people have adopted. I like a good curmudgeon and a sharp tongue. I don't want us to degenerate into bitter gossips, but come on, let's tell the truth about how we feel. I know someone who continually makes people feel bad and unworthy, but because she is well-known and powerful, no one will say a word against her. It's only when I tell people how she has treated me that they respond that she's done the same to them. How else are we going to defeat the demagogues if we don't tell the truth? We can't become that boring, sterile Roman I mentioned earlier. I bet he didn't have a bad thing to say about any one.

Thoreau expresses it well:

> Men are very generally spoiled by being so civil and well-disposed. You can have no profitable conversation with them, they are so conciliatory, determined to agree with you .... I am never electrified by my gentleman; he is not an electric eel, but one of the common kind that slip through your hands, however hard you clutch them, and leave them covered with slime.

It's not easy to be real in this society. Being authentic takes conscious effort and energy. But it also permits exuberance and flow to revitalize our life. Those of us who question the consumer society sometimes think we're above it, but we're affected just the same. One of the saddest stories I know is of a woman who has been unable to declare herself as a lesbian. She is highly educated, well-read, and a wonderful person. But she cannot brave the sanctions against homosexuality. She can't declare who she is. I don't blame her. I think I would have a very hard time myself. But it shows how strongly we are affected by our society.

This isn't easy. Every time we tell the truth, we take a risk that someone will draw back and look at us as if we're strange. For instance, over the past 20 years I've used alternative medicine almost exclusively. Whenever I tell people that I go to a homeopathic physician, I brace myself, waiting for that look that often says, "Are you crazy? Why are you going to a quack?" And I always have to explain that, of course, I'd go to an emergency room after an accident, but that conventional medicine is always my second choice. Obviously, this is getting easier to talk about as more people turn to alternative health methods.

So authenticity is not just something you do for your own sense of dignity and integrity, it's also a way you make a difference in the world. Sometimes you can be most effective by telling your story.

You're not trying to convince and manipulate others to do what you do, you're just telling your story. You tell how you feel about the right wing, but you don't insist that people agree with you. You express your views, even if they're unpopular, but you don't do it in an unpleasant way. As we'll see later, caring and community depend on feeling accepted and valued, something that we forget when we try to argue others into agreeing with us.

The most basic step toward regaining authenticity is to learn from your own experiences, to listen to that small voice within. Learning from your experiences means taking time to sit and mull over your day. It means keeping a notebook with you to record your thoughts and feelings. It means behaving like a detective, looking for clues to the real self, watching for patterns and ruminating about what they mean. It means having a friend you can talk over your experiences with, a friend that you can tell anything to.

It's hard to have a friend like that. And it's hard to find time to be authentic. I'll be talking about both of these issues in the sections on community and leisure. But you never really experience depth and enjoyment unless it's real. Just like plastic flowers can never give the joy that real flowers do, nor a CD convey the excitement of a live concert, so a thought or feeling that doesn't really come from you can never really allow you to live deeply.

Speaking of plastic flowers makes me think of another eloquent writer about authenticity — not someone I would have expected. Most people writing about authenticity are psychologists or educators or theologians, but some of the most profound statements I've read come from an architect — someone who is concerned about such things as plastic flowers! These ideas are in a book I had been hearing about for years but never read (an architect — what relevance could that have for me?). I realized, after finally reading the book, that, like anything wise, it had ramifications not only for its subject, but for our lives. It's Christopher Alexander's *The Timeless Way of Building*. He shows how authenticity is at the core of all of life.

I've suggested that authenticity is being true to your emotions, feelings and thoughts: It's saying what you think or feel about your experience. Alexander sees it as being true to one's *nature*. At first he talks about architecture, saying that when a room or a building is true to what it is used for — its nature — it creates an aliveness that can't be mistaken. But he moves beyond architecture. He says we are always searching for the moments and situations in which we are most alive, and to find these, there is a *way* that we must follow. First, he says, we must move beyond our fears that people will laugh at us. When we coddle such fears we "make places which are dead and life-less and artificial."

Most of us, Alexander says, are not fully true to our own natures — we're not fully "real." But when you meet someone who is true to him or herself, you feel immediately that this person is "more real" than others. So, he says, everything has a division between the real and not real, and the more real something is, the more alive it is. But Alexander isn't satisfied with just the word "real." He finds "free" closer to what he means. When you free yourself of the expectations of others, you can be more authentic. Then he determines that even the word "free" is limited, so he talks about the "eternal." Finally he gives up and calls it "the quality which has no name," a quality that involves realness, freedom, and the eternal.

This "quality which has no name" is something we search for all our lives — and we are experiencing it when we feel most alive. It's a feeling of freedom and passion. "This wild freedom, this pas-sion, comes into our lives in the instant we let go," Alexander says.

> Our letting go is stifled, all the time, so long as we have ideas and opinions about ourselves, which make us hug too tightly to our images of how to live, and bottle up these forces. So long as we are still bottled up, like this, there is a tightness about the mouth, a nervous tension in the eyes, a stiffness and a brittleness in the way we walk, the way we move. And yet, until one does let go, it is impossible to be alive.

But how do we do this? How do we overcome our fears and let go? It is "when we forget ourselves completely: playing the fool perhaps among a group of friends, or swimming out to sea, or walking simply, or trying to finish something late at night over a table with a group of friends, cigarette stuck to lower lip, eyes tired, earnest concentration."

What Alexander is describing is another way of talking about authenticity and flow. You let everything go: your to-do list, your anxiety about how intelligent you sound, your worry that others will laugh at you. You are focused on the activity in front of you, and you laugh easily. You walk in a leisurely way. Your speech flows — you forget about the impression you're making! For me, his most striking image is the one of swimming out to sea. You are in the heart of nature, you're buoyed up by nature, you're conscious only of life around you. (No one worries about how they look swimming in the sea!) Being submerged in nature is to connect to your own nature. You realize that both you and the sea are expressions of the evolution of the universe.

"A man is alive when he is wholehearted, true to himself, true to his own inner forces, and able to act freely according to the nature of the situation he is in," Alexander writes. "In our own lives, we have the quality without a name when we are most intense, most happy, most wholehearted." This is the core: We are being true to ourselves! It is integrity! First, we have to respond honestly to our experience, then we have to express it honestly and, finally, we have to live up to what we say. Then we have the roll call for aliveness.

## The inauthentic culture

I heard about a new product the other day. A Reuters brief says, "Singapore scientists looking for ways to transmit the sense of touch over the Internet have devised a vibration jacket for chickens and are thinking about electronic children's pajamas for cyberspace hugs." Parents, via the Internet, can touch a button that is supposed to make kids feel like they've been hugged? Can this be for real? Could people be suckered into buying this? Can people really be human in a falsely marketed world?

Most people, when they're looking for ways to become more acceptable, blame themselves and their own inadequacy. We must teach people how to read their culture! This was a key lesson in the early women's movement. Women who felt lacking in self-esteem blamed themselves until they discovered all the cultural forces influencing and channeling them. Until you realize how cultural forces operate on you, your efforts to change are next to pointless. Who we are is not just a result of how our parents treated us. Who we are depends on the society we live in. If you live in an uncaring, intensely competitive society, you are going to suffer doubts of self-worth and weaknesses of identity. You are going to have a hard time being authentic. If your society predicates a successful image on materialism and extrinsic rewards, there is no self there.

*Until you realize how cultural forces operate on you, your efforts to change are next to pointless. Who we are is not just a result of how our parents treated us. Who we are depends on the society we live in.*

But can we self-authenticate in our society? Christopher Alexander says that a person cannot feel alive when he lives in a place that is not alive: "The fact is, a person is so far formed by his surroundings that his state of harmony depends entirely on his harmony with his surroundings." How much authenticity are we surrounded with? Our TV friends aren't real. Those aren't real experts on the airwaves telling us what drugs to take. Those people in commercials aren't really happy! Those talking news heads don't really know what they're talking about. Newscasters aren't telling you what has actually happened. Right-wing politicians can't stop lying.

Most people in restaurants who wait on you don't *really* like you. Your boss is more concerned about covering himself than he is supporting you. Athletes aren't as good as we've believed — they've been taking steroids! Evangelists asking for your money have no connection to God. I read a newspaper story that actually said Congress passed tougher bankruptcy laws because it was concerned about people not saving money. Correction, please: Congress passed those laws so the credit card companies could make more money!

Our environment isn't real. You must have some contact with nature for that. What does it mean when you go into your garage from your house, click the garage door open, drive in your car for 20 miles listening to talk radio (which is not real conversation), slide into your corporate garage, take the elevator up to your little cubicle and work on the computer for the rest of the day? Maybe you have a meeting where the division head says you're all one big happy family but they have to lay off 10 percent of the employees. And then you repeat your morning trip in reverse and spend the night watching television or surfing the Net. We're not in touch with real life — real-life people and flowers and conversation and making music!

A funny yet profound Australian movie *Love Serenade* shows how inauthenticity stains the fabric of contemporary life. In the movie Ken Sherry, a hotshot DJ from the big city (Brisbane), comes to little Sun Ray to run the local radio station. Sherry starts playing love songs and spouting fatuous bromides on the meaning of romance and life while beginning simultaneous sexual relationships with two sisters who live next door. Both are searching for emotional meaning and true love, but Sherry is just out for gratification and, in a series of pompous New Age rationalizations, tells them so. Sherry becomes a symbol of status and wealth and its incompatibility with the humble, honest ways of life in a small town. In a shocking ending both Sherry and the sisters return to their true natures, and the phony posturing of celebrityhood is in the process eradicated.

Once I was teaching a group of kids in an alternative high school and wanted to illustrate the difference between real and counterfeit. So I took them down to Seattle's downtown Farmer's Market and asked them to compare shopping there with going to the mall. Now, the Pike Place Market is not just a once-a-week setup like a lot of farmers' markets. It's a building — a warren of three floors of little businesses built on the side of a hill that looks out over Puget Sound. It was founded in 1907 just west of Seattle's downtown. The Market's street level has real farmers, real produce, and stalls for jellies, flowers and crafts. Other floors have antique shops, used bookstores, small clothing stores, herb shops, candle shops, and on and on. Many people know the Market from seeing pictures of fishmongers throwing salmon. You ask for a fish and the front guy calls back for it, and in a minute it comes ripping through the air, the fish-monger catching it like a football.

I recommend Googling it to get a feel for the place. Periodically there are Big Thinkers who want to tear it down and put in something modern. But civic activists have preserved its funky countercultural zeitgeist. One of its defenders was internationally celebrated artist Mark Tobey who spent time painting it. It's been described as "an honest place in a phony time."

I've spent many, many happy times wandering through the market, buying flowers or stopping at one of the cafes or getting "strolling" food from one of the ethnic shops run by Russians or Japanese or Ethiopians. There's one grassy section where I've watched many Democratic presidential candidates, including Bill Clinton, address the liberal stronghold of Seattle.

But what my students noticed were the real people selling real goods. They talked to the stall regulars and could sense that they loved what they did. These weren't the cashiers at a big department store who didn't know or care who you were. These people ran their own little businesses and sold their own creations. The kids recognized a vitality and energy that they didn't see at the mall. Further, the kids could see that being outside with a view of the water and sky made a tremendous difference in vitality. And the market has no piped-in Muzak. Instead there are street musicians —buskers — who sing protest and folk songs. On the corners are men selling the local "homeless" newspaper, *Real Change*, and always lots of people asking you to sign petitions to legalize something or passing out flyers urging you to vote. None of these people would even be allowed in a shopping mall.

This is the way shopping — going to the "market" — is meant to be! And who understands this? Who understands the vacuity and inauthenticity of the mall? Cut off from nature — no street people or activists handing out flyers allowed! Walled off from anything real. And a chief design feature is to make it difficult to find your way out. They want captives! The irony is that here in Seattle we have the first shopping mall ever built — Northgate. I used to go there in the '50s when I lived in a Seattle suburb and didn't know the difference between real and counterfeit. (Most everything in the suburbs was counterfeit.) It was only after I was an adult and I started experiencing real life rather than "suburbanimity" that I began to understand the importance of places like the Pike Place Market. And now as I think back to my mall visits when I was young, I realize I have absolutely no real memories. Each visit blended into the next. There was nothing meaningful to hang onto.

Thomas Moore, in *Care of the Soul*, says that it's not easy expressing your true self because

> we are pleasantly sedated by the flatness and predictability of modern life .... You can travel far and wide and have a difficult time finding a store or restaurant that is even mildly unique. In shopping malls everywhere, in restaurant districts, in movie theaters, you will find the same clothes, the same brand names, the same menus, the same few films, the identical architecture.

One way to shake up the flatness and sterility is to examine the ancient art of Play.

## Play
*All life should be lived as play.*      — Plato

Not long ago, we played Hearts with some friends of ours. It would never have occurred to me as a way to spend the evening, but our friends' oldest daughter was leaving soon for college, and she was an ace at Hearts. I was surprised when it turned out to be great fun!

All of us around the table had always been high achievers and were well known in Seattle, but here that was irrelevant. I particularly enjoyed the fact that my super-competent husband just couldn't figure the game out. In the old days he would have taken it all very seriously and put his mind to winning, but as he wallowed in last place he joined in as we laughed and laughed.

Playing cards is something that's disappeared in our lives. A few years ago I would have thought, What earthly good is it to play cards? In fact, I remember when I was young and sneered at my mother for playing bridge. (What a nasty child I could be!) But now I'm beginning to understand the importance of play.

A lot of self-help books talk about learning to be more playful — about being bright and cheery and playing silly practical jokes. I've always found such trifles to be irritating. They trivialize something important. Consider the work of Johan Huizinga, particularly his best-known book, *Homo Ludens* — a study of the play element in culture. I found him even more fascinating knowing that he had been in a Nazi prison camp. Alive from 1872 to 1945, Huizinga was an acclaimed Dutch philosopher imprisoned by the Nazis after he gave a public speech criticizing the German influence on Dutch science. (Shades of the right wing in this country!) He was arrested in 1941, released in 1942 and then kept in detention. He died in 1945, just a few months before the war ended. Here was an academic who stood up for his beliefs.

In *Homo Ludens*, published in 1934, Huizinga set out to prove that play was the most important thing in life. To him, it was the source of all of civilization. Culture, the arts, weapons — all developed because of humanity's instinct to play. Today psychologists see many benefits to play in terms of a child's development and adjustment to the world, but Huizinga resisted this kind of interpretation because he was anxious for us to understand that play is so much larger than games, and that it extended throughout life, not just childhood. To him it was an approach to life in which everything is done purely for its own sake, purely for the joy of it.

It's easy to see why play is anathema to us as a culture. We do nothing except for secondary benefits. We walk for fitness, develop contacts instead of friends. We join boards to help us move up. We go to school to get a good job, read books that make us look intelligent. We do almost nothing for fun! We must not forget psychologist Tim Kasser's findings that people who are motivated by extrinsic goals such as status and wealth never score as high in measures of happiness and well-being.

So, let's take a look at how Huizinga saw play.

Play is purposeless. It's not done for money or status or health (although you might get those, but then it's probably not play any more). It's something done for the pure pleasure of the experience. If it's no fun, you're not playing. One way to think of it is to remember that pleasure and enjoyment are pure energy, and so play is a way for us to connect with the larger energy of the universe (of the big bang).

Play is absorbing. I remember watching my daughter when she was a baby. She was just able to sit up and manipulate things with her hands, and she would spend hours absorbed in either a deck of cards or a piece of string. Her breathing would slow, her features would grow intense. I have always felt that this sort of absorption was central to psychological health, and yet we so seldom experience it in our culture of constant interruption and multitasking. (Why do only one thing when you could be doing three?)

Play is time away from ordinary life. It's something that has nothing to do with real life — like a game. You can escape your usual emotions of anxiety, impatience, and irritation. You forget about efficiency, productivity, and the bottom line. You're free.

Play is intense and often dramatic. When you play a game, it's exciting to see who wins. When you watch a play, you are swept up in its drama. (Note that these dramas are called *plays!*)

*Play is, more than anything else, the expression of the pure joy of being alive, an expression of our true nature.*

In play you forget about self-consciousness and express yourself freely. That was the joy of playing Hearts with my friends. How often do you get to whoop it up or raise your fist in victory? When do you get to make rude noises when the other person does something (plays a card) you don't like?

Play is, more than anything else, the expression of the pure joy of being alive, an expression of our true nature, of the big bang, that original flowing forth of the burst of life and light that we recapture when we give ourselves over to pure play.

Probably the most egregious violation of play's vital characteristics is, ironically, sports — either amateur or professional. When do kids these days get to organize an informal game of kick the can? Who starts a game of work-up baseball? Kids' sports are all organized, with practice times cutting into family time and meals. Youngsters are under intense pressure to win. As one person said, you don't just "play" tennis, you work on your backhand. And I don't need to say a thing about professional sports. There's no play there. It's all about money, fame, and status.

Are video games examples of play? Is there healthy play and unhealthy play? It seems that healthy play should bring you joie, it should make you laugh and shout, it should make you want to throw your arms around each other as you fall over laughing. It should take you into nature, into movement, into connection with yourself, with others, and with a wider life. It should make you feel free. Do video games do this? Are they play or an addictive escape from life?

And I hate to say it — knowing this violates its purposelessness — but play is good for us. Psychologists find play to be important for healthy relationships, strong families, and even spiritual growth. Play can make you forget about anger and worry and anxiety. What a wonderful relief! But at least if we know the benefits maybe we will be lured into play, and then we will play for its own sake. I remember when I used to teach classes to women returning to college, and I would try to encourage them to branch out and pursue some of their own interests. The only way I could get them to do something was to tell them that if they developed their own interests they would be better mothers and better wives. So by pointing out the benefits of play, maybe I can get people to take it seriously.

For me, this all comes back to letting joy be our guide in life. I know there are some things we have to do that we don't want to do, but at least we can try to figure out what we can do to make them more enjoyable and more fun. But here's the crucial question: How can play exist in a culture in which we're all striving to get ahead, in which we want to win all of the time, in which everything is measured in terms of money? How can we play when we have no free time? We'll only make changes when we realize the importance of play and reject our indoctrination that happiness lies in money and power. In *Exuberance: The Passion for Life*, Jamison reminds us of the centrality of play. She describes the life of Snoopy, the infamous beagle in the Peanuts cartoon. Snoopy has a celebration for every day of the year and for every special occasion, ranging from a "First Day of Spring" dance to a "Suppertime" dance to a "Be Kind to Animals" dance. We need our own special dances and celebrations! In particular, Jamison reminded me of a phrase that always comes to me at some joyful moment — the cry when the Jabberwock was slain in Lewis Carroll's *Through the Looking Glass*: "Oh frabjous day! Callooh? Callay!"

What better way to express your joy!

## Laughter

*Wearing a rubber nose wherever I go has changed my life. Dullness and boredom melt away. Wearing underwear on the outside of your clothes can turn a tedious trip to the store for a forgotten carton of milk into an amusement park romp. Humor is the antidote to all ills. People crave laughter as if it were an essential amino acid. I believe that fun is as important as love.*

— Patch Adams

If play helps to undermine our consumer society, laughter does so even more effectively. Laughter is the wick of joie de vivre. It redeems everything. The times I've tripped while walking up to make a presentation or worn the wrong dress to a wedding have been humiliating at the time, but they gave me such good stories they were worth it! Laughing about embarrassments makes you glad the embarrassing episodes happened! There's no joy without laughter. When you laugh, you feel transported and free and expanded. You fall in love with life. People returning from visits to other countries tell me they are astounded at how much more laughter there is in other cultures. When they return home the people they see on our streets look grim and angry — the poet William Blake's "marks of weakness, marks of woe."

### LAUGHTER BOOSTS HEALTH

Patch Adams's rubber nose is literally just what the doctor ordered. Research has shown that laughter increases the secretion of natural chemicals, endorphins, that make people feel peppy and good. It also inhibits cortisol secretion and lowers the sedimentation rate, which implies a stimulated immune response. Oxygenation of the blood increases, and residual air in the lungs decreases. Heart rate and blood pressure at first rise, but then the arteries relax. Skin temperatures escalate as a result of increased peripheral circulation. Laughter also relaxes. Physiologists have shown that while anxiety and muscle relaxation cannot occur at the same time, a hearty laugh can induce a relaxation response lasting as long as 45 minutes.

I paraphrase Adams in order to confirm what we should all know — there's no question that laughter is good for you. Study after study in health fields confirms it. Laughter helps prevent heart attacks, boosts your immune system, reduces stress — in so many ways it helps you live longer.

And of course laughter is a bond to other people, helping form relationships as the best way of all to improve your health. Laughter helps your health indirectly as well, because it gives hope: One study found that humor may significantly boost a person's level of hope, which in turn, researchers feel, stimulates a person's ability to solve problems creatively. We are in such downtrodden times that laughter is more important than ever, but we rarely see it as essential to solving our problems.

So once again, science has confirmed what wise people have always known. Take a look at some words of wisdom from the ages. Nietzsche said, "You must laugh 10 times during the day, and be cheerful; otherwise your stomach, the father of affliction, will disturb you in the night." And Mark Twain wrote in *Tom Sawyer*: "The old man laughed loud and joyously, shook up the details of his anatomy from head to foot, and ended by saying that such a laugh was money in a man's pocket, because it cut down the doctor's bills like everything."

Of all the subjects I'm considering in the realm of joie de vivre, laughter is the most complex. Exuberance, flow and play can be fairly easily described and classified. But laughter serves so many purposes. It's a gesture of conviviality, a tension reliever, an expression of delight or courage.

A GESTURE OF CONVIVIALITY
*In conversation, humor is worth more than wit and easiness more than*
*knowledge.*                                    — George Herbert

When someone laughs, you feel safe. It's the person with a sour look and rigid face that we hate to approach. Who knows how they will respond! But when someone smiles and laughs easily, particularly over absolutely nothing at all, she is telling you that she will be kind. (I used "she" here because it is much more often to be a woman who uses this kind of laughter. Men still try to signal their status — by being unsmiling — more often than do women.)

So a woman might say, "Wow, it sure is hot in here — I'm going to have to start taking off my clothes!" Now, that's not really very funny, but a group of women friends would laugh at that. Laughing easily is a gesture of conviviality, an invitation to approach, a promise to be hospitable.

LAUGHTER AS TENSION RELIEVER

When something is tense, and someone makes an even slightly humorous comment, people laugh — and the tension is released. One of the funniest examples of this is recounted by Robert Drennan in *The Algonquin Wits: Bon Mots, Wisecracks, Epigrams and Gags*. It contains cute little stories about members of the roundtable at the Algonquin Hotel, among them legendary writers Dorothy Parker, Robert Benchley and Robert Sherwood. One story involves Franklin Pierce Adams and George and Beatrice Kaufman. The incident, as Drennan tells it, happened at a dinner party where Beatrice Kaufman sat down on a cane-bottom chair and broke through the seat. There she was, stuck, with her feet in the air, her derrière firmly wedged. Adams looked at her, and instead of hurrying over to help her out and probably cause further embarrassment, he said, "Beatrice, I've told you a hundred times, that's not funny!"

What a gift to be able to respond like that! You can imagine how embarrassed silence was shattered with a thunderclap of laughter. Nothing frees people like laughing. Nothing connects people like laughing together. The stresses of the day are released, and life looks a little more promising.

## An expression of delight

Laughter is at the core of joie de vivre because it is an expression of delight. Think of seeing something that lifts your spirits — like a little baby taking its first steps. Our response is to laugh with joy. When we're out walking Maggie and run into a group of bystanders, she will plop herself down and refuse to move. It cracks up everyone on the sidewalk. Maggie knows what she's doing — her breed used to be the performing dogs in the circus.

This kind of laughter happens among groups who just enjoy being together. I taught a college class at Seattle University that became so close and caring that if anyone would say anything light-hearted at all, the whole class would erupt in laughter. It was an expression of the pure joy of being together. It was a class in which, when the students had to give oral reports, the other class members not only applauded wildly at the end, but also when the person got up to begin! (Incidentally, it was a class in which I had de-emphasized grades and competition. It was an upper-division five-credit course on the subject of Voluntary Simplicity, so how could I be a hard grader? Nonetheless, I was truly astounded at how the students were just bursting with joy and delight when they came together. I think the lack of competition is what did it.)

## Intimacy

*Among those whom I like or admire, I can find no common denominator, but among those whom I love, I can: all of them make me laugh.* — W.H. Auden

I like to tell people that my marriage is always on the brink of collapse — we're just hanging on by our fingertips, that I've been planning to leave every week for over 30 years, but he no longer believes my threats! I know I can never leave because there's no one else I've ever laughed with as much. No one shares an exact same sense of humor as people who love each other. In one way we discovered this early on: We loved the same comedy, in movies and TV series. If there is one ingredient for marital longevity that you read over and over again in the articles on 50th-wedding anniversaries, it's being able to laugh together.

## COURAGE

Laughter is a refusal to be overcome by life. It's a commitment to persevere no matter what the circumstances. Failures only occur, really, because you have not lived up to society's expectations of what success is. I've found that the very best way to deal with failures is to put them into perspective and to laugh. Again, it's saying, "I reject your standards. I'm not going to be daunted by what society wants." Writer Katherine Mansfield says, "When we begin to take our failures non-seriously, it means we are ceasing to be afraid of them. It is of immense importance to learn to laugh at ourselves."

*Laughter is a refusal to be overcome by life. It's a commitment to persevere no matter what the circumstances.*

So much of our energy goes into the unimportant things, like trying to get ahead or to appear important and impressive. In the long run, these don't count! It's enjoying the day-to-dayness of your life. Laughter is an expression of the realization of that wisdom.

All wise people say that we must learn to be detached about our successes and failures. Thoreau's reaction to the failure of his first book always inspires me to laugh. He had paid to have *A Week on the Concord and the Merrimack Rivers* published. It didn't sell very well, and the publisher finally sent the remaining 706 copies (out of 1,000 printed) back to him. That night he commented in his journal that he had "a library of nearly nine hundred volumes, over seven hundred of which I wrote myself."

## INTEGRITY AND HONESTY

Probably the most satisfying laughter is when someone says something true that no one would say out loud. Dorothy Parker did a lot of this, particularly since she knew that everyone was talking about how outrageous she was. So why not say outrageous things! When she said, "It's a small apartment, I've barely enough room to lay my hat and a few friends," she was playing to people's suspicion of her being promiscuous.

The early 20th-century comedian Artemus Ward uses this kind of honesty in his comment, "I have given two cousins to war and I stand ready to sacrifice my wife's brother." He plays on the idea that first, none of us wants to go to war ourselves, and second, that our in-laws are often a pain. It is the honesty expressed that makes people laugh.

## UNPLEASANTNESS ANTIDOTE

Again, a story from Dorothy Parker: In 1925, Harold Ross was struggling to keep *The New Yorker* magazine alive with a tiny, inexperienced staff and an office with one typewriter. Running into Parker, Ross said, "I thought you were coming into the office to write a piece last week." Parker replied, "Somebody was using the pencil."

A friend who is a professor at Stanford told me a similar story. During a faculty meeting, the dean was droning on about all the money he raised. One of the English professors raised his hand and asked if that meant the faculty would no longer have to keep buying their own pencils. (Humanities departments tend not to be as well funded as the business schools!)

## OVERCOMING STATUS ANXIETY

Slipping on a banana peel is the perennial gag. In our status-obsessed culture, we're all worried about making fools of ourselves. If you slip on a banana peel, you feel pretty foolish, and if you yourself don't laugh, there will just be an uncomfortable silence. But if you laugh, you're saying that you are really not that concerned about making a fool of yourself — that you have enough self-esteem for something like this not to bother you. Now at one level, of course, it does bother you. But choosing to laugh instead of getting embarrassed puts a whole different spin on the experience.

My funniest stories are about times I've made a fool of myself. I even welcome these events now because I know I'll have a good story. For instance, something happened recently that I could hardly wait to call my daughter about. We were at a potluck, a neighborhood picnic, and I had brought a green salad — made out of all-organic materials, of course. Well, my salads are so good that I always make a beeline to them before anyone else. So there I was, eating away, and suddenly in my salad I saw an odious green worm-like creature. It was an inch and a half long with lots of little feet. Aaaargggh! Luckily I was outside so I surreptitiously dropped it on the ground. Then I tried to look through the bowl to see if I spotted anything else. My daughter laughed and laughed. I knew she would think it was hilarious, and it was worth having it happen to get to laugh with her.

## LAUGHTER FOR FREEDOM AND DEMOCRACY

But laughter has an even deeper significance in a society with a large gap between the rich and the poor. It is a path to greater equality and a gesture of defiance to the powers that be. Part of the reason we laughed so much in the Simplicity class I describe above is that I reduced the experience of competition. We were all equals, and as equals we could more easily laugh together. Research on conversation shows that the person with the most power makes the jokes, and the followers do the laughing. In other words, making people laugh is a gesture of power. So when the jockeying for status is reduced, you have more laughter — when someone says something funny and everyone laughs, you have achieved a new level of equality.

It's also a defiance of the powerful. On being told that Calvin Coolidge was dead, Dorothy Parker remarked, "How could they tell?" Mark Twain asserted that, "The human race has only one really effective weapon, and that is laughter." Einstein said, "Whoever undertakes to set himself up as a judge of Truth and Knowledge is shipwrecked by the laughter of the gods."

The funniest humor of the Bush presidency has come from Jon Stewart. His humor rests on the refusal to be cowed by Bush and his minions. Stewart's method? He tells the truth about their lies. He plays today's tape and then juxtaposes it with a contradictory statement made previously. The result: They're exposed as fools. "Heck of a job, Brownie." "We do not torture." "No more than six months" in Iraq. Stewart punctures their dissemblance and superciliousness. For Stewart, laughter is a subversive gesture: He's going to laugh at the people in power because they are ultimately ridiculous. They think we can't see through them, but it's very clear that they're not fooling us.

A *Salon* commentary on a protest against the Bush administration describes how the right wing dismissed it as rabble-rousers in a carnival atmosphere, but the article went on to say that throughout history protests have used clowns and fools to ridicule the powerful: "Carnivals of protest create their own bubble of consciousness, in which the unspeakable can finally be shouted, the powerful parodied, and the status quo turned upside down." Theologian Harvey Cox talks about a holiday in medieval Europe known as the Feast of Fools. It was celebrated around January 1st, and even the staid priest and serious businessmen would dress up in costumes and sing outrageous ditties that ridiculed the powerful. Even though the Feast of Fools was never popular with the ruling class, it could not retaliate. The Feast showed the public that the rich and powerful were not necessarily superior to them. As Cox explains,

> Unmasking the pretense of the powerful always makes their power seem less irresistible. That is why tyrants tremble before fools and dictators ban political cabarets .... People elected a harlequin king: he was King of the Bean in England and the Abbot of Unreason in Scotland. This attitude is expressed in more formal terms by the psychiatrist Thomas Szasz: "When a person can no longer laugh at himself, it is time for others to laugh at him."

The Protestant Reformation changed all this and used sobriety, thrift and ambition to replace mirth, play and festivity. And of course forced on us a whole new attitude about work that we continue to suffer from today.

Humor is a way to *refuse to be daunted by fate*. As Bill Cosby says, "Through humor, you can soften some of the worst blows that life delivers. And once you find laughter, no matter how painful your situation might be, you can survive it."

## Build a sense of humor?

Sometimes I think it's impossible to foster a sense of humor. You either have it or you don't. You certainly can't will yourself to be funny. It's pretty painful to watch people try. There seems to be lots of silly advice on the Internet telling you to do things like "take a laugh break instead of a coffee break," or keep a "humor first aid kit" with disguises and costumes. Suggesting that we watch funny TV shows or read jokes isn't so bad — just a little sad that our humor has to be manufactured. But the really pathetic piece of advice is, "Remind yourself to have fun." Whoa! A person would be in a really sad state to have to do this. Actually, maybe having to remind ourselves is a reflection of the state we're really in.

Some people join laughing clubs where one person starts to laugh and it spreads. Again, this seems a little sad, but it does show that laughing is something people want. And it expresses a truth about laughter: It's catching. So first, you have to try to become an easy laugher. Don't hold back. Don't worry about saying something funny yourself. Be ready to laugh freely at what others say. Everyone loves an easy laugher.

You can start by smiling. Smiling is the natural human gesture of congeniality. This sounds silly, but people in the corporate world learn to suppress their smiles. They try to look serious and businesslike and in control. Once I thought I would try it, just to see if people took me more seriously at work. But after one day I decided it was a stupid idea! When you don't smile, you just don't enjoy yourself as much. So try smiling and laughing more readily. (I know this advice verges on the stuff in silly self-help books, but it's also true.)

Probably the best way to develop a sense of humor is to hang around people who are easy laughers themselves. The more someone laughs at what you say, the funnier you get. Humor is truly like a plant that needs a lot of water and sun.

But laughter comes from a philosophical grounding. It's a releasing that questions and challenges authority. Laughing comes from being a person who is free and easy and convivial and informal — someone who rejects the conventional and enjoys people who don't conform. So you have to learn to challenge convention. You can't be uptight and worried about doing the "right" thing. You can't believe that authorities and experts are always right; you can't believe that someone else has the right to control you or manipulate you. Laughing is an act of emancipation from everyone who doesn't value life — stuffed shirts as well as demagogues.

*Laughing is an act of emancipation from everyone who doesn't value life — stuffed shirts as well as demagogues.*

So you can start now by questioning what you hear and questioning conventional expectations about behavior. Quit repeating others' words — only say what you think or feel. I hate to hear a cliché coming out of people's mouths. Think about the words you use. Like "bottom line." It's a horrible expression. You only hear it used in a pompous or uncaring way: "We're one big family here, but the bottom line is that we have to start working more efficiently and productively, and so we'll be laying some of you off." Wouldn't it be great to carry one of those klaxon horns that Harpo Marx had and honk it every time someone used the term "bottom line"?

Maybe what's most important is for you to decide that you are who you are and you will express it even when not everyone approves. There's nothing else to say but "This is me." People without a sense of humor are egotistical, always focused on self-promotion and impressing others. Sometimes they are people who only want to change your mind, to convince you that they're right. One woman described humor as "the importance of not being earnest."

## AFFIRMATION OF LIFE

Humor involves a basic acceptance of life, an affirmation of life. It's the belief that people are basically good and that we're supposed to be enjoying life, even though there are a lot of problems. When you become more caring about others you laugh more easily because you can laugh out of delight. Judgmental people don't laugh. Rigid moralists don't laugh. Extremists don't laugh. Most right-wingers have phony smiles and wooden faces. They are rigid, uncompassionate automatons. Demagogues and dictators don't have a sense of humor. How many photos have we seen of Hitler smiling? Despots are filled with the need to have power and control over others; they are people who don't care what happens to others, people who are willing to kill and destroy. They easily fly into rages and have little flexibility and always blame everyone else for misfortune. Maybe the proof of the importance of humor lies in this: that dictators have none. Ultimately, I'm asking people to learn to trust their own emotions, particular their ability to enjoy life, as a way to resist the manipulation of the consumer culture. So the final analysis, as mysterious as it might be, is that laughter is important because it makes us feel good.

## Forces undermining joie de vivre

### THE WORKPLACE AND OUR DEFINITION OF SUCCESS

We've already explored the forces of the consumer society that constrict us — the commandeering of our time, the extreme competitiveness, the commodification of our relationships and the chilling, cold hand of the corporation. There's no jumping for joy in the corporate consumer society. But it's not just our present that undermines joie de vivre — it's also our past.

### PURITANS AT PLAY

We can start with our cultural-religious heritage. I recently came across a book I just couldn't resist — *Puritans at Play: Leisure and Recreation in Colonial New England* by Bruce Daniels. Most of us have heard of Max Weber's views in *The Protestant Ethic and the Spirit of Capitalism*, and to many of us it rings true. Puritans believed in predestination, so there was really not much one could do about whether one went to heaven or hell. Naturally, though, people were curious to know where they would end up, so they started looking for signs that would let them guess their fate. They reasoned that those favored by God would probably have success in this life — so material success meant you were going to heaven. Not surprisingly, anything that got in the way, such as fun and play, was reviled.

The Puritan work ethic was also influenced by the fact that people had to work very hard to survive. And there was a vast continent to conquer. Both elements would conspire to create a strong work ethic. But many of us identify with the fear that Christianity instilled in people because we ourselves experienced it growing up. So blaming our Puritan heritage makes sense.

One could conclude that even though we seem decadent today with our emphasis on materialism and creature comforts, it's not really enjoyment that we're experiencing. It's instead an escape from fear, guilt and harsh judgment. Daniels, in *Puritans at Play* argues that Puritans had a profound ambivalence about pleasure: Whenever the ministers preached about relaxing, or enjoyment, there was always a caution: Don't go too far! Puritans believed in "sober mirth." Jesus, a 17th-century writer reminded people, was a "man of sorrow." In 1684 Increase Mather, a member of the elite clergy, said: "Lawful recreations ... moderately and reasonably used are good and in some cases a duty." But people "often spend more time therein than God alloweth of. And, too many indulge themselves in sinful sports and pastimes .... The Scriptures commend unto Christians, gravity and sobriety in their carriage at all times; and condemn all levity." Then he gave a list of all the sinners God had struck down!

The truth is, America was founded by religious extremists, and it happened comparatively recently. What jumps out at me even more is the utilitarian belief system — that everything is supposed to serve God's intention. The ministers didn't warn people just about being sinful, they inveighed against being unproductive. Leisure was particularly suspect, and the Sabbath laws were very strict. "Sabbath laws forbade many practices regarded as proper and lawful on other days," Daniels writes.

> Social custom proscribed sexual intercourse, unnecessary traveling, and any type of frivolity .... Magistrates punished crimes regarded as minor, such as using profanity or stealing

apples from a tree, with more severity if they were committed on a Sunday. Brandings and mutilations for crimes
committed on the Sabbath were not unusual, and a few ministers and civil leaders believed the death penalty appropriate
for Sabbath breaking.

Brandings and mutilations! (That sounds familiar, except that
we're using them in Iraq!)

Further, all child-rearing advice advocated harsh, repressive
training. Puritans saw the child as evil. This may be our biggest
legacy — seeing human nature as evil and not trusting it to be able
to decide for itself. Remember, Kasser's research showed that harsh
child rearing tends to create materialists! So our Puritan ethic did not
make us just into workaholics, but addicted shoppers as well.

Ultimately, joy is always a source of subversion. The Puritans
knew this and admonished people to avoid joy. They knew people
needed some play, but they wanted to control it. We should remember this — maybe if we get people to play more, play will undermine
our cruel economic system.

## The counterfeit life

"I did not wish to live what was not life," Thoreau wrote in his
famous "suck the marrow out of life" passage. What does this mean?
What is "not life?" To me it means experiences that are fake. We are
overwhelmed with the counterfeit life.

What first comes to mind is, of course, television. A friend
whose husband was chatting at a dinner party said, replying to someone else's story, "Oh yes, that happened to some friends of mine." His
wife looked at him strangely, then told him later: "That didn't happen to some friends of ours. That happened to some TV characters
we were watching!" Reality TV is not "reality." Laugh tracks aren't
real people laughing.

But it's not just TV shows that are inauthentic. It's almost
every part of our lives. Who can say that we're experiencing real life
at work? People sitting in front of screens and trading imaginary

money around the world? Scientists working to find medicine for diseases that the drug companies invent? (For example, ADD for adults.) Insurance companies swamped in paperwork designed to deny people's claims. Toy manufacturers creating tons of junk that amuse kids for only a second. Reporters aren't reporting real news any more but transcribing press releases from those in power, whether corporations, government, or right-wing think-tanks. And the rest of our lives? Driving on a freeway for an hour isn't exactly an experience of aliveness. Pornography isn't real sex. Scoring well on tests isn't real learning.

Isn't real life a deep connection with another person? Or with a book, music, nature — with an idea? When do we have time for that?

## THE SHAM

Similar to the counterfeit life is the experience of life as a sham. In the counterfeit life we're being manipulated to think we're having just as much fun with fake friends as real. In the sham experience, we're being fooled so external forces can control us.

So much of American democracy is a sham. There's the doublespeak of the people at the top. Bush's government pays phony "journalists" to write stories for them to hype right-wing policies. Bush runs fake town meetings: Everyone admitted has to be vetted. No one can speak freely. Bush lies about the reason for the Iraq War. It's impossible to cover even a fraction of the sham in our government. But I recently had a direct experience of it myself.

I live close to a major metropolitan zoo. But like so much else, it is being privatized because the city supposedly can't afford to continue supporting it. (This is the city of Microsoft millionaires and billionaires, remember.) They decided they needed a parking garage and worked with the surrounding neighborhood to come up with an acceptable plan of a low-profile, mostly underground structure. But when the city cut their funding, instead of just making a smaller garage, they decided to move its location to a less accessible, more sensitive site and build it above ground. And they deliberately conspired to withhold any information about their "switcheroo" from the public till the last minute (required by law), with just a couple weeks' notice. When neighbors discovered the tactic and protested, officials said it was a "done deal."

This was not a public process! They were not interested in what we had to say! Public process was just checking off another box on their to-do list. We even found e-mail under public disclosure showing the head of the Parks Department predicting that the "neighbors will come unglued" if they heard about the new location, so officials had better "do high-level strategic thinking" on how to subvert public oversight.

It's hard to feel alive when you're immersed in a counterfeit reality and trapped in a plastic existence. The artificial surrounds us:

- The petrochemical industry has injected at least 80,000 synthetic compounds into our lives. (Causing cancer, birth defects, disease and disability.)
- Our cities have cut us off from nature — we can rarely open windows in our office buildings; we spend more and more time encased in our cars.
- Our foods are pumped with chemicals and scientists are eager to genetically modify anything that grows.
- The emotional atmosphere in work is laden with pretense and posturing.

We have an epidemic of lying and dishonesty, harrowingly described by David Callahan in his book *The Cheating Culture: Why More Americans Are Doing Wrong to Get Ahead.* This is a society of corporate scandals, constant lying by the government, and plagiarism by journalists.

The immensity of our unreal society strikes us when we read newspaper stories like the two in the March 12, 2005 *New York Times.* One recounts how our soldiers sexually abused and humiliated prisoners in Iraq, while the other tells of President Bush hiring someone to push a public relations effort in the Middle East to try to quell the growing hate toward Americans. Public relations as a response to torture!

You can't be fully alive when you're encased in an artificial society. As Thoreau said, "Reality is fabulous" and "shams and delusions" can't compare.

## TRIVIALIZATION

You come home from a long day at work where the boss has been sniping and your coworkers sarcastic, everyone complaining but no one willing to speak up. Of course you want psychic numbing! A drink and a sitcom on television. But researchers have found that after you watch a sitcom, the most common response is a mild state of depression. I'm not someone who has thrown out my television. Until I can find another real source of laughter in my life, I'll keep going back to some of the tried and true like Seinfeld or Jon Stewart.

I often feel it's an elitist putdown when someone announces that they don't have a television. So I won't rant and rave about television in general, and I think it's a mistake to denounce TV before we give people some alternatives. But who would argue that most TV trivializes our experiences — in particular TV commercials. Commercial time used to be strictly limited, but today more and more ad spots are crammed into a half-hour programming slot. It's got so bad that people are buying TiVo and DVR boxes just for the convenience of fast-forwarding commercials.

My favorite trivial TV was a program we stumbled across while brushing our teeth before bedtime, *Elimidate*. Here was a cheap version of the already cheap idea of reality shows. The basic concept was consistent with other shows: Vote people off by being unkind and cruel. In this case, one man was presented with three women, all but one of whom he would have to "eliminate." (Sometimes it was a woman with three guys.) They went on stupid dates together, with each woman trying to outdo the others. The highlight of the show was to pull one of the women off and ask her opinion about the others. The more snide, the better.

It's obvious that our experience of television leads us to expect less of life. It sets a low bar for us to judge all of our experiences by. In particular, it has trivialized our expectations of what relationships can be. Guys are shown choosing a beer over a beautiful woman. A woman spends the night in a hotel room with her car.

REFUSAL TO UNDERSTAND WE'RE MORTAL

One of the reasons we do not fully engage with life may be because we avoid facing death. One of the most alive places I ever lived in was the South. I lived next door to a funeral home in North Carolina, and every day the kids stopped by to view the body. I, on the other hand, did not see a dead person until I was with my mother when she died. I've always suspected I'm attracted to Thoreau's vision because my father died when I was eight years old. I never again took life for granted. Being aware that I will die, I try to live every moment to its fullest.

DIMINISHMENT OF OUR EXPERIENCE

The result of all this is that we're experiencing just a fraction of what we really could experience. Our feelings are shallow and trite. We have few original ideas that emerge from our own experience. Jingles from advertisements echo in our heads. Vaclav Havel's words say it best:

> In everyone there is some longing ... for free expression of being
> and a sense of transcendence .... Yet, at the same time, each
> person is capable, to a greater or lesser degree, of coming to
> terms with living within the lie. Each person somehow succumbs
> to a profane trivialization of his or her inherent humanity.

We should be laughing more often, telling the truth more, speaking up more, feeling elated more, experiencing the suffering of the world more deeply, feeling a profound connection with nature and the universe. But we have bland, tepid lives. People either aren't smiling or they have phony smiles. How many take anti-depressants? I'm not blaming them; our culture has trivialized our existence by getting us to care about silly things like the latest fashion, the newest makeup, the fastest car, the biggest house.

Joie de vivre is the attempt to trump the conventional, to expand our definition of success to something more alive. Theodore Roszak expresses it this way:

> But when the transcendent energies waste away, then too the
> person shrivels — though far less obviously. Their loss is suffered

in privacy and bewildered silence; it is easily submerged in affluence, entertaining diversions, and adjustive therapy. Well-fed and fashionably dressed, surrounded by every manner of mechanical convenience and with our credit rating in good order, we may even be ashamed to feel we have any problems at all.... But it needs the next revolution too, which is the struggle to liberate the visionary powers from the lesser reality in which they have been confined by urban-industrial necessity.

Abraham Heschel writes:

The stirring in our hearts when watching the star-studded sky is something no language can declare .... The ineffable inhabits the magnificent and the common, the grandiose and the time facts of reality alike. Some people sense this quality at distant intervals in extraordinary events; others sense it in the ordinary events, in every fold, in every nook; day after day, hour after hour.

Enjoyment must be our guide. One of the saddest things I heard a middle-aged physician say was that he never really wanted to become a doctor. He just wanted to say that he had gone to Harvard Medical School (which he did). Sometimes I've decided to be on a board because I thought it would further my career. When the board experience wasn't any fun, I always dropped off. The only way to decide something is to observe your level of joy. You know you are on the right path when you feel joyful.

Figure out how to enjoy your life, whatever your lot. I know one man, the maître de in a restaurant, who is also a wonderful singer. Periodically he bursts into song during dinner, singing a special aria for a table of customers. I once saw a young black woman directing traffic on a ferry, and as she pointed right or left, she would be dancing and whirling and making everyone laugh. When I taught women who were returning to school, I would ask them to make a list of 10 things they like to do.

Sometimes they could not even think of one!

# CHAPTER 7

# Visionary Leisure

*You don't need to leave your room, remain sitting at your table and listen. Don't even listen, simply wait. Don't even wait, be quite still and solitary. The world will freely offer itself to you to be unmasked. It has no choice. It will roll in ecstasy at your feet.* — Kafka

*The capacity for reflection comes from a state of mind, made possible by the physical habit of doing nothing at certain hours of the days.* — Lin Yutang

On Sundays during the summer, my husband and I get up early and take Maggie to the arboretum, a lush haven of dogwoods and rhododendrums and azaleas along Lake Washington in Seattle. It's beautiful and peaceful, still cool as the sun begins to filter through the trees, forming dappled patterns on the water and the grounds. Flora bracket a grassy corridor, romantically called Azalea Way, and you can stop at lily-padded ponds with benches tucked away in shady spots and just sit and gaze.

One day we sat down by one of the ponds after hearing the ribbit of frogs. At first we saw only one, a little tiny green creature, but as we sat, looking, we spotted more and more, just sitting there on the lily pads. And so there we all were — my husband and I, our dog and the frogs — just sitting and looking. It seemed that just sitting and looking and waiting to see what would happen was enough for all of us.

*The real meaning of leisure has to do with a near-mystical experience where time stops and you feel connected to life, expanded by life, transformed by life.*

Throughout most of my life, I would have felt impatient with a morning like that. I would have been anxious to get back to my projects — a book I was reading, a paper I was writing. I would be restless to get back to my real life, my productive life, the important part of my life.

But now I know that this kind of reflection in time is the real part of my life, and it is just as important as — maybe more important than — my projects. So this time, we not only didn't go right home, we stopped at the local organic bakery and had a cinnamon roll and tea, sitting outside with our ever-present bichon watching the sailboats float languidly by. And then, continuing to defy the gods of work, we stopped to visit with some friends to meet their new puppy.

There was nothing productive or efficient about this morning, nothing really useful about the day. I crossed nothing off of my to-do list, but it was pure delight. It made me feel, as Thoreau writes, "grateful for what I am and have. My thanksgiving is perpetual." It was indeed the very best way I could have spent my time.

How did I change in my attitude toward time? What made the difference? Where did this new vision of life, of leisure, come from?

First, let's explore what I'm talking about. What is leisure? To most of us leisure is a pejorative term. It sounds like wasting time. We think of overweight men in polyester sports coats with white shoes and heavily made-up women with tightly permed hair, smoking cigarettes, gossiping and heading for Wal-Mart. We think of cruises and beaches and golfing vacations, all stuff you have to pay lots of money for to derive the privilege of "relaxation."

The real meaning of leisure has to do with a near-mystical experience where time stops and you feel connected to life, expanded by life, transformed by life. As I've studied the concept in the past several months, I've been overwhelmed with what leisure really means and how the term has been a wicket of controversy over the years. If people really understood the idea of leisure, this society would be transformed. It's crucial to understand it, because if we don't, we won't value leisure enough to commit to it; we won't care enough to work for policies that will allow more true leisure.

How did the concept of leisure become corrupted? We have all kinds of images floating around in our consciousness, and we rarely bring them out to look at and challenge. It reminds me of when I went to Europe in the '60s, the days when the Berlin Wall and the Cold War were still in full sway. Like most liberals, before the trip I had scorned our government's propaganda about communism. I hadn't felt that I was influenced at all by its silly attempts at scaremongering. But I remember very clearly the moment I realized how beholden I was. I was taking a train into Czechoslovakia and in my compartment were a Czech mother and her five-year-old son. I remember watching them closely and thinking, "Wow, they're no different from us!" I was actually surprised that they weren't some sort of monsters! My next thought was, My goodness, look at what I'm thinking, I'm more brainwashed than I suspected! It was a moment of understanding how strongly our culture affects us, how easily popular ideas seep into our brains.

The subject of leisure is similar to my experience in Czechoslovakia. We've been brainwashed without realizing it. So let me ask you, which of these things would you consider to be leisure: Reading, sitting in the sun, gardening, studying, walking, writing a poem, having a coffee at a cafe, shopping, watching television. I'm sure I've made my bias fairly clear, so anyone who has come this far would probably guess that I veered off in another direction when I got to the end of my list. Shopping and watching television are our primary non-working activities, but I'm not including them in my definition of leisure. The rest of the list belongs.

Think about what the others have in common. What is similar about reading, gardening, studying, walking, writing a poem, or hanging out in a cafe? They are reflective and joyful. They involve an openness to life, to the universe. They are a commitment to a rich inner life, a commitment to grow in wisdom. Others would probably expand this list. For instance, I haven't listed any sports, pastimes that could be considered reflective and joyful. I'll let others explore that side, because I have only second-hand knowledge of sports. Sometimes I wish I did enjoy watching baseball or basketball because people seem to have so much fun, but whenever I try, a voice in my head just keeps saying, It's only a ball! How can they get so worked up over it? I also think it's important that we differentiate between leisure activities and escapism. Escape activities get our minds off our problems, but they do nothing to deepen our ideas or our experiences. We may need to have some escape activities, but not at the expense of leisure.

While I feel strongly that we need to explore true leisure activities, this admittedly is something new for me. My unexamined assumptions about leisure led me to do what most others are doing: focus my goals on my work. When I say work, I don't just mean something I'm paid for. I regard community education as my life work, even though I make very little money from what I do. There is nothing I like more than leading a discussion or making a presentation about Simplicity or the Slow Life. If there's ever a time I experience flow, it's in front of an audience. We can enjoy our work, but we have to remember it's still work, and whenever we work, we're not totally free. Certainly it's easy to see that we're not free when we're in a paid job in the workplace, and as we discussed, the workplace is getting worse. But it seems that whenever we have a project, we're not really free because it's essentially a utilitarian approach to life. We're not doing it totally because we're drawn to do it, as in true leisure.

My excitement over re-examining leisure reminds me of my early experiences in the feminist movement, exploring women's history. Part of us worried that maybe women accomplished less because women really were inferior to men. And we suspected women hadn't been able to do as much because of their homemaking duties. But we were overwhelmed in our discoveries of how much women actually had done — it just had not been recognized in history books and popular culture.

Reading about women's activities and accomplishments throughout the ages changed me in a dramatic way. I realized that at some level I really had believed that women were inferior and existed only to be men's helpmeets. But reading about their history changed that feeling and affected my own vision of the possibilities in my life.

The same process occurred as I read about what people have said about leisure. I felt that I had been hoodwinked! I had been cheated! Here I was, working my whole life to get good grades and to write articles and books, and I discovered I had been missing something essential not only to my own happiness, but to my ability to contribute to the common good.

And why? Why has this history of leisure been hidden from us? Why has the concept been trivialized? It's just as we explored earlier: When an idea is threatening to the powers that be, it is marginalized, reduced and made to disappear.

Simply put, leisure threatens the corporate consumer society. Corporate consumerism adopts a cunning strategy of making people feel that work is the most important thing in their lives. Then, when their whole identity is invested in work, it threatens them with losing their jobs. That way a corporation can control people, keep their wages down, and make more money. What power!

On that morning when I sat looking at the pond, I was in awe of life. I would not have felt anything if I had walked on by, only briefly noting the lily pads in the flat water. I had to sit and look. I had to be open to seeing the frogs. The essence of leisure for me is awe, and according to Heschel, awe leads to insights, insights about life, wisdom.

So I have the zealotry now of the convert. I've found the scriptures of leisure and I want people to know about them. Let's explore what some great thinkers have said about leisure.

## Time away from work

Leisure is time away from work. That should be obvious. But what isn't obvious is how rare and essential it is. As Whybrow notes in *American Mania*, we're pushed to our physical and psychological limits in the amount of time we spend at work, or even the time we spend thinking about work. It's sapping our joie de vivre, ruining our health, separating us from our families and friends, undermining our chance for an inner life and destroying the environment. (Remember, the more we work, the more we consume.) We're in dire straits, even though on the surface things might look OK.

The danger of framing leisure in terms of work is that we begin to assume that leisure exists merely to refresh us so that we get back on the job. But as we'll see over and over again, true leisure transcends work. We work to have leisure, Aristotle proclaimed — we don't have leisure in order to work.

*The danger of framing leisure in terms of work is that we begin to assume that leisure exists merely to refresh us so that we get back on the job.*

## No commercials!

To enter a true leisure state involves avoiding commercialism. It doesn't mean that leisure precludes spending some money. It does suggest avoiding prepackaged entertainment. Leisure implies a sanctuary and repose devoid of consumer frippery. Part of leisure's corruption springs from big business seeing it as a bonanza for selling stuff, from athletic clothes to home-entertainment centers.

## A direct engagement with life

Any leisure activity is something we do because it brings us joy and delight. It's not something we do to get something else. It's not working out on the treadmill in order to get fit (unless you're crazy about the treadmill, and in that case you're just plain crazy).

Mirroring our exploration of status, almost everything we do these days is in service of another goal. We work to make money; we join groups to make contacts that will help us get ahead. We exercise to look good; we read to impress people. We groom to show off to people; we buy houses to one-up the Joneses. We buy cars to impress people. In the process, we lose the ability to enjoy through sheer neglect, just as we'd lose the functionality of a limb if we never moved it.

I think of the way I spent a half-hour recently. I had hung my sheets out to dry on a perfect Seattle day. The sun was out, but it wasn't really hot; there was a mild breeze that gently billowed out my sheets. I realized, after about a half-hour had passed, that I had spent the whole time literally watching my sheets dry. Maybe there's something to the old cliché, as exciting as watching grass grow. In a state of pure leisure, watching sheets dry can be rapturous.

Reflection time is important for reliving and deepening the joy of our experiences. If we consume thing after thing, have one appointment after another, nothing really sinks in. It's only when we have time to reflect on something that it really becomes a deep memory, that we can retrieve its emotions and insights from our memories. To get the full enjoyment out of anything, I need to replay it over and over in my mind. When I'm absorbed in doing something, it's only half the joy. The other half is the remembered joy, the pondering, the ruminating, the mulling over.

It also means moving at a leisurely pace, a pace that allows us, as in the parable of Eyes and No Eyes, to be aware of what is happening and what we're feeling. We have to take notice as we're going along, not just when we're sitting still. We have to watch the cues from life that tell us what is happening. We have to watch how we're feeling, to alter our plans. If we feel a cold coming on, we should take a nap. Instead, we're taught that we "haven't got time for the pain," and we take a pill that muffles our ability to hear our body's messages. Only when you stroll along and talk to yourself about how beautiful the trees and the sun are will you really experience them. Speed walking won't do it. You'll finish the whole route, and you'll only have thought about work.

Leisure often is also the way we learn. We must give the opportunity for that still, small voice to speak. It's the only way to resist the standardization of life. To change, to evolve, we must consciously choose, take action and try our ideas out and then return to reflect on the results of our actions, asking ourselves, Do I choose this? Otherwise we just stay blindly on the same path, never learning from our experience. We live a second-hand life.

## The core of a democratic society

We have almost no time for reflection, contemplation, meditation, pondering, rumination, musing, mulling over, cogitating, studying, deliberating, considering, wondering about, speculating about, examining, envisioning or thinking about life. I'm surprised we have that many words! It must reflect their importance in our English speaking cultures — or should I say past importance.

The reflective life is looking at your own experience, thinking about your own values, examining your own emotions and making decisions for yourself. Reflection and deliberation are the only ways we will save ourselves and save the planet. So much of what we do — driving our cars here and there — we do because we have not stopped to think. We aren't destroying our planet deliberately; we're doing so because we don't stop and ask about the consequences of our actions. And this is particularly true in the areas of long-term consequences. We've been trained by our quarterly stock reports (or daily updates) to think only in the short run. So we fail to see the true costs of our actions.

Leisure, then, is an activity that connects you to life. You're absorbing life. It can look like you're doing nothing, of course, but you're really doing the most important thing you can do. The images that come to me often involve a connection to nature. You're sitting at the beach watching the sun go down. You're sitting around the campfire listening to the logs crackle and snap. You're walking by a lake gazing at the clouds. You're on your hands and knees in your garden slowly pulling up a weed and getting the whole root. You're connecting with the energies of that first fiery explosion at a deep, quiet level.

Leisure often involves solitude. You're reading a book before the fireplace. You're sitting in a cafe writing in your journal. You're walking through a park watching the leaves drop off the trees. You're sitting in a cathedral in England. It's solitude, but you feel connected to life.

And leisure involves connection to others. You're sitting at a cafe with your friends drinking a glass of wine, laughing about the movie you saw the evening before. You're working with a group of volunteers cleaning up after the Katrina hurricane. You're walking with a partner leafleting homes in the political campaign. You're singing in the community chorus.

And leisure involves the arts. You're walking through the Louvre, stopping to look at the *Mona Lisa*. You're carrying your sketchpad with you as you sit in a cafe and draw the interesting-looking person at the next table. You're taking a class in watercolors.

It involves travel. You're floating down a river in England, getting ashore periodically to explore a village pub. You're looking up at Notre Dame in Paris. You're trekking the Himalayas.

And my favorite: It involves studying and thinking. You're indulging the basic instinct of humanity: wanting to know more, wanting to understand, wanting to develop your own philosophic system. You're sitting with others in a study circle. You're sitting in the library reading. You're bent over your morning *New York Times*.

Leisure allows you to think, to enjoy, to protest, to plan. No surprise that it's a threat to the powers that be!

## The classics

A wonderful book on classic leisure is *Leisure, The Basis of Culture* by Josef Pieper. A more accurate title would have been, *Leisure, the Basis of Happiness and Wisdom*. In any case, it transformed my life. And it snuck up on me. I thought I knew something about leisure. I knew we needed it; I knew our free time had been shrinking. But I saw leisure mainly as time to refresh energy levels for returning to work. Instead, leisure, as Pieper envisions it, is the whole point of life.

This is not necessarily an easy book to summarize. It must be read several times and very slowly! Not just because it's complex, but because his language is so beautiful. To try to summarize it in my own words will diminish its impact, so I want to use his phrasing as much as possible to give you a flavor of the book and encourage you to read it yourself.

Pieper depicts our world as being one of "total work" and laments leisure's near-forgotten stature. "Can the world of man be exhausted in being the 'working world'? Can the human being be satisfied with being a functionary, a 'worker'? Can human existence be fulfilled in being exclusively a work-a-day existence?" His answer is a resounding No! You cannot live fully if work dominates your life. Why? Because you are never free. You are never in tune with the world. You are always reduced to being a functionary and you miss living deeply. Even as his book was published in Germany in 1947, work was indeed taking over and "the whole life of the working human being is consumed."

Pieper explains his idea by contrasting two different ways of knowing. The first is what we are all used to: In Latin it is called *ratio*. It is like what we do in school: We read something, we discuss it, we try to find errors in logic, we pull an idea apart, we come to conclusions, we prove our idea.

Then Pieper describes a second kind of knowing: It's called *intellectus* — definitely not something we learn in school! It is "the ability of 'simply looking' ... to which the truth presents itself as a landscape presents itself to the eye." When we do this, says Pieper, we connect with reality. It brings "a higher bliss, a healing, and the fullness of existence, and thereby the fullness of happiness."

And this comes with no effort.

> It is an inner absence of preoccupation, a calm, an ability to let things go, to be quiet .... Leisure is a form of that stillness that is the necessary preparation for accepting reality; only the person who is still can hear, and whoever is not still, cannot hear .... Leisure is the disposition of receptive understanding, of contemplative beholding, and immersion — in the real.

Pieper sees leisure as opening up, a letting go, similar to the experience of falling asleep:

> The surge of new life that flows out to us when we give ourselves to the contemplation of a blossoming rose, a sleeping child, or of a divine mystery — is this not like the surge of life that comes from deep, dreamless sleep? .... In just the

same way, do the greatest, most blessed insights, the kind that could never be tracked down, come to us above all in the time of leisure. In such silent openness of the soul, it may be granted to man for only an instant to know "what the world holds in its innermost."

Leisure to Pieper is so much more than the way we spend our weekends and vacations, both of which we tend to jam with frenetic activity. So it's not surprising that Pieper's ideas have amazed and overwhelmed me. I've been trying to say that we need to move from the consumer society to a culture of connectedness. Pieper gives us a direct example, almost an experience of what it means to be connected to the universe. He observes, "The power to be at leisure is the power to step beyond the working world and win contact with those superhuman, life-giving forces that can send us, renewed and alive again, into the busy world of work."

Being fully ourselves is a central theme for the Slow Life, one I'll keep returning to over and over. When I talked earlier about the metaphysics of joie de vivre, I argued that we are expressions of that first fiery explosion at the birth of our universe, and that we are part of a universe that continues to evolve. We need to express our true selves because it is the universe expressing itself through us. Pieper puts it this way: "There can only be leisure, when man is at one with himself, when he is in accord with his own being." When we are at work, we are only functionaries; when we are at leisure, we are fully ourselves and it comes from "the gift of contemplative self-immersion in Being."

*"What do you do?" we ask when we meet someone. Even though I always try to substitute "Tell me about yourself," people still respond by telling me their occupation.*

"What do you do?" we ask when we meet someone. Even though I always try to substitute "Tell me about yourself," people still respond by telling me their occupation. And of course we pigeonhole people by their jobs. We think most lawyers are jerks, that elementary school teachers are a little silly, that a secretary isn't very smart, that a dentist is dull. And think about accountants! (I once met an accountant who asked me if I knew the difference between an introverted accountant and an extroverted accountant. The introvert looks at his feet as he talks to you. The extrovert looks at *your* feet.) So right away, we have trouble connecting with the real person because we see him or her in a narrow, stereotyped way.

And then we start assigning people status points. We may think lawyers are jerks, but they get more status points than a schoolteacher. If we meet a secretary, or an administrative assistant, our status meter goes down a few notches. If someone is a doctor or a professor, the points can go through the roof. Even if they are unpleasant, unscrupulous people, we gather around them! And so, instead of wanting our children to grow up just to be decent, caring people, we want them to grow up and get an important job. We don't say that we want them to be ethical people or kind people. We want them to be somebody rich and important!

Now some will object to what I've just said, and hopefully some of you have moved beyond pigeonholing and status-mongering. But it's not the way people act. Our work decides so much more than our paycheck. It gives us an identity and our place in society.

So Pieper laments, as do many others, the way work has taken over. But there is one point he makes that I have not heard elsewhere. He says that our attitude toward work is part of another belief — that we're the sum of our own efforts. He thinks we should recognize that we receive something as a gift from life, and that our arrogant belief in our own power hardens our hearts and closes our minds: "The hard quality of not-being-able-to-receive; a stoniness of heart, that will not brook any resistance — as expressed once, most radically, in the following terrifying statement: 'Every action makes sense, even criminal acts ... all passivity is senseless,'" — a quote he implies comes from Hitler. (I have a feeling that he could not have quoted Hitler openly because his book, published in 1947, was being written while Hitler was in power.) Perhaps leisure was a subtle way to resist Hitler. Perhaps work without end lays the foundation for a fascist society.

Pieper says that workaholics have no feeling for justice, celebration or poetry. In fact, what came to mind when I read him was that workaholics rarely have a sense of humor, and if there is anything that we receive as a gift from the universe, it is humor. When we make people laugh, we have no idea where our words come from; they just pop into our mind. So we see even more clearly why leisure is necessary for freedom.

## Making leisure possible

What can we do to implement leisure into our lives? According to Pieper we need adequate wages, limited power of the state and avoidance of internal poverty. We need adequate wages because we don't have time or the emotional capacity to be still and listen to the universe if we are always anxious about money. Of course, as we have discovered since he wrote his book, even those with enough money have difficulties. We spend so much that no one feels any income is adequate. Our goal, as we need to say time and again, is to reduce the gap between the rich and the poor.

And as to limiting the power of the state, certainly that still applies. But in America we also need to limit the power of corporations who control not only our lives, but the actions of the government.

Wages and freedom from the corporate state are issues we need to work on together. What we can do individually is address internal poverty.

Pieper's concerns about ways of knowing, *ratio* and *intellectus*, have obvious ramifications for education. Education, he says, should be concerned with the whole:

> Whoever is educated knows how the world as a whole behaves. Education concerns the whole human being, insofar as he is ... able to comprehend the sum total of existing things ..... For it is in leisure genuinely understood that man rises above the level of a thing to be used and enters the realm where he can be at home with the potentialities of his own nature, where, with no concern for doing, no ties to the

immediate, the particular, and the practical, he can attend to
the love of wisdom, can begin leading a truly human life.

Pieper wants education to be concerned with wisdom — to
figure out what reality is and to connect to the essence of reality. He
sees the goal of wisdom not as mastering knowledge, but being forever
in search of understanding. Wisdom is a "putting-oneself-into-relation
... knowing as the power to place oneself into relation with the sum-
total of existing things ... to be in relation to the totality of being."

And this means teaching people to become philosophers (all
of us). The goal of philosophy is not like that of science. "In the
philosophical act, the human being's 'related-ness' to the totality of
being is realized; philosophy is oriented toward the world as a
whole." To create a culture of connectedness, we must take the time
to experience this "related-ness," to absorb the world as a whole.
Then we understand how we are connected to ourselves, to others, to
nature, to the universe.

Pieper ultimately extends even this vision of connectedness.
He says something that brings all of my thinking together:
"Philosophy begins in wonder" — where "wonder" is the realization
that life is "greater, deeper, more real" than we can ever suspect.
Remember how Underhill puts it: We want to become Eyes instead
of No-Eyes. To look at life with wonder is to be amazed that anything exists. Goethe, when he was 80, said, "The highest state to
which humanity can aspire is wonder ... the sense that the world is a
deeper, wider, more mysterious thing than appeared to the day-to-
day understanding." This to me is the basis for the slow life, for
community, leisure, and joie de vivre.

Approaching life with wonder means that we try to keep alive
the feeling that life is wonderful — to never feel that we have the
final answer, but to keep searching and to experience a connectedness
with the whole. If your approach is one of wonder, you never close
yourself off to a new form of wisdom or aliveness. "It therefore
belongs to the nature of philosophy that it only 'has' its object in the
manner of a loving search," says Pieper. It is going through life seeing

more — seeing the beauty in people and in nature and in everyday acts. Feeling connected with the essence of life. Pieper says, "So this is the goal, to which philosophy is directed: understanding of reality in terms of an ultimate principle of unity."

So this was how I changed. This is why the high point of my day is sitting in my back yard and tilting back my lounge chair so I can lie there and watch the breeze moving lightly through the trees and the branches waving like dancers' arms. This is why leisure is essential in our lives. Without it we are cut off from life and our culture is in danger.

I always return to my joyful day of sitting and watching my sheets dry. A few years ago I would have felt that I had wasted that time — I could have read the paper more thoroughly, written a letter to the editor, prepared a talk. But now I know that the time spent watching my sheets dry was the best way I could experience my time. And it felt wonderful!

## Jacob Needleman

Philosopher Jacob Needleman, writing toward the end of the 20th century, comes to similar conclusions about leisure, with a slightly different approach. He says that time is our psychic energy, but that time is only an illusion, as are so many other things in our lives — such as fame, wealth and power — that are expressions of the ego, the secondary self. Because behind the secondary self is the real self — our minds are expressions of the divine mind. Your real self is outside of time, while your secondary self is within time.

Sometimes, he says, we experience the real self breaking through. It's an expression of "I am" from a deeper source.

We often feel this self emerge when we're young — Needleman says it hit him at 15. Reading him made me recall the summer when I was 12 and walking along outside of the courthouse in the small town where I lived. I remember the streets being lined with big leafy trees and having this strong feeling of amazement that I was alive, and that I was I. I've always remembered this, even though, as I said, nothing really happened. It makes sense to me to think that it was the emergence of the real self from my child self.

Needleman says that as we get busy with the world as we grow up, competing and striving, the real self visits less and less. Then, when we begin to lose ambition, envy and pettiness, usually as we get older, the real self begins to visit again. This, he says, is why most cultures have honored elders, because they could see the real self present. As Thoreau says, "It's surprising how contented one can be, with only a sense of existence." With a true sense of existence, time slows nearly to a stop.

Needleman says something that takes me back to the beginning of this book — the importance of authenticity and being true to the real self:

> Is the stress of time, the famine of time, the result of living a life that is not my own? Could I possibly be driven mad, as we are driven mad, except by a life that is not my own, that is not occupied by my own intimate self, that is not felt and respected in my blood and bone?

And so as we rush around, we cannot connect with ourselves, and we cannot build a culture of connectedness. Because with no real self, there can't be connection with others, with the Earth, or the universe, the real self, or (as Needleman quotes Emerson) the "Over Soul."

> The problem of time in our world is not due to technology in itself. It is due to the fact that our inner sense of time obeys the machine and acts with the tempo and rhythms of the machine. If we could use the technologies invented by the mind and at the same time retain a relationship within ourselves among all the principal parts of our being, the body, the mind and the feelings, we could make use of technology and still retain our humanness, our real time, our real past and our real future.

So leisure is not just slowing down, it is another kind of time. We have stepped out of time because we are absorbed in life. We become timeless.

## Bertrand Russell

If I need more leisure for anything, it's to read and discuss with others my favorite classics of the past. Atop my list under leisure would be Bertrand Russell's *In Praise of Idleness*, written in 1932. Russell makes several suggestions in his little essay. First, that the Protestant work ethic evolved as a way to get the lower classes to work without making a fuss. When you make something a "duty," people feel good about doing it. But it is often a form of false consciousness. Most of us who participated in the women's movement discovered this: We had grown up learning that our purpose in life was to sacrifice ourselves for our families. Our needs were subservient to the needs of our husband's and our children. Of course there were other offshoots of that belief system — in particular, that women weren't as smart as men. It took us a long time to challenge those two belief systems and to see that they perpetuated male power.

In the same way, the idea of moral duty to work perpetuated the power of the upper classes. It is not to say that the upper classes consciously created this belief system to repress the workers; it is simply the way human self-interest works. We create dictums that are beneficial to our own interests, and then we rationalize them so that we can live with them. Many slave owners did this with slavery. It's hard for us to realize that people once thought slavery was acceptable — the supreme rationalization.

In fact, Russell links our ideas about the duty to work with rationalizations of slavery: "The morality of work is the morality of slaves, and the modern world has no need of slavery." During medieval days serfs were forced to give their surplus to lords.

> Gradually, however, it was found possible to induce many of them to accept an ethic according to which it was their duty to work hard, although part of their work went to support others in idleness. By this means the amount of compulsion required was lessened, and the expenses of government were diminished .... The conception of duty, speaking historically, has been a means used by the holders of power to induce

others to live for the interests of their masters rather than for their own.

Modern technology has made it possible to reduce the amount of labor needed to support basic survival. In fact, Russell says that World War I, when so many workers were in combat, proved that just a small part of the labor force could produce enough. Russell believes we should have adopted a four-hour workday. That would have allowed people to earn enough to survive and greatly reduced unemployment.

Russell anticipates the argument that people would not know what to do with all that leisure time. In truth, some experiments in the '30s, such as Kellogg's six-hour day, show that given extra time, people quickly find ways to use it. It's only when we have limited time that we turn to television; true creativity and pleasure take time.

Russell says that we used to have a "capacity for light-heartedness and play which has been to some extent inhibited by the cult of efficiency. The modern man thinks that everything ought to be done for the sake of something else, and never for its own sake." And Russell sees that, of course, education would be needed to change our attitudes and help people learn to live more fully with leisure. Russell gives us a stunning portrait of what life could be like:

> In a world where no one is compelled to work more than four hours a day, every person possessed of scientific curiosity will be able to indulge it, and every painter will be able to paint without starving, however excellent his pictures may be. Young writers will not be obliged to draw attention to themselves by sensational pot-boilers, with a view to acquiring the economic independence needed for monumental works, for which, when the time at last comes, they will have lost the taste and capacity. Men who, in their professional work, have become interested in some phase of economics or government, will be able to develop their ideas without the academic detachment that makes the work of university economists often seem lacking in reality. Medical men will

have the time to learn about the progress of medicine, teachers will not be exasperatedly struggling to teach by routine
methods things which they learnt in their youth, which may,
in the interval, have been proved to be untrue.

Above all, there will be happiness and joy of life, instead of
frayed nerves, weariness, and dyspepsia. The work exacted
will be enough to make leisure delightful, but not enough to
produce exhaustion. Since men will not be tired in their spare
time, they will not demand only such amusements as are passive and vapid. At least one per cent will probably devote the
time not spent in professional work to pursuits of some public importance, and, since they will not depend upon these
pursuits for their livelihood, their originality will be unham-
pered, and there will be no need to conform to the standards
set by elderly pundits. But it is not only in these exceptional
cases that the advantages of leisure will appear. Ordinary men
and women, having the opportunity of a happy life, will
become more kindly and less persecuting and less inclined to
view others with suspicion. The taste for war will die out,
partly for this reason, and partly because it will involve long
and severe work for all. Good nature is, of all moral qualities,
the one that the world needs most, and good nature is the
result of ease and security, not of a life of arduous struggle.
Modern methods of production have given us the possibility
of ease and security for all; we have chosen, instead, to have
overwork for some and starvation for others. Hitherto we
have continued to be as energetic as we were before there
were machines; in this we have been foolish, but there is no
reason to go on being foolish forever.

On December 1, 1930, W.K. Kellogg, owner of the highly
successful cereal company, inaugurated the six-hour day at his plant
in Battle Creek, Michigan. It was an instant success and was covered by
the national media as well as studied by universities and government
agencies. All proclaimed it the wave of the future.

But following World War II, the company officially ended the experiment. It had begun to reduce unemployment by sharing hours among a larger number of workers, and workers loved it even to the point of reducing their salaries. Many held on as long as they could, but by 1985 the last remnants of the program were gone.

Few know the story of Kellogg's great experiment. I had never heard about it until a few years ago, when I discovered the work of Benjamin Hunnicutt, professor of leisure studies at the University of Iowa. He tells the fascinating history in *Kellogg's Six-Hour Day*, a more detailed follow up to his book *Work Without End: Abandoning Shorter Hours for the Right to Work*. These two books are part of a hidden history in the United States, and when you read them you realize how we have once again been hoodwinked into believing things that militate against our best interests.

In the early '20s, a strange thing happened. The country started to worry that American workers were now so productive that they would produce more than people would buy. The '20s were also the culmination of a century of effort to reduce the workweek. During the first two decades of the 20th century, working hours fell from 60 to 50 hours a week. During the Depression they fell as low as 35.

But what people discovered was a new reason for living. You didn't work just to survive; you worked to become fully alive through your own creative powers and your involvement in community. The exuberance in the reports of the Kellogg workers makes you realize exactly what we're missing today with our long hours of work. People saw the shorter work hours campaign as a "miracle of welfare capitalism," claiming that, says Hunnicutt, "workers would be liberated by increasingly higher wages and shorter hours for the final freedom promised by the Declaration of Independence — the pursuit of happiness."

The word most often used was "freedom." The women interviewed by the Women's Bureau in the Department of Labor talked of free time, free evenings, freedom to pursue one's own interests, freedom to help their neighbors, freedom to make things and give neighbors gifts. They talked about choice and control over their lives.

And they talked about caring: They told stories about how much fun they had together (this during the Depression) going on trips and walks, playing baseball and other games, sitting on their front porches and talking.

Reporters noted how happy people were to have lives of their own, and that their family life was better, their homes' appearances improved as they spruced up their lawns and gardens. They were healthier as they participated in parks and recreation facilities. People were reading and studying more. Women returned to traditional activities like canning, which brought families much closer than today's sitting around the TV together.

But then the tide began to turn, and we started our long death march to increased work hours. What happened? The essential message in both of these books is that employers realized that if workers were allowed shorter hours, the corporation would ultimately lose control over them. If leisure became the center of their lives — if they had time to think and talk and find satisfaction in other ways — they would be much harder to subjugate. Productivity would decline; profit would suffer.

So Hunnicutt documents the insidious ways that people's minds were changed. Some of it was very conscious and deliberate; some of it was just an automatic response of the powerful to protect their turf. But people's minds were changed without their being aware of what was happening.

The story of this change reminds me of what I learned when I did my dissertation. The most effective way you control people is to get them to buy into their subjugation. When it's done in an obvious, overt manner, people will rebel. You have to convince them that it's for their own good. In my dissertation I explored the ways that women were kept out of the male workplace. Essentially, they were led to believe that if they became carpenters or bank presidents, they would be unattractive and no man would want to marry them. When women entered these fields they often left — not because they were fired, but because the men were cold and inhospitable, not speaking to them, not responding to them. In some cases there was violence or dirty tricks, but at least those cases could be taken to court on charges of discrimination. Yet how could you complain to a court that no one said good morning to you? That no one welcomed you, that you were ignored and had no one to eat lunch with. Subtle discrimination drove many women out of male fields.

A similar story line was used to convince people that shorter work hours were wrong. In one aspect the gender card was played, portraying men who would work shorter hours as being feminine and weak. Manly men worked eight hours! Many of the hobbies that people had taken up, such as birdwatching and gardening clubs, became the butts of jokes.

Leisure became the subject of a cultural debate. In 1936 and 1937, H.G. Wells introduced two films to the American public in which he took up the theme — *Things to Come* and *The Man Who Could Work Miracles*. His essential question was, Whither mankind? He echoed Charles Beard's question, The stomach being full, what shall we do next? In *Things to Come*, the protagonist says,

> What is all this progress? What good of this progress? Onward and upward. We demand a halt; we demand a rest. The object of life is happy living .... We thought this was to be the Age of Leisure. But is it? ... We gain the whole world — and at what price!"

Gradually leisure's defenders got worn down. The Depression didn't help matters much. Roosevelt decided that the best path to confront unemployment was work-creation by the government instead of work-sharing by the people. Advertisers began broadcasting the "gospel of consumption," seducing people into spending more money, forcing them to work longer hours instead of working less by living more simply. Hunnicutt shows how the human-relations industry helped trivialize leisure by invoking Maslow, arguing that work was the way to become self-actualized. Social reformers began to talk more about people finding themselves in the workplace instead of in leisure. And all these worked together. As people began spending more money on leisure activities they became less fulfilling.

Consequently, workers were less likely to fight for shorter hours. Unions started asking for more money instead of fewer hours.

Some suggest that the free time people had in the Depression may have been too scary. That free time came to be associated with financial worry. During World War II, people's productivity was pushed as well. In the '50s Erich Fromm published *Escape from Freedom*, talking about the fact that true freedom was alarming to people. Academics of the time talked about the importance of educating people for leisure, but their voices were soon ignored. One of the reasons leisure became threatening was because people had lost their traditional communities and pastimes and did not know what to do any more.

What all of this shows is just how significant and important leisure is. Yet few of us have even been exposed to its history and debates. (Of course it's not part of our official history.) In 1979 Representative John Conyers of Michigan sponsored a bill to set the standard work week at 35 hours in order to reduce unemployment. The bill went nowhere.

For most of us, the notion of progress involving a nonmaterial "higher life" through shorter work hours isn't even on our radar. The subtle addictions of corporate consumerism have persuaded us that longer work hours will give us a better life, despite a full weight of evidence to the contrary.

# CHAPTER 8

# *Slow Together: Exuberant Community*

IT'S STRANGE HOW INSIGHTS OCCUR. You mull over a problem long enough, and answers seem to emerge.

It all started a few years ago when my husband and I joined a book discussion group. We were searching, as so many are, for an experience of community. We quickly discovered, however, that ours was a dysfunctional book group! Instead of the goodwill and camaraderie we were looking for, we often left a meeting feeling slighted — thinking that everyone thought we were stupid and shallow and dull. How did this happen? All we were doing was discussing a book! But somehow our discussions fell victim to our whole American culture. We became competitive and judgmental. We became what we were taught to be in our college English classes — warriors of the word, pouncing on any utterance and hacking it to pieces. We wanted to win!

This wasn't community. When you experience community, you feel expanded and joyful. You become more witty and wise, and so does everyone else. You feel new ideas blossom and you feel as if you can say anything and people will nod their heads in agreement and understanding. We began to wonder if the problems in the book group were our fault — something we'd done. Then I saw a story in the *Wall Street Journal* about the anguish and suffering of book discussion groups. The story said that a whole new profession had emerged — therapists treating survivors of book groups! One man said that the members in his group were some of the meanest people he had ever met. I felt a little better after reading that. I could see it was a bigger problem than I had imagined. We dropped out of the book group, but I still yearned for community.

*When you experience*

*community, you feel*

*expanded and joyful.*

*You become more witty*

*and wise, and so does*

*everyone else.*

Next I tried going to church. I prodded myself to attend Sunday morning services, even though I really don't like church services, no matter how universal. We were still sitting in uncomfortable pews, facing straight ahead with the leader in the front of the room talking down at us. Large groups with an authority figure in the front almost never create community. After the service, during the coffee hour, I just couldn't really get good conversations going. There wasn't much time, and I felt like I had to keep mingling. I even got involved in some of the other activities — something I know you need to do if you really want to meet people. I became a member; I paid dues. After three years I finally gave up. I never succeeded in feeling I belonged to a community, or that a real community was even there.

I kept searching. I went to a meeting of the Green Party. No one welcomed the new people, and once again there was a man giving a lecture with formal discussion. I went to the Democrats, and the meeting was the longest, most boring talk-athon I've ever sat through. Again no one took the simple courtesy of welcoming new people. I decided to give up. It's only community, I told myself; not like it's a cure for world hunger.

## Other, more important problems

In fact there were other, seemingly more important issues I felt I should be focusing on. I've always been involved in social change, and I've long realized that if we are to solve our massive problems, we need people's involvement. But how do you rouse someone to action; how you ignite concern? I've always wondered how people can read stories in the newspaper day after day and not want to take action — stories about kids killing kids or species passing into extinction. In a way I understand the paralysis, because I've felt it myself. Some of the devastation happening to the environment, for instance, is so depressing that it's difficult not to repress it or sink into despair. A few years ago I read a newspaper story that was particularly upsetting. It was about an animal I'd never heard of before — something called Miss Waldron's red colobus monkey. The article said that the monkey was now extinct. The September 12, 2000 *New York Times* reports, "For the first time in several centuries, a member of the primate order, the taxonomic group to which human beings belong, has become extinct …."

Extinct. Completely gone. This "loud-mouthed, red-cheeked monkey from the rainforest" has disappeared forever because human beings hunted it, ate it, *consumed* it. In the past this monkey could have escaped the trappers because it could flee deep into the wild. But logging and road building shredded its habitat and stranded monkeys in isolated thickets.

The article must have caught my eye because the name was so human sounding, and I realized that indeed it was a very human monkey — one of our ancestors. But I kept feeling worse as I read on. The scientists said this monkey could have been saved. Now, the report says, the forests where this vocal monkey lived are silent: "You don't hear anything, you don't hear birds. You stumble over snares and shotgun shells." And of course environmentalists have long been warning that the same could happen to the human race.

This is the kind of tragedy that saps your initiative. What can I do? you wonder. It's better to just ignore such stories and get on with the day's business. Worrying won't help anything.

But it's not just the plight of nature that upsets me. There's the sadness I feel when I see a homeless person begging on the street or discover how many of my friends take anti-depressants. The terror I feel when a friend discovers a lump in her breast or tells me of another friend being killed by a drunk driver. The despair I feel when I read about a child being hospitalized for asthma. The anger I feel when I read about a for-profit prison that makes teenage boys labor under a hot Texas sun.

I've spent many hours wondering how to rouse people to act, and then one day I remembered an experience I had one summer many years ago, when I was young and just out of college. Thinking about it gave me a new idea.

It was the summer of '64, and I was sitting in a schoolroom in a small village in the south of France, listening to a Canadian boy teach Bob Dylan's "Blowin' in the Wind" to a group of students. I thought the guy was stuffy and overbearing, but I wanted to stay on his good side because we were hitchhiking together when the program was over, and I didn't want to travel by myself.

The other students were from France and England. We had spent the day renovating an old woman's house, throwing out the garbage and painting her kitchen a clean fresh white while she sat and beamed amidst the clutter. The weekend before, we had celebrated Bastille Day at the ocean. I remember it as a glorious day — the sun was hot, the sand blew into our faces, the waves were high. As we watched a roasting lamb turn on the spit, we passed around a bottle of wine, and that night, when we returned to our dorm, we sang rousing, jubilant songs.

I was participating in a tradition started after World War I, when college youth took to the country to restore people's homes and villages. Ever since, students have flocked to these summer work camps throughout Europe, experiencing the delight of joyfully making a difference. As I look back on that summer, it seems to me that this experience holds the key to social change. We can't just rant. We must help people experience joy and meaning and a sense of belonging. We must help the public transcend ordinary, barren lives and experience the aliveness I felt that summer. All of us yearn for a profound engagement with life: We're searching for a sense of sublime exhilaration and intoxicating reality, a life that is vital and engaging. That's what I remember from that summer. I was making a difference and experiencing a magnificent intensity and sharpness of life. And the chief delight of it was that I was experiencing community!

Maybe this is the answer to social transformation — people need to experience joyful community. It addresses two needs: solving the world's ills and letting people feel part of something bigger. Maybe we can only have community when we're involved in something really significant, and maybe we can only bring about social change when we experience joyful community. But there's something else. At the heart of both community and social change is conversation. Certainly it's obvious that conversation is central to community, but we don't necessarily associate it with social change. Sociologist Amitai Etzioni says that we bring about social change by creating a national conversation. He calls it, distinctively, a metalogue.

## Conversation

Some of my most transformative moments have been in conversation. An evening of good talk and laughter can be blissful and intoxicating. What could be more engaging than sitting at a French café with good friends talking about life, nursing

*Maybe this is the answer to social transformation — people need to experience joyful community.*

a bottle of wine, laughing and commenting on the passersby? Who hasn't imagined themselves catching sight of Sartre and Simone de Beauvoir in the '50s or wished they could have listened in at the Algonquin Round Table in the '20s? Today, unfortunately, most of our conversations are mundane or even antagonistic. We're surrounded by anger on the streets and on the talk shows. By the same token, a lot of conversations are trivial — they're about the weather or a new restaurant.

It seems obvious to say so, but we forget how much conversation can make a difference. It can be something very small. I remember how I felt when my mother died, how a few brave souls had the courage to tell me how sorry they were. Our tendency is to fall mute when someone is suffering, but I learned that even a few words can bring great comfort. I remember how I felt when I encouraged a friend to present her work at a poetry reading, or when I helped another friend decide to go back to school.

Conversation in the workplace can make a startling difference in morale. As a community college administrator, whenever I felt burned out, I would walk around the campus talking to people — not about anything particularly important, just chatting about their lives. I felt renewed and committed once again. To be sure, conversation in the workplace often is more negative than positive, competitive and divisive rather than uniting. Sometimes I think that no one enjoys work because relationships are so dreadful. In fact, research bears it out — your relationships with your coworkers are a primary source of work satisfaction and vice versa. I remember when I was working at a juvenile detention hall and the superintendent called me into his office and told me I was too emotional in my work. "No, I'm not!" I blurted out. And then I burst into tears.

It's not what people say but what they don't say. Seldom do we feel appreciated at work, or feel that others recognize the value of what we're doing. Why? Because no one tells us! Recall how in my study of women being trained for traditionally male work, I found one of the biggest obstacles to their success was the fact that none of the men spoke to them in an encouraging manner, or even spoke to them at all! It wasn't that the men were outright sexist — they just ignored the women.

The manager's basic tool is still fear, even though the alternative is so much more effective! I remember something my daughter told me. One of her coworkers had gone on a business trip, and the company laptop was stolen when she left it unattended. The coworker was a young woman new to the job, and she knew the company was struggling financially, so she was doubly distraught. My daughter, her supervisor, sat down with her and told her that it was OK, that it could happen to anyone, and that they really valued her services. The young coworker was terribly relieved. She began working with more confidence and commitment. But here's the key — not only did the young coworker feel better, so did my daughter. She felt enlarged by the experience.

In fact my daughter may have derived even more good will from the experience — because of something that had happened to her when she was in high school working in an ice-cream shop. She had asked for a 10-cent per-hour raise, and the owner had screamed at her for 10 minutes. By behaving differently as a supervisor herself, she helped heal an old wound.

Yes, these are small examples, but when you begin to think about it, many of us have taken a new step in our lives after a conversation with someone. Countless numbers of young people have committed themselves to saving the environment after talking with Jane Goodall. During the '60s I committed to opposing the Vietnam War after a conversation with a young man on a bus who was being shipped off to fight there. I had protested the War before, but that conversation firmed my involvement.

Ultimately, conversation flowers when it is in search of the truth, when we have a chance to talk with others about the meaning of life or explore ideas that have transformed the world. Socrates will always be our ultimate guide — even though we will never really know what he thought, since Socrates himself never wrote a word. But Plato's picture of Socrates has inspired humankind throughout the ages to search for truth through dialogue. The philosopher Karl Jaspers explains that Socrates thought the point of life was to discover truth, and that truth emerges from dialogue among people: "Truth comes to us in dialogue. It is still unknown to both participants, but it is there. Both of them circle around it and are guided by it."

Such is the transformational potential of conversation. It's strange — Socrates is probably the most (maybe only) recognized philosopher. Almost everyone in the Western world has heard of him, but still, we totally neglect what he did — spark conversations! Certainly encouraging conversation is not one of our government's goals. And how many churches make it a priority? What classes in school focus on conversation? Few worry that we've lost the art of conversation, even though we admire Socrates.

*Ultimately, conversation flowers when it is in search of the truth, when we have a chance to talk with others about the meaning of life or explore ideas that have transformed the world.*

How can we elevate the idea of conversation and get people to see what it is capable of, get people to take it seriously — to see that every exchange they have with others has the potential for an experience of exuberance and meaning?

Three elements of togetherness are intertwined in the pursuit of Slow: social change, joyful community, and conversation. Where do we go from here?

## Neighborhood community

The key to understanding something is often experience. A few years ago, I discovered something that seemed very promising!

For years, following Labor Day my husband and I would begin strategizing over how we could avoid the approaching Seattle winter. Summertime in Seattle is magic, but Seattle's winters are dark, dark, dark! You get up in the dark, and then by 4:30 p.m. it's dark. And all day long is a dark monotone — the "grey duvet," a friend calls it. It's wet, too — not that the rain pours down, there's just a perpetual mist. People in Seattle have serious issues with SAD, seasonal affective disorder.

We decided to try living part-time in the San Francisco Bay area. We have lived in Seattle for many years, but we had also periodically (but temporarily) lived in the Bay Area and have lots of friends there. One winter in particular, after the sun came out on 3 of 100 consecutive days, motivated us to try something different. And so we spent three academic years in California — first in Palo Alto and then in San Francisco — while maintaining our home in Seattle during the summertime.

The weather in the Bay area during the long winter months was certainly an attraction. But over the course of our stay, we gradually realized something was missing. We realized that we missed what we came to think of as an "invisible" layer of neighborhood community we had built up in Seattle — something we possessed only by living here for many years and being involved and engaged.

Of course we kept in touch with our Seattle friends while we were away, but it wasn't enough. We missed the little things that we took for granted — running into people we knew grocery shopping, or waitresses knowing our order at our favorite restaurant or our wonderful conversations with the owner of our favorite bookstore. None of these experiences are earthshaking. They don't seem that significant in the great scheme of things. But we realized that we really, really missed the feeling of belonging to a community. It was something we felt we could never attain in San Francisco — partly because the city is so big, and partly because community takes such a long time to create.

So we came back home enlightened and somewhat surprised. I had always been interested in community, but not necessarily in my neighborhood. Community typically focused around my interests. When the women's movement was strong, most of my friends were in feminist activities. When I became involved in the Simplicity movement, a lot of my community experience revolved around that. But I had never considered my physical neighborhood a "community." Community comprised people of my choosing. As I read more about community, however, I realized that there was something to be said for "unintentional community" — community with people that fate, not choice, brought into your life. The concept meshed nicely with something I'd discovered in the Bay area, focused both on community and conversation.

It was called Oakland EcoVillage. It involved a group of people who live around Lake Merritt in Oakland and have created a community that revolves around self-education and self-entertainment — and in particular, conversation. Two or three events are scheduled for a typical evening, and they have a constantly updated calendar on the Web. So if you feel like going out some night, you check the calendar and choose among maybe a health-support group, a simplicity circle, a video get-together, or a Middle East discussion group. Once a week the community gathers in a local pizza parlor to just hang out and talk. Once a month they get together to assemble the calendar.

This sounded so exciting to me! It was not only community personified, but people organizing their own educational and entertainment experiences — taking back their lives from the consumer society! As I looked over the offerings, I wondered why they called themselves an EcoVillage, given there was no particular focus on the environment. Their response: We thought we would focus on meeting people's needs, and then maybe we could get people to focus on the planet's needs. Perfect, I thought. If people learn to care for each other by gathering together, they can't help but care more for the planet. It's as if caring is an ability that we all have, but is either nurtured or withered.

And we learn it primarily through conversation.

So here was a way to focus on neighborhood community and on creating opportunities for people to join together and talk. Some neighborhood communities may focus on building parks or putting in a traffic circle. In the EcoVillage, the focus was on conversation!

So when I came back to Seattle, I threw myself into starting such a village in my own neighborhood: the Phinney EcoVillage. My husband set up a Web site with a calendar, and we began posting mission statements and events under the banner, "Simpler, Slower, Smaller." I call it "EcoVillage Lite" because all we intentionally have in common is living in the same metropolitan district. Otherwise the EcoVillage is an accident of location.

We're still getting rolling. But we've established a core group of regulars and have an e-mailing list with more than 500 names. We have neighborhood stroll nights, video nights, discussion groups. We've even thought of projects like backyard chicken coops and neighborhood kiosks. We coordinate with other Seattle groups such as Sustainable Seattle and the City Repair Project. We've led the battle to save the zoo from a garage and other construction. We're even fairly high up on Google searches: You can find us on the Web at <www.phinneyecovillage.net>. It's been an exhilarating experiment, enabled by just a half dozen or so committed neighbors. It isn't the apotheosis of community organizing yet, but it's a great start.

## The importance of community

One of our standout campaigns in the Phinney EcoVillage is something we call "stop 'n chat." We were inspired by Larry David's "Curb

Your Enthusiasm" episode where he rails on and on about how he hates "stop 'n chats." And yes, he's right about those meaningless "résumé exchanging" encounters. But for the EcoVillage, a stop 'n chat is the fabric of community ésprit. It's amazing how much bonding can happen in the few moments it takes to catch up on people's lives. And how much interdependency in a neighborhood can spring from a few chance encounters. So now when my husband returns home from errands, he's full of stories about stop 'n chats. A Gen-Xer in our neighborhood likes to make fun of the concept but has dropped by several times with his girlfriend. He calls their unannounced visits his "stop 'n chat revenge."

Besides stop 'n chats, the Phinney EcoVillage project has given birth to several principles of community heuristics. Here are some we've culled:

> Don't try to conform it to some preconceived notion of an "ecovillage." You should research what's out there (our PhinneyEcoVillage website contains links to several), but each ecovillage should be by nature different from all others. The coordinating themes are always sustainability, ecology and community. But villagers need to feel free to evolve as the project advances.

> Work in partnerships with other groups. Find out what other activities happen in the neighborhood and coordinate with them. We have a Phinney Neighborhood Association and City Repair "Placemaking" project we work with. We also work with the Save Our Zoo coalition, Phinney Ridge Community Council, local Democratic precinct and Phinney Neighbors for Peace and Justice, a peace group. We're partnering with the Washington Toxics Coalition to persuade neighbors to post pesticide-free signs in their yards. And don't forget church gatherings where relevant. Before we did the EcoVillage we had no idea how much stuff was going on in the 'hood.

> Coordinate resources with other groups. We share mailing lists and announcements with other groups. My poor overworked

husband's web skills come in handy in getting the word out
for a variety of causes.

Be mindful of the long haul. Nothing in life ever really happens overnight, even if it sometimes seems that way. The
EcoVillage has taught us to be patient with community
change. Some things work quickly, some things never work;
most take months or even a year or two to really gel.
"Ecovillagery" is a slow process, and why shouldn't it be?

Get everyone involved in some aspect. People love to have a
project or event to call their own and shape in their own
interests. An EcoVillage organizational structure should be
as flat as possible, encouraging full participation in decision-
making. That doesn't mean it's cat-herding time. But
responsibilities need to be shared to involve everyone.

We have to remember that happiness research shows that relationships with other people nurture the lifeblood of well-being.
Building community may indeed be the most effective way to elicit
caring and concern for the common good. You
can't just read about caring, you have to experience it. In particular, community can teach us to
care about people beyond our immediate selves.
Yes, we care about our friends and family, but if
we've never experienced community, will we
care about people halfway around the world?
Will we care about the people who will be alive
a hundred years from now?

*Community is so vital
to a fulfilled life, yet
building community is at
the bottom of consumer
society's list. As we run
short of time, community is
where we cut back. Why?*

Community is so vital to a fulfilled life,
yet building community is at the bottom of consumer society's list. As we run short of time,
community is where we cut back. Why? First,
we don't realize its importance. We don't recognize what an incredible impact it can have on our lives. Further, building community is
not something that yields instant rewards. The rewards come from
staying in for the long run, not a value our society cherishes. Next, I

think that because we have experienced community so rarely, we don't really even know what it is. How can we value it if we've never experienced it? Unless we develop a vision of what community can be we cannot move to create it. Finally, our community-building skills, in fact so many of our people skills, are stunted due to neglect.

I like to ask people when they've experienced community in their lives. I get all sorts of stories: the experience of community in college when living in a group house, the community you felt when marching in protest parades, even the feeling of community when taking the same bus every morning. I particularly hear about the community that is created in a crisis situation — an earthquake, a flood, a fire. A time and place when people are forced to come together because they know they really need each other. This description seemed to apply perfectly to neighborhood community.

So this is the big challenge: We really do need each other, but somehow we don't realize it. We are in a crisis situation in so many ways, and the only way to solve them is through community, learning to work and share with others. People always recall what it felt like to help each other out in a crisis, but somehow they're unable to keep the spirit of community going. In fact, I think my main role in life now is to try to get people to understand how much we need community and help them learn how to create it. We are, after all, living in perpetual crisis. Nature is sending us the message through the Los Angeles wildfires, the Malaysian tsunami, the Afghanistan earthquake, and Hurricane Katrina. And the biggest SOS of all, global warming, looms ever more critical. If a global community doesn't pull together soon, planet Earth is finished.

I realize community is something I've been working toward all my life. A friend, when she saw me forming yet another small group, said, "Cecile, you're doing it again! Trying to bring people together! You must have been a sheepdog in a former life." (I thought, Yes, it's true. How nice to know your true self!)

But I had never really understood how important community was. Most of us didn't until Robert Putnam published *Bowling Alone*. (What an incredible title — the sort most writers wish they'd thought of!) We may still be bowling, says Putnam, but we're not bowling in leagues. Then he goes on to trace the decline in "social capital" (an admittedly awful consumer-economy phrase) via different categories:

- Entertaining friends: decline of 45 percent
- Picnics: decline of 60 percent
- Family dinners: down 33 to 50 percent
- Full service restaurants: down 25 percent while junk-food outlets doubled
- Bars, nightclubs, discos: down 50 percent
- Greeting cards: down 20 percent
- Playing cards: down 50 percent
- Increases in video games and casino gambling, which are competitive and solitary.

It's like finding out how many species of animals are going extinct! Just as we haven't realized the value of many of these species, so we don't realize the value of activities like playing cards or having people over to dinner.

"We must learn to view the world through a social capital lens," says Lew Feldstein of the New Hampshire Charitable Foundation. "We need to look at front porches as crime-fighting tools, treat picnics as public-health efforts and see choral groups as occasions of democracy. We will become a better place when assessing social capital impact becomes a standard part of decision-making."

When I talk with people about community, there's an immediate response. I like to relate what a German woman said in one of my workshops: "You know the main difference between our cultures? In our country, when we have a latte [and she raised the paper cup she was holding] we spend a couple of hours talking to our friends. But you, you use coffee for fuel, drinking alone in your car as you rush to work." When I mention her comment, others chime in with their own stories. One friend told me about being in Denmark and asking for a coffee to go. The woman behind the counter had no idea what she was talking about! "Well," the waitress said, sounding confused, "we make the coffee here." It just didn't occur to her that anyone would drink coffee on the run.

People know that it's missing in our lives. But what strikes me is that we really have no idea what community is. As with everything important, our sense of community has been diminished. Some like to argue that going to the mall is an experience of community. (You mean you think these vendors are nice to you because they like you? Could it be that they're on script?) If we have no sense of what community means, we just go along with pre-packaged, shallow, ersatz experiences.

## Community in the past

A good way to understand what community is might be to see how it was described in the past. The book *We Had Everything But Money: Priceless Memories of the Great Depression* provides a moving record of people's recollections from that era and sheds fascinating light on what community is. Its flyleaf reads, "Love and sharing saw America's families through the Great Depression." The prologue hearkens to a time when "banks closed and hearts opened." Memories don't necessarily reflect reality, one could argue. But memory and reflection are how we learn from our own experiences, so we need to consult them. "This book is the true story of how things were in the Great Depression," editor Deb Mulvey notes.

Thirty-five percent of Americans were out of work; in 1932, 10 million lost their jobs. World War I veterans had been promised a bonus payment, but it never came. The stock market crashed, banks closed, insurance companies failed, and people lost any money they had not hidden under a mattress. Businesses disappeared. People lost their homes as banks foreclosed. To make matters worse, 1934 and 1936 brought extreme droughts, forcing people to migrate, searching for any way to survive. Fires swept the prairie, and people took long journeys across the continent looking for work.

Many men who had worked all their lives became hoboes. They were forced to leave their families trying to find work so they could send money home. They rode boxcars and slept in abandoned buildings and in hobo camps under bridges. Some visited their families when they could, but some just disappeared and were never heard from again. People spent hours in breadlines to get food. I would expect everyone to know (but perhaps they don't) that there was no unemployment insurance and no Social Security. All that came later, mostly as a result of the Depression.

People made do. "Use it up, wear it out, make it do, or do without" was the slogan. They transformed yards into gardens and gathered nuts from woods around their houses and sold apples on the street corner. They milked cows and made their own butter. They sold the fish they caught, but that could be expensive because with no refrigeration, they had to pay to have a block of ice delivered by the iceman in his horse-drawn wagon. Mothers made everyone's clothes. They walked the railroad tracks to find coal. Kids went to work, selling tomatoes at roadside stands or papers on corners — the papers sold for three cents, and the kids kept a penny for themselves. They caught fish and shot rabbits and squirrels for dinner. They trapped animals for their skins. They collected pop bottles and redeemed them for a few cents, which they turned over to their mothers. They shined the apples their dads sold. They picked blackberries and sold them door-to-door. On Saturdays they got a dime to go to the movies. Their shoes had holes, and they wore only hand-me-downs. Girls worked in people's homes for $2 or $3 a week, plus board and sometimes room. Some brought their cows and horses into the house to keep them from freezing to death in cold winters when there was no fuel. Children took turns going to school to share their clothes and shoes.

Families made sacrifices for each other. One story recounts a boy coming home from school one afternoon in 1933 to find his father crying and holding hands with his mother. "Son," he said, "I lost my job today, but we have nothing to worry about. We will get through this together." The father didn't find work for another two years, but because he had made his son feel so safe and secure, the son, when he retired years later, attributed his good life to his father, who had never let himself be defeated. Another man said that he, too, had received his most valuable possession during the depths of the Depression. He had been in high school and wanted the class ring more than anything. His mother, who made quilts and sold them, set out to make a quilt that she sold for $9, the price of the ring. "I still have that ring," he remembered as an adult. "It will always be a prized possession."

Over and over the stories reflect how the key to survival was helping each other out. Families moved in together with aunts and cousins and grandparents all sharing one bathroom. People bartered — trading extra produce for someone else's eggs, or a chicken for part of a slaughtered pig. A doctor was paid with homemade cakes and pies. Grocery stores gave credit.

People thought of imaginative ways to help each other: One group of girls formed a club they called The Secret Helpers. They gathered weekly, bringing their pennies and nickels and creating food boxes. Then they would take the food box, put it on the front door, ring the doorbell and run — hiding close by to watch the reactions. Almost all the stories tell of people feeding hoboes who came to their door. If they had food, they shared. Some let the men sleep in their barns. Some kept a big table set up in their back yards and a pot of beans on the stove.

One story told of how the mother of a family had hurried to the bank to deposit over $1,000 one day — all the proceeds from that year's crop. She had kept out $5 for groceries, but in the next hour that's all she had. The bank had closed for good. Then her house burned down, and the family moved in with relatives for a while. Then a caravan of cars came driving up the street, full of mattresses and dishes and everything the family needed. Women held quilting parties, and people helped them rebuild their house. The family lived the rest of their lives on the farm they thought they'd lost.

Another family was getting by with only a daughter working as a saleswoman in a department store; her salary bought food for eight people. One day something happened: The Swedish Society showed up at the family's door with about 120 friends, bringing all sorts of food that would last for days. They presented the family with an envelope containing $157 — a lot of money in those days.

There are so many stories in this little book, and at the end of each story there is always a coda like these:

- "We not only survived; we may well have become better and stronger people for the experience."

- "It made us appreciate everything we have now."

- "There may have been a shortage of money, but there was never a shortage of love and caring, and for that I'll always be grateful."

- "I'll never forget those years: Neighbors helping neighbors, sharing whatever good fortune came their way; doctors rendering services regardless of patients' finances."

- "The Depression was terrible in some ways, but it taught many Americans a better way to live. We began to not only think more about others, but to help them. The Depression helped me grow up."

One woman found an account her father had written in the 1930s about his experience:

"I like the Depression. No more prosperity for me! I have had more fun since the Depression started than I ever had in my life. I had forgotten how to live, and what it meant to have real friends."

## Defining community

The Depression reminded Americans that community is about caring for people, feeling safe, feeling accepted, feeling like you belong. Maybe most of all it taught us that spending time with people, as one of the men quoted above said, is not wasting valuable time.

And that pretty much sums up today's attitude: We feel like we're wasting time hanging out with people. We feel we could be doing something more productive. Even if we don't consciously think that time is money, it's at the base of our belief system. If nothing else, when you develop "social capital" you really are putting something away for a "rainy day," or a day when the banks close, or a day when you are struck by a hurricane.

Reading about the Depression helps us see how important community can be in times of a crisis. We begin to understand that we really do need each other. When affluence goes up, community goes down. Why? People begin to believe they don't need other people — that whatever they do need, they can simply buy. So perhaps one way to get people to care about community is to re-educate them about eras like the Depression, when having community was essential.

*Reading about the Depression helps us see how important community can be in times of a crisis. We begin to understand that we really do need each other.*

## The Great Good Place

We also need to re-learn how joyful and fulfilling community can be. The person who has done this the best for me is Ray Oldenburg, author of *The Great Good Place*, one of my favorite books. He tells the story of what he terms "the third place." The first place is home; the second is work. Oldenburg says it is essential to have a third place.

Basically it's a place to gather and talk and just hang around. Unfortunately, most of us know about these kinds of places only vicariously from the TV show *Cheers* — the place where "everybody knows your name." Urban areas are exploding with corner coffeehouses — not just Starbucks — where people go just to be with other people. The downside is that many bring their laptops to log onto wireless Internet connections. Still, logging on in a crowd is better than "bowling alone."

Having a public place that welcomes you is important. Some might argue, "Well, we've got our homes." And yes, a home can be a third place for others. We need a "take back your living room" campaign. We need to revive the drop-in option. Today having friends over seems so formal: Cleaning your house, deciding what to serve, cooking for a crowd. We once had a neighbor who made a big pot of spaghetti or soup every Wednesday. You could drop in or not — no obligation. But we always had wonderful food and conversation.

Oldenburg compares us to chickens. He says that chickens used to just roam around (and some of us eat only "free range" chickens now), pecking and investigating whatever they wanted, but now they are hatched and kept under controlled conditions. Artificial light destroys night and day, and the chickens eat tasteless formula food. They get very little exercise and are highly anxious because of the crowded, stressful conditions. All this makes them very vulnerable to disease, so they're shot full of antibiotics as well as growth hormones.

It sounds like he's describing contemporary man. Our food is tasteless, our lives highly controlled and we live in artificial environments — workplaces where the windows won't open and you can only reach your floor by riding in an enclosed, windowless box. Like chickens, we get little exercise, and we certainly don't have much chance to range freely, particularly if our exercise comes from a treadmill or a stationary bicycle. And you can argue that, again like the chickens, we're highly anxious, our health is vulnerable and we have to be pumped full of antibiotics and hormones. Unlike the chickens, nobody locks us up; we just stay "cooped up" on our own. (Perhaps that's not totally true. Our economic system does indeed lock us up, but we have a little more ability than chickens to rebel.)

The Great Good Place gives us a chance to break out and experience real life. We need this kind of secondary level of community to feel we belong to something bigger than ourselves. It builds trust — something else that has declined in this society. Without trust, we don't expand our horizons and are dominated by fear. And further, almost everything we do is utilitarian — done for another purpose. We do very little just for the fun of it, and being social should always be fun.

It's a leveler. Work status and the pecking order (chickens again) drop away. One of the biggest causes of unhappiness is low status. As the gap between the rich and poor widens into a chasm in the US and the middle class dries up, the competition for status has become cruel. Everyone is trying to scratch their way up — even those with lots of money — because there is always someone richer. There is usually someone with higher status that treats you like a nobody.

And most of our "places" these days are structured to make us feel like nobodies. Oldenburg refers to them as non-places — so big and impersonal that you feel insignificant. We are a shopper, a con-

sumer, a client — not a person. Part of it, of course, is that we have made everything speed up to generate profit. Think of the way physicians rush their time with patients because they're pressured by HMOs to make a profit. Think about the large classes children have because schools don't get adequate funding. When you order some- ·
thing from a drive-through fast-food place, you give your order over a loudspeaker! You're just an anonymous, disembodied voice. A third place has human scale. People recognize you and know your name. You can become a person.

You get to shed your role as worker or spouse or parent or politician or whatever. At work we're the most constrained: When I was a community college administrator, I felt like I had to act like an "administrator," whatever that was. I could see that I shouldn't laugh too much, wave my arms around a lot, rant about the Republican Party, or swear. Being an administrator required me to become a bland, unstimulating person.

Usually we're more free to be ourselves in our families, but that can be a role we need to shed as well. I've seen drastic changes in women when they're around their husbands or their kids. They feel like they need to act like a wife or act like a mother, and they rarely relax as themselves. A third place can liberate them from society's stamp.

Even when you're at home, you're not necessarily seen as who you are. Oldenburg makes the point that neither the workplace nor marriage work as well without third places. Certainly I can see it in my marriage. When my husband and I are out with others I start thinking, Oh, I see why I fell in love with him. At home we both can become irritable and irritating people. Is it a coincidence that America's divorce rate reached 50 percent just as the number of places to hang out declined by half?

You can relax at a third place. Certainly stress is one of our big problems of well-being. In a third place you can step out of the striving and competing and super-organized mode. You don't have to pay attention to what you're wearing. You don't have to worry about your image. You don't have to make an appointment to come in. You just drop by and hang out.

It's something you do for enjoyment alone. You go to the third place only because you simply want to! This very important — not only because enjoyment contributes to happiness, but because we do almost everything today in order to get ahead. In fact, some people experience enjoyment so seldom, they don't even know what they enjoy, as my experiment showed asking returning women in my classes to list 10 things they enjoyed doing.

This is important in terms of personal happiness and health, certainly. If you no longer pay attention to your feelings, you can't make changes in your behavior because you have nothing to guide you. Emotions developed in our evolution were a tool to help us survive. We enjoyed being with other people because being with others made life easier. We enjoyed food because we needed to eat to keep alive. And it's still true for us today: All too often, ignoring physical feelings can mean we don't discover a disease or health problem until it's too late. Perhaps that is why cancer, the physical metaphor for long-term neglect and imbalance, has become so widespread in American society.

When we no longer know what we feel, we're open to being manipulated by Fast culture: advertising, marketing, consumerism, status, power. In our emptiness, we adopt the responses they want us to feel. The manipulators are able to make us get excited about all sorts of things, like a pair of jeans or a diamond ring or a get-rich-quick candidate.

In fact, Oldenburg says, societies with a third-place culture are less affected by advertising. For one thing, they're not watching TV. But the third place also inoculates them against needing to impress people because they feel accepted for who they are.

## Variety and diversity

The third place allows you to meet people you might not have met. Usually the friends you have over to your house are often pretty much like you, but in a third place you might meet people that could surprise you. Oldenburg feels that third places allow for the possibility of eccentrics. You say anything you want in a third place. The "real" world, on the other hand, tries to sterilize us: "The mundane world subdues us, especially the modern urban one, which dislikes idiosyncrasies and will not tolerate 'characters.' It encourages us to be image-conscious and self-conscious. It prefers a 'cool' individual, and 'cool' individuals don't kick up their heels."

## Non-commercial

A third place is not necessarily free: you're usually paying for your coffee, a glass of wine, or maybe books. But third places don't demand that you spend a lot of money. Further, you are generating your own entertainment — a powerful way of resisting commercialism, because most of our entertainment is prepackaged, from TV to video games.

## Informal and casual

Most things we do are more formal, and we have to be careful about what we say, how we act, what we do. We need to make sure we're showing enough deference to the boss and exuding authority to the people who report to us. We have to dress for success and keep our desk neat and under control; we have to try to talk intelligently, but not be too radical or we'll be put in the "troublemakers" camp. None of these help us feel wild and free and exuberant. We need informal and casual for that! A side benefit is that you can meet your friends without having to clean house or make dinner!

## Political freedom

Third places protect against demagogues and dictators. Hitler banned gatherings of more than three people on the street corners of Germany. England and Sweden forbade drinking coffee in the 18th century because rulers thought coffee houses were darkened dens of subversion and revolution. I remember during the early feminist movement of the '70s, when men would see three women standing talking together, they would say, "What are you plotting?"

Political change doesn't come unless people get to talk with each other. Political talk helps make connections: Everyone has a little piece of the puzzle about what is really going on. We particularly need to talk, given information overload these days. We just can't all know everything! And finally, sometimes it's only when you hear others express their outrage at something that you have courage to express your own dissatisfaction. Gatherings give you inspiration and courage to challenge the status quo.

*Political change doesn't come unless people get to talk with each other. Sometimes it's only when you hear others express their outrage at something that you have courage to express your own dissatisfaction.*

*The Great Good Place* is incredibly exciting to read — but it's also sad, because the book in essence says that these convivial gathering places are dying out. There are many reasons, but once again I want to return to that ever-recurring theme, the imbalance in wealth in this country. Great good places don't make lots of money and so cannot pay high rents. As chains move into a neighborhood, they raise the rents, forcing mom-and-pop places to close down. This is true for groceries and bookstores and barbershops and novelty stores. But more often, the great good place is a café. Starbucks may indeed be a third place to some (the chain has adopted that term), but I feel strongly that it's almost impossible for a Starbucks to be a true third place. No matter how hard they try to disguise it, they're just too corporate. A real third place stands against everything a corporation stands for.

### Forces that undermine community and conversation

The social binding experienced in the Depression, and the informal gathering spot of a great good place, give us some feeling for what community is. But to create more community, we need to be clear about what is undermining community and conversation.

#### STATUS

We've talked about status before, but the increasing gap between the rich and the poor means there are more and more ways to rate people, and we usually only want to be friends with people at our own status or above us. I remember returning to Stanford a few years ago to be a visiting scholar. The air was cool, the sun was hot — there was that different slant of light that always evokes the excitement of fall. I was sitting at an outdoor café on the Stanford campus, meeting with a mentor from the institute I would be working with.

Her job as a senior scholar in the program was to welcome me, explain the ropes, put me at ease. But as we talked, I found my spirits drooping. The woman scarcely paid attention to me — she kept glancing around, periodically calling out to people passing by.

I wanted to take her face in my hands and hold it — as my son used to do as a baby when he wanted to get my attention. I had visions of grabbing her by the lapel and jerking her across the table! What was wrong with this woman! Didn't she have any concept of hospitality or politeness?

What I learned was how demoralizing it is to be invisible — how hard it is to have low status. When I was a graduate student at Stanford, I didn't feel that as much. But when I came back to Stanford as a "visiting scholar," people quickly realized that I was a nobody, and I became invisible. I was a nobody for one reason: I was not a professor at a prestigious university. In fact, by that time, I had quit my position as a community college administrator (which wouldn't have given me many points anyway) and described my profession as "community educator" (not many points there!).

Now, if there is any place where you can almost smell status, it is Stanford. This does not mean that there aren't lots of great people there who are fighting the ranking system, but it's very hard not to be affected by it. As one of my friends there says, "When you meet someone at Stanford, you spend your first five minutes summarizing your résumé." Even though it was a painful experience, I learned first-hand how important it is to make people feel equal and valued.

## BIGGER IS BETTER!

Another barrier is our belief that bigger is always better. Community only really occurs in small groups. I continue to be flabbergasted at how hard it is to get people to understand this. I worked for a long time to find the best size for my simplicity study circles, and after much experimentation the answer was nothing mysterious — it's the size of a good dinner party: six people. Any more than that and only a few people get to talk. Conferences usually break up into small groups of 12 people. What quickly happens is that a few dominate, and the others sit silently. When I do workshops, I typically have people break up into small groups of three. You want to give people a chance to talk, because being listened to can transform you. Being listened to makes you feel valued and appreciated. When I break people up into small groups, the level of excitement in a room just explodes. People love the chance to talk to just a few people, partly because they hardly ever get it — not at work and not in schools. In fact, think about when you go to a banquet. The tables are always too big. They usually sit 10 people, and the person across the table is too far away for you to talk to. You can't talk to people on either side of you while you eat, so you're usually stuck with talking with just one person. Community blossoms only in a small group. In fact, large groups are more prone to influence and cultism. If Hitler had used his histrionics on a group of six people, they would have laughed him out of the room. It was the large group, the crowd psychology, which gave him his power.

## THE BUILT ENVIRONMENT

By now people understand that getting rid of our front porches and substituting back patios was wrong! People are beginning to understand that if you open your garage door with an automatic device and go straight into your house, you undermine community in your neighborhood. To be neighborly you have to be out on the streets! Further, city planners are discovering that community in a neighborhood is almost directly correlated to the level of traffic. More cars mean people don't come out of their houses as much. It's only when people are out on the streets that they can meet each other and talk. So the built environment matters to community.

I discovered this in the South during the '60s. I was working with an American Friends Service Committee anti-poverty program and living in a black neighborhood. Since the people were poor, their houses were small and close together, meaning that they ran into each other more easily. Further, since it was hot and people didn't have air conditioners, they sat out on their porches and could easily call out to one another.

With affluence, our houses have gotten bigger and further apart. Even family members aren't required to share the same space. When we grow up without people around us, what does it do to us?

## RUDENESS AND THE DECLINE OF CONVIVIALITY

A few years ago, some good friends invited us to come along with them for a New Year's Eve dinner party. Within 10 minutes I wanted to leave, but of course I couldn't. I had to stay until midnight! I felt like I had just walked into a family feud where no one was speaking. I pride myself on being able to lead a good conversation, so I kept trying. But sooner or later, when you feel like all you hear is your own voice going on and on, you start to get discouraged. I tried questions and funny stories, but nothing worked. I was glad when it was time to sit down to dinner. At least we could focus on the food.

But once again, conversation lagged. So I cast about for topics to introduce. This was in the day when the stock market was booming, so sooner or later people began discussing their investments. I piped up that Whole Foods was doing well because people were starting to see the importance of natural and organic food.

Well, I might as well have said I favored abortions at a born-again Christian's house. I immediately got taken to task for naïveté about organic food. "There is absolutely no evidence," they said, "that organic food is any better for you than traditional (pesticide-treated, hormone-injected, biogenetically altered) food." They cited various tests and were scientists at Stanford, so how could I argue?

My doctorate from Stanford is in lowly education, and I can rarely remember facts, so my confidence was pretty low. I immediately wracked my brain to change the subject. But the slight against organics got my usually quiet husband's dander up. He started talking about how important alternative health care was becoming. Talk about dousing a fire with gasoline! They didn't even attack on this one. There was just total silence. Undoubtedly images of witch doctors and snake-oil salesmen were dancing through their heads. I can't remember how the rest of the evening went. But we left at five after midnight.

Let's ask that old question: What's wrong with this picture? Certainly these people had a right to their opinions, and they were a lot smarter and better versed in scientific fact than I was. But I was a guest! They should have been concerned about my feelings and done whatever they could to make sure I was having a nice time! At the very least, they could have commented to me, "That's an interesting viewpoint!" Even if they had me categorized somewhere between The Juice Man and Dr. Kevorkian.

The evening struck me, once again, how we have lost old-fashioned conviviality. The online dictionary says that conviviality means "relating to, occupied with, or fond of feasting, drinking, and good company." The key phrase for me is "good company." Conviviality is the old-fashioned way of welcoming people and making them feel comfortable. It is taking delight in others and enjoying things with them. Conviviality is the culmination of joie de vivre and leisure experienced with other people, the balm of Slow.

I don't mean a fake bonhomie. We get too much of that. Even curmudgeons like Mark Twain and Kurt Vonnegut are models of conviviality. It's simply a basic approach to life in which you stop and take time for people and enjoy them. You greet them; you welcome them. You pay attention.

*Conviviality is the old-fashioned way of welcoming people and making them feel comfortable. It is taking delight in others and enjoying things with them.*

Yet conviviality is declining as rudeness eats away at friendly culture. In a survey taken by research group Public Agenda in 2002, almost 80 percent of respondents thought that lack of respect and courtesy was a serious problem in American society. People are upset about cell phones in public places, about foul language they hear constantly. People blame the speed and selfishness of our society, and particularly the reckless way people drive. My worst experience of rudeness was in a grocery store parking lot when a woman got angry because she thought we had taken her parking spot. After parking she elbowed her way past us to the shopping carts and spat, "Thanks so much for taking my spot!" In this case, my husband, his usual calm and restrained self, ignored the comment. But I hurried after her to explain that we saw there was another spot opening up closer to her than we were and that we wanted to park to let others into the lot. Her response was to ram my shopping cart with hers and scream, "Out of my way, bitch!"

In a convivial setting, the tone is of mutual interest and respect. One day I was riding the bus home, and a couple of scary-looking skinhead types got on. One wore a spiked collar and had all sorts of metal piercings. I heard him address an older man getting off the bus with an "Achtung!" Their conversation was about as vulgar and violent as you get, and they were talking as loud as they could, so no one could miss it. I was ready to get off and take the next bus.

As luck would have it, they sat down behind someone who might have been Miss Conviviality of 2004. They started harassing her — a young woman of about 18 or 19. The one with the spiked collar began with a "Hello there, you're sure beautiful! You got a boyfriend? I'm looking for a new girlfriend!" He proceeded to ask her all sorts of questions about her personal life, including her sexual experiences. I had to conclude these guys were scum. My approach would have been to look disgusted and ignore them. Instead, I learned a new lesson.

The woman began talking to them politely and nicely — as if they really were people whose thoughts she valued. She answered most of their questions and even asked them a few, such as, "Where are you from?" In response to the personal questions she said, "If it's all right with you, I'd rather not discuss that."

When it came time for her stop she said brightly, "Here's my stop. Nice talking to you!" and she hopped off the bus. Right before that, Mr. Stud Collar had asked her if she was going home now, and she said, "Yes, my boyfriend is waiting for me." She was obviously smart enough not to put herself in a vulnerable position.

As I thought about what I had just witnessed, I was amazed at her presence of mind. I would have communicated, no matter how silently, that I thought they were low-lifes. But she treated them like people, with firmness and directness but nonetheless respect.

This was just another reminder that being engaging and putting people on equal footing not only enhances relationships, it defuses potentially uncomfortable or violent situations. Who knows what might have happened if they had been ignored or made to feel inferior?

## Civic life

It's easy to see that community, conversation and conviviality are important for our own health and well-being. But they're also important for the health and well-being of our society. When we hear about the decline of civic life, we start thinking about organizing lectures to inform people. Our tendency is to think that if we just give people enough facts they will become more involved in change. But linguist George Lakoff, author of *Don't Think of an Elephant!*, argues that lectures and information will only go so far and even become self-defeating after a point. Instead, one must find ways to really connect with people.

Robert Putnam discovered that neighborhoods where people talk over back fences tend to vote more. Conviviality feeds civic life. We need more people to vote, we need to get people talking about social issues. But we have to start with conviviality to lubricate the gears.

Conviviality also means that you create opportunities for people to enjoy each other. I've felt for several years that if I did nothing more than have lots of potlucks, I would be contributing more to social change than any of the protest marches that I've been in. We need to create experiences where we can laugh and enjoy each other. That's conviviality.

## Dark side

As I talk about conversation, community and conviviality, I'm aware that there's a downside. Why did so many of us flee our small towns and come to the big cities? It's true that community in small towns can be constraining and judgmental. If you have conventional ideas you might do all right, but if your beliefs are different, you can be ostracized or shunned. One of the most horrifying failures of social capital is the number of school shootings we've had in the last few years, often in small or suburban communities, as analyzed by Harvard researcher Katherine Newman in *Rampage: The Social Roots of School Shootings.*

The first surprise is the settings, which tend to be model examples of Putnam's high social capital. Most people in these towns know each other. Organizations such as the Elks, PTA and Masons are alive and flourishing. Church attendance is high. In the places Newman looked at in depth, most people stay in the community to live after graduating from high school.

For kids who went on shooting sprees, there weren't even the usual warning signs — issues like violent backgrounds, dysfunctional families, chaotic schools, or distracted adults. The shooters were always white boys, and usually they were simply on the margins. They weren't popular. They were often teased and made fun of. Sometimes they were physically abused by other kids. They were often small and nerdy and failed to make the sports teams. They were neither popular nor cool. (The author suggests that one of the main reasons these boys go on rampage is to prove their masculinity and to take revenge on the popular kids who rejected them.)

The things Newman didn't say also surprised me. She notes that most people go to church:

> Social life revolves around faith. Churches buzz with activity seven days a week. People gather for singing, suppers, and special revivals. Adults participate in mentoring programs and Sunday school groups, even when their children have grown out of these activities. Churches connect people even in nonreligious contexts, running social groups for mothers of preschool children, picnics and potlucks, sports teams, charity drives, Boy Scout groups, youth groups, and volunteer groups, and the list goes on. Although attending church is somewhat less popular among the teenagers, it is nearly universal among adults and young children.

The phenomenon begs the question, is there something in the religious community that undermines caring and acceptance? In a shooting at Heath High School in West Paducah, Kentucky, the target was the prayer meeting, something held regularly in the center of the school. And what about the shooters' political orientation? Many of these were small Southern towns usually associated with right-wing Republicans. Much of the hatred throughout our society has come from right-wing fundamentalists with their messages of rigidity, conformity and hatred. Newman does not elaborate on these factors, but they would seem to be highly connected.

Another point worth analyzing was the coincidence of many rampages when the economy was booming and consumerism was flying high. Other kinds of violence had dropped, as they usually do when an economy is good, but school shootings exploded.

Somehow communities hosting rampages had all the vestiges of small-town connectedness and sharing. But they lacked the key ingredients of true conviviality: acceptance, diversity and openness to different points of view.

Another dark side of community can be cultism. Arthur Deikman, author of *The Wrong Way Home: Uncovering the Patterns of Cult Behavior in American Society*, says that we usually think of cults only as something weird and far out. In fact, he says, cult behavior is on a continuum from low to high — and most of us are involved in cult behavior, however mild it might look. Whenever we don't speak up because we're worried about reprisals from the leader of a group — whether it's at work or in an organization — we're exhibiting cult behavior.

And how many times have we witnessed this! How many times have we seen a leader silence someone with a put-down or something cutting? Every day right-wing talk shows practice this kind of derogation. How many times have we hesitated to speak up for fear of getting on the wrong side of the "leader"? How many times have we failed to speak for fear of ostracism from a group? In particular, I've seen this in academic circles, where people are so wary of saying something that isn't blessed by the current academic star. Academics have put down feminist and black scholars, saying that

they are forced into political correctness, but there have always been
strict party lines in the academic world as well.

## Change

We all know we need a new reality — one in which we feel valued,
cared for, respected. We know we need to learn to care for the common good, to find new challenges and new delight in our everyday
lives. This new reality is one that you see
through your neighbors' eyes when you take
time to talk, as you laugh with them over the
muddle they've made of their day, as you try to
make sense out of life. We get a glimpse of that
new reality when we take time to stop and talk
to the man who owns the grocery store on the
corner, when we stop and talk to passersby when
we're out walking our dog, when we ask the
risky question after someone's speech, when we listen to the person
who disagrees with us, when we get together with friends just for the
pure joy of it.

*We all know we need*

*a new reality — one*

*in which we feel valued,*

*cared for, respected.*

We need to know that creating opportunities for convivial
conversation and community are vectors of social change. We also
need to know that it's important to start small. (Small is still beautiful,
too!) We'll talk in more depth about creating community in our
neighborhoods, but you can begin tomorrow: Spend more time in
your front yard; walk in your neighborhood. Ask to borrow the prover-
bial cup of sugar. Stop and chat. Welcome the new people. Find out
if there's a neighborhood watch (anti-crime) program and attend.
And whatever you do, make sure it's filled with fun and conviviality.

CHAPTER 9

# *Slow Is Beautiful*

*We have lost our sense of time .... We believe that we can add meaning to life by making things go faster. We have an idea that life is short — and that we must go fast to fit everything in. But life is long. The problem is that we don't know how to spend our time wisely. And so we burn it .... Ultimately, "slow" means to take the time to reflect. It means to take the time to think. With calm, you arrive everywhere.*

— Carlo Petrini, *Slow Food: The Case for Taste*

AND NOW FOR SLOW. We've discussed some of the obstacles to the Slow Life and offered alternative visions for achieving Slow. But you, dear reader, are probably wondering just how you leave the fast lane for the slow path, the fast track for the slow go. As Petrini suggests, the strategy is both easy and hard. We cherish life and want to pack all the enjoyment we can into it. But we try too hard and move too fast, and as a result we're experiencing life like some MTV video, in split-second bursts of images and sound with no meaning or absorption or spirit. Look back on your week some time and count the memorable experiences you had, if any. Is this the way you expected to live your life? What can you do to recapture the anticipation you once held for your days on Earth?

### Taking back our time for things that matter

First of all, and most basically, the Slow Life means taking back our time for things that matter. And what matters is clear: We need joie de vivre, leisure and community, joyful, leisurely times with other people, talking and thinking about the events of the day. Or, put another way, relationships, reflection and revelry. Ironically and unfortunately, these activities are always at the bottom of our to-do lists or not even on the lists. They're the first to go when life revs up.

   To give attention to relationships, reflection and revelry, we need more time — in particular, shorter working hours and fewer hours at the shopping malls and in front of the television. The Take Back Your Time campaign has been focusing on this, advocating shorter work hours as well as guaranteed paid parental and sick leave. More and more people know that Europeans have a guaranteed four to six weeks of vacation, and they've begun to understand how poverty-stricken we are in terms of time.

   So we need policies. We can begin with ourselves. In the Slow Life, you try to strip your life of the inessentials so that the essentials can come through. It means constantly asking yourself, Do I want to do this? Does it need to be done? Can I get out of it? In many areas I've cut back to the bone — particularly what I do only to "get ahead." My favorite suggestion to someone is, Cancel something. You may just make a lot of people happy! My husband and I discovered this once when we were planning a party but changed our minds. When we called up people to cancel, we noticed a sound of relief in their voices. Like, Oh, a free night. If you really want to build good morale at work, call a meeting and then cancel it!

   Then you find more time for what you really want to do.

   It's not just what we do, but how we do it. Many of us have cut back on our work hours and spend little time shopping or in front of the TV — but we're still rushing around. Often we're trying to save the world, so we feel justified, but we're fooling ourselves. When I give workshops to activists or professionals, they always respond strongly to Thomas Merton's words from his book, *Conjectures of a Guilty Bystander*:

There is a pervasive form of contemporary violence to which the idealist ... most easily succumbs: activism and overwork. The rush and pressure of modern life are a form, perhaps the most common form, of its innate violence. To allow oneself to be carried away by the multitude of conflicting concerns, to surrender to too many demands, to commit oneself to too many projects, to want to help everyone in everything, is to succumb to violence .... It destroys the fruitfulness of one's own work, because it kills the root of inner wisdom which makes work fruitful.

We can derive some definition of the Slow Life by looking in more depth to where it all started — the Slow Food movement. This movement is not only fascinating in itself, it's highly symbolic — because food is at the core of life. You might say that the way we engage with food is the way we engage with all of life. In the Slow Food movement, we're urged to savor our food. Just as we learn to savor our food, so we must learn to savor our lives.

Imagine an evening of having good friends over to a Slow Dinner. When you sit down to the big bowl of chicken stew, you don't just gulp it down as if it's fuel. You first notice the taste. Wow, taste that garlic! And the cumin and coriander! What an incredibly flavorful dish! In the same manner, you notice your friends. You see that Sara has an attractive new haircut. You notice how tan and relaxed Jeff looks since he returned from his vacation. You're not reading or watching television or talking on your cell phone or checking your Blackberry for messages; you're paying attention to the food and to your friends.

Then you verbalize your appreciation. You comment on how good the stew is. You don't just say, "Great stew." You go "Mmmmmm, this is soooo good. I'm so hungry. Homemade is just so much better than anything you can get in a store." And so on. You compare it to other stews and remark about the freshness of the vegetables and the tenderness of the chicken. In a similar fashion, you appreciate your friends — you tell Sara how much you like her new hairstyle; you show your appreciation of Jeff's wit by laughing. When you appreciate something, you feel a conscious sense of satisfaction.

Further, appreciation seems to be more heartfelt when you verbalize it out loud, with real verve and gusto. In *A Life of One's Own*, Joanna Field (Marion Milne) recommends verbalizing your appreciation to yourself when you're alone. Let's say you're walking by a lake, you say to yourself, "The waves are so pretty today, and the sun so warm," and you optimize your sense of satisfaction and appreciation.

And then you enjoy your setting. You turn to your dinner companions, commenting how wonderful it is to have such a good dinner with such good company. Express your exuberance! White middle-class people have a lot to learn from ethnic groups — we always seem so quiet and repressed! Express your good feelings and laugh easily! When someone makes a joke about old-fashioned stews or about the intelligence of chickens, you all laugh. Not necessarily because the comment was funny — you laugh because of the sheer enjoyment of the evening. Laughter always increases enjoyment. A Mozart sonata is playing in the background, snow is falling lightly under the clouded glow of a full moon, your dog is curled in front of the fireplace. You're not just gobbling down your food by yourself in a stark kitchen with a bare light bulb. You realize that an evening like this is an incredible experience and should be enjoyed to the hilt!

Then, you reflect. After dinner you sit with some tea and reflect on the dinner and the evening. Maybe you reflect as you talk with others about the people in the world who are hungry and how lucky you are to have this good food; or maybe you sit quietly, watching people smile and laugh, and you remember stews that your mother cooked and the good times you had with your family and how glad you are that you keep in close touch with friends and family. You feel grateful that you've given up your hectic lifestyle and switched to a less demanding job. In the past, you would never have enjoyed cooking a stew. But now, serving food to your friends has a new significance. This is what it's all about, you think as you listen to the laughter: gathering with friends and creating community. When you take the time to reflect, it deepens your experiences.

Later, you remember.

The evening is over, the guests have gone, you replay the evening in your mind. Your husband laughs as he recalls something Jeff said, and you chat together as you clean up the kitchen. You comment on how reluctant people were to leave. Kathleen said she would be sending out an e-mail to set something up for next month. Remembering — recalling and replaying — an experience makes it a true memory that you can relive again and again, contributing to a rich inner life. When we move fast and have no time to recollect an experience, it stays on the surface. Just as a long, slow simmer brings out the flavor of the stew, remembering deepens experiences.

*To savor your life, you not only need more time, you also must learn to move in an unhurried fashion. Slow isn't just a reduced pace. It's unhurried.*

Finally, you imagine.

Later on in the week, you continue to think about the evening, and you begin to imagine what kind of a society it would be if we really cared about coming together to savor life. You begin to imagine what the effects would be on people's health, on the nation's greed, on our national selfishness. Can we create a society in which people savor life by noticing, appreciating, enjoying, reflecting on, remembering, imagining, and creating new visions of what life could be?

So we begin by learning to savor our food, the source of life, but we go on to savor all of life. We savor a walk in the woods, we savor a good book, we savor a visit to the art museum. In all cases, we're going slowly enough to notice, appreciate, enjoy, reflect, remember, and imagine.

## Moving in an unhurried fashion

To savor your life, you not only need more time, you also must learn to move in an unhurried fashion. Slow isn't just a reduced pace. It's unhurried. Someone who is depressed or sick or scared or angry might move slowly. Being unhurried is a conscious choice in this culture, a choice that helps you experience life more fully. To be unhurried is to be relaxed, reflective, patient, intentional, leisurely, calm, unruffled, composed, and peaceful! (Don't you feel calmer just reading those words?) When you're unhurried, you're relaxed and focused, yet open to and aware of what's around you. When you're unhurried, you can enjoy the moment and put everything else out of your head. When you're unhurried, you're not worrying about everything you need to do. You're not fretting about all the crises you need to confront.

Recall how you feel when you're hurried. You're anxious, worried and tense. You don't take time to notice anything. If you're walking quickly around a lake, you don't even see the water or birds or the sun or the trees. You've as much as spent that hour in your office — even though only in your mind. Think about a hurried pace at work. You're striding down the hall, your eyes on the floor, not noticing anyone — again, you're miles away. You're missing out on connecting with the life that's right in front of you.

Think how you feel around a person in a hurry; it's almost a slap in the face. You feel dismissed, you feel ignored. You feel belittled. It brings shame and anger. My college president — the one who caused me so much anguish that I quit my job — was someone who could never sit and talk with you. He checked his watch, he took phone calls, he adjusted his desktop, he kept his eyes down. There was absolutely no connection at all.

Savoring life and moving at an unhurried pace is the way you begin to transform your personal life. It means you will feel connected — that you engage life as you move through your day — complimenting your receptionist on her new dress, enjoying the artwork in the café, stopping to chat with the grocery cashier, watching the birds in your feeder, studying about ancient Rome. An unhurried pace helps you feel connected to life.

Even if we did nothing else but reduce our pace, there would be an effect. If we slowed down at work we would reduce the stress and anxiety that are decimating people's health and well-being. If we slowed down in our neighborhoods, we would get to know our neighbors and incur the healthy benefits of friendship and conviviality. If we slowed down in our homes, we would have time for each other. If we slowed down our own pace, we would have fewer accidents, we would get sick much less, we would enjoy ourselves more. All these would happen automatically. But slowing down won't happen automatically — it has to be a conscious choice.

Being unhurried allows other things to emerge: When you're unhurried, you can be more thorough, more patient, more determined and perseverant. Fast implies a sudden, unsustainable burst of energy that flares and then quickly burns out. It's like a tornado instead of a strong wind. A tornado is destructive, while you can use a strong wind for sustainable energy. It reminds me of how I behave when I can't find something. I'm frustrated and I rush through the house, looking for but never finding what I've lost. I go back to the same places, over and over, finding nothing. Then, once I slow down, it seems to pop out — right in front of my eyes, where it always was. Or I think of our car mechanic — very slow, very dependable, very thorough. He's been in business for himself for years, takes pride in what he does and takes time to chat with his customers. He's not like a Jiffy Lube sort of place, a chain that hires inexperienced workers, puts your car through an assembly-line approach and all too frequently messes up the job.

Most of all, if we move at an unhurried pace, we experience the ultimate in contemplation that we experience in true leisure: The universe breaks into our consciousness. We begin to respond to life with awe and wonder. As Abraham Heschel explains, we experience life as sublime:

> The sublime may be sensed in things of beauty as well as in acts of goodness and in the search for truth .... The sublime is not necessarily related to the vast and the overwhelming in size. It may be sensed in every grain of sand, in every drop of water. Every flower in the summer, every snowflake in the winter, may arouse in us the sense of wonder that is our response to the sublime.

At the core of the slow life, then, is the decision to enjoy life — to affirm that life is beautiful and people are good. To create an acronym by taking a cue from Heschel — S-L-O-W stands for Sublime Life Of Wonder.

## From consumer to connection

It's important to resist the consumerist approach and avoid accumulating "tips" for the slow life. We need to see that the Slow Life involves a belief system. Since our belief system determines the way we act and experience life, we must consciously choose it. Central to the belief system of the Slow Life is the rejection of values inherent in the consumer society — in particular, our American definition of success. Success in the consumer society is defined as more money, status and power, and this definition festers with our acceptance of, as we discussed earlier, competitiveness, commercialization and corporatization of our lives. The consumer society is a fragmented, destructive lifestyle fueled by speed. The Slow Life engenders a "culture of connection," a connectedness to life — to yourself, to others, to the planet, to the universe.

When you're connected to yourself, you live with integrity — you act on your values and you are committed to truth and honesty. Your values have been tested in your own experience instead of adopted as "second-hand" from the experts. You know that you are an expression of an evolving universe and that you must exercise the creative powers that the universe expresses through you. To live with self-realization, you have to slow down, take time to listen to your inner voice and find ways to act on what you hear. You are obedient to that voice, instead of the voice of the consumer society.

When you are connected to others, you commit to living in community, to caring for the common good, and to working for equality, justice and democracy. You commit to living joyfully with family, friends and the wider community. When you are connected to the planet, you try to live more sustainably, not using up or destroying nature. When you are connected to the universe, you commit to living with joie de vivre; to living with leisure and to affirming that life and people are good.

To do all of this, you must learn to take your time for what matters, move in an unhurried manner and savor your life — all done with a consciousness of your belief system. To recall our opening story, if the SUV driver had been connected with herself and with her community, she would have willingly and gladly backed up for the driver in front of her to park. She would have noticed the driver wave in cheerful acknowledgment through her window, and she would have left the situation feeling better about herself, about her life and about others.

So we have two prongs defining the Slow Life — the personal and the cultural. But there's a third and more complex element. The Slow Life also invokes social change. It is an ingenious way to begin to transform a lifestyle that is destroying the well-being of people and the planet.

## A catalyst of social change

We must be absolutely committed to changing not only our own lives but society as well. Personal changes cannot be sustained unless they are accompanied by parallel changes around us. You may yourself transform, but all about you people are driving fast, blowing their horns, responding with anger and impatience. You cannot help but be affected by your culture. Personal change requires political change. We need new policies favoring shorter work hours and guaranteed paid vacations, sick leave and parental leave.

By the same token, you can't just throw your hands up and say, What's the use? when everyone around you moves to the spinning disco ball of corporatization and consumerism. Public policy incubates in personal change. Activists argue that political change precedes personal change. But to bring about political change, you need a movement. Lawmakers won't act unless they feel there is a sizable group of people demanding change. And it's important to remember that movements are built by individuals who have transformed their lives.

So we're back to the personal. We must work both sides of the street, the personal and political.

How do we go about building a movement? The Slow Food movement offers a good model. It attracts people in a positive, welcoming way. This is very important because our usual approach is to go about hitting people upside the head like donkeys! We lecture them, shake our fingers at them and demand that they get moving. This approach may have worked with college demonstrations in the '60s, but today is a different political dynamic. We progressive activists can learn a lot from the Slow Food movement about how to attract people to get involved with us.

As we've discussed, we really need to welcome people; to greet them when they come in the door or show up for a rally; to ask them questions about themselves, and why they decided to come; to get their names and e-mail addresses for follow-ups. Remember that for most people it's not easy to come as a stranger to an event. They don't know what's going to happen or what the people are like. They're worried they've stumbled into a seething den of extremists. If they're ignored, they just sit and wait until they can escape!

At a Town Hall meeting recently in our neighborhood over the Zoo parking-garage controversy, we had welcomers positioned at the parking lot and main entry to thank people for coming and direct them to a sign-up table with flyers and other materials outlining our cause. It worked wonders. More than 100 persons signed up for follow-up, with several volunteering for committee work. Most donated money to cover expenses and ongoing publicity. Those kinds of numbers are invaluable to building a sense of momentum and solidarity, especially in an area united only by mailing address (rather than predetermined political bent or social values).

Another pitfall: Activists often bore people to death. If it's a meeting, it's usually too long and chaotic. If it's an evening presentation, it's often simply a talking head or two lecturing the group, with little audience involvement. Recall George Lakoff's first principle of organizing: Just giving people information does not change them! We need to find ways to engage them. We may let them ask questions, but we rarely involve people in effective discussions. I always have people turn to a few others to talk about their own ideas, and I always feel the buzz in the room ignite.

Too often we also focus on the negative, the many wrongs. After a certain point, however, people can't absorb a negative message. They feel overwhelmed or despairing. They look for an escape. Fear can help motivate people to a point, but inspiring them can be even more effective. We need to let people know about positive actions — particularly by ordinary people just like them.

Again, drawing on our Zoo campaign: In the first public hearing 30 people showed up, and that was considered a real breakthrough.

So we sent e-mails around congratulating everyone and asking them to spread the word. At the next meeting, more than 200 people appeared, and we repeated the process. Eventually we compiled a mailing list of some 2,500 persons from all over the city and beyond, simply by collecting names, thanking everyone and asking them to carry the torch forward. The Zoo was forced to cancel plans for a certain type of construction process and then abandon its efforts to persuade neighbors into adopting pay street parking (to force Zoo-goers to use the new garage). The Zoo's energy consistently was negative, telling the neighborhood: You don't matter, we won't listen, it's a done deal. Our energy was positive: We can "Save the Zoo."

Often activists send people away without giving them ideas about what they can do. And of course, the attendees forget about the information in a couple of days. (Nobody has a decent memory these days.) Not only do I try to give people concrete ideas, I have them talk about what they have already done — because almost everyone has done something, and it gets reinforced when they talk about it. Further, I try to finish up the evening by having people raise their hands and tell what specific action they will take. People feel enlivened as well as enlightened! You can tell how effective a workshop or presentation has been — just listen to people as they leave. If they're talking animatedly with one another, you've won them over. If they file out silently and head straight for their cars, you need to revise your format!

Robert Putnam's follow-up book to *Bowling Alone*, called *Better Together,* cites a number of effective community-building projects. One is Saddleback Church, an evangelical church in Orange County, southern California. The Web site gives you good directions and tells you where to park (first-timers get free valet parking). They let visitors know they can dress informally; they have personal testimonies and pictures of people who look interesting and non-threatening.

In other words, they make the first visit — always the hardest — totally non-threatening. Their tips seem trivial, but how many times have we arrived at an event anxious and exhausted because we had worried about what to wear, got lost and frantic over the time and didn't know where to park. Too often we don't go someplace new simply because we don't know what the people will be like! When talking to people about Voluntary Simplicity, I first show them that I'm really a very normal person, very similar to them. Statistics show that trust has declined in our country, and part of it comes from feeling uncomfortable around new people and worried about what kind of people you're getting involved with.

Saddleback is a huge church with membership (at one count) of around 30,000. So it would be easy for someone to go and never come back after the first time. But central to people's involvement is the small group of six to eight persons. (I always love it when I see my vision of small groups validated, partly because it's so effective and yet usually dismissed.) They have groups for everything from geeks to mountain-bike riders.

When people are meeting others and enjoying themselves, they feel good about themselves and new ideas they're exposed to. Alas, progressives often have the opposite effect! For instance, how many times have you heard progressives lament the electorate's stupidity for supporting right-wing policies? When we talk that way, we scare people because they fear they, too, will be attacked for being stupid. It can be intimidating coming to a political meeting because progressives are often armed with facts and data, but short on warmth. Newcomers can feel like they don't know enough to even come to an event, lest their stupidity be revealed. Further, we're not often kind to people who disagree with us, so people may be afraid to open their mouths. When we attack anyone who disagrees with us, newcomers will be hesitant to say anything lest they get attacked. I once invited a twenty-something friend to an evening of political discussion at my house, and when he said that he might vote for Nader in the 2004 election, people just jumped on him for throwing away his vote and handing the election to Bush. Afterward he was literally shaking! He's a very thoughtful, well-informed young

> *When people are meeting others and enjoying themselves, they feel good about themselves and new ideas they're exposed to.*

man who will never come to another of my — or even *any* progressive — political meetings.

   As a teacher I've learned that if you treat even one student
badly — with derision or sarcasm — it scares all of the students. So
everyone clams up and fails to get involved. To get anywhere with
progressive change, we must always treat people with care and dignity.

   After all, in a democracy we must believe in people. Certainly I've
wondered how anyone could support right-wing policies. But the fault
lies in the fact that people have not had the opportunity to be citizens.
They haven't had the chance to come together and reason together.
People need time to reflect and reason, but they also need encouragement
to take a stand, to take action. They don't get that if they attend a lecture
(after driving around in the dark looking for a place to park) and then feel
ignored and dismissed (and bored to death) at the end of the evening.

   So the Slow Life movement can help foster social change. The
Slow Food movement has banquets, inspiring community and joy. It
brings people together to enjoy good food and good company and at
the same time educate them about caring for the land and food. The
Slow Life movement doesn't just call people together for a lecture; it's
much more interesting than that. In Japan it supports a Sloth Society,
a group dedicated to moving as slowly and living as sustainably as a
humble sloth. One of their campaigns, which I just love, involves
encouraging people across the country to join with friends on
December 22nd, the winter solstice, turn out their lights for two
hours and use candles. They provide a whole list of Slow things to do
by candlelight — reading, thinking about peace, having a quiet dinner with friends, thinking about your own life. All reminiscent of
that starry night my husband and I watched the meteors. People have
an interesting, moving experience that helps them to begin to think
about their use of energy as well as their use of time.

   The Slow Life movement also transforms via a sense of humor
— so crucial in policy arenas where people tend to become holier-
than-thou. It begins with the name of the group in Austria and
Switzerland — the Society for the Deceleration of Time. In London,
a group sponsored a "very slow walk." A Web site is devoted to "slow

thinking." If we want to bring about change, we need to be more provocative and fun.

The Slow Life movement is convivial and caring. It enlivens as well as enlightens. It doesn't just throw facts at people, it inspires them. Certainly this kind of joyfulness has always been the most effective approach to social-change movements. I'll never forget, during the late '60s, standing in a black church with people who had faced down the dogs and guns of the racist South, singing "We Shall Overcome." Or the marches in the last few years against Bush's policies, particularly in San Francisco, where people dress up, make huge, outrageous walking puppets and invent clever slogans. One guy on Market Street in downtown San Francisco, dressed like a Secret Service agent, stood alongside marchers saying, "There's nothing to see here, everyone just move along. Just move along people, there's nothing here to see." We carry our small white dog in a baby backpack with a sign that reads, "Bichons Against Bush." People race up to video her.

In the Slow approach to societal change, instead of people feeling depressed and guilty — as we often do when we hear a lecture on the environment or war — people feel positive, hopeful and valued. Instead of feeling bored and overwhelmed by a deluge of facts, people feel involved and engaged. Further, social change involves more than marches and protests. We also need to just live differently in our daily lives, creating and testing new models for living. People in the Take Back Your Time campaign work for policy changes like guaranteed vacations, sick leave and parental leave, but they also encourage people to make personal pledges. People pledge to take back their lunch hours, leave work on time, turn the television off, have dinner with the family, play card games with their friends. When people are following these pursuits they're not out shopping (which destroys the environment) and they're not watching television (which sends them out to shop). Making people feel guilty about watching television or shopping doesn't work. We have to provide something that is more fun and more inspiring!

When the quality of people's experiences begins to change, they become engaged and involved instead of passive and compliant. They're awake and alive, instead of drugged and dead. This suggests an even more complex definition of Slow: The Slow Life is a subversive countercultural movement that resists the dominant corporate consumer society.

## Subversive

*There is a time when the operation of the machine becomes so odious, makes you so sick at heart, that you can't take part, you can't even passively take part. And you've got to put your bodies upon the wheels, and the gears and all the apparatus, and you have to make it stop. And you have to make it clear to the people who own it, and to the people who run it, that until you are free their machine will be prevented from running at all.*
— Mario Savio, Free Speech Movement Leader (1964)

Let's look at that word "subversive." Many years ago, searching for my direction as an educator, I found *Teaching as a Subversive Activity*, by Neil Postman and Charles Weingartner. Although the dictionary defines subversion as "a systematic attempt to overthrow or undermine a government or political system by persons working secretly from within," Postman and Weingartner see it as an "inquiry" approach to education in which the students learn to think for themselves and question conventional ideas that cannot help but crumble under analysis. Under their approach, subversive activity becomes a method of social change not reliant on direct attack or even policy change, but aimed at persuading people to question conventional ideas and develop their own truths.

I always try to think of my work as subversive. It seems so benign on the surface: Look, isn't that sweet? Those people are trying to slow down! What a quaint idea! When you appear benign, you don't threaten the powers that be. But you ultimately subvert the dominant paradigm by getting people to think differently. It's flying under the radar system — it's building a new Trojan horse. You make changes nonthreateningly, step by step, subtly but surely. And before you know it — bam! The system has collapsed!

How is the Slow Life subversive? Postman and Weingartner see the subversive teacher's role in teaching students to be "crap detectors" — to be able to recognize when people are trying to deceive, bamboozle or lie. Slow enables crap detecting because it gives you time to reflect and notice. So much of what we hear from the right wing is deceptive, but no one has the time to check out their claims. We just rush on to the next deception. The same holds true for patently false advertising claims. Only when people die (if even then) do marketers get challenged on misleading claims. In most cases, no one who really slows down to analyze advertising hype would ever want to buy the product.

Slow is subversive of the consumer society. It's not that you have to give anything up in the Slow Life; it's that the old material-ism and consumerism fall away when you engage in slow activities because you're taking your time and enjoying yourself. When you have meaningful experiences you don't get bored or lonely, so you don't hang out at the mall or spend your evenings sprawled in front of the TV.

Slow is subversive of the artificial society. Going to a farmer's market rather than the chain grocery store not only provides you with better food, it's more real. Your food isn't all shrink-wrapped. The vendors interact with you, and since you're outside, the light is real rather than artificial.

Slow is subversive of the commercial society. When you do something yourself instead of paying for it, the satisfaction is much greater: Think what people used to do: They cooked, they canned, they sewed, they built their houses, they grew food, they had town meetings, they read out loud, they played cards, they educated their own kids, they helped each other give birth, they treated themselves with remedies passed down through the ages. We can do these again!

Slow is subversive of greed. When you take the time to buy the street paper from the homeless man instead of walking on by, you experience a special kind of fulfillment that undermines greediness.

Slow is subversive of fear. When you stop and chat with peo-ple as you go through your day, you feel more trusting. We live in an age of free-floating anxiety — will we get mugged on the streets, will a terrorist act blot us out? One of the best ways to ease that anxiety is to slow down and take time to talk with people throughout your day.

You can do your own slow subversions just about any day of the week. Instead of finishing that office memo while you eat a sandwich over your lunch hour, take a leisurely walk with a coworker in the sunny spring day. You are subversive of a society that says time is money, that you had better hurry, because the person next to you is working harder and faster. You are helping create a new reality of leisure and enjoyment.

Listen patiently to a neighbor or relative rant and rave, denouncing the activities of peace demonstrators, and then say, "Well, I can understand how you might feel that way, but in my experience…" You are subversive of a society that tolerates only mainstream ideas and tries to silence dissent. You are creating the reality of a strong democracy that values everyone's opinions. Without this vision, all our freedoms are gone.

Spend your day chopping vegetables, checking on your slowly simmering stew, cleaning the toilet and anticipating your potluck guests. You are being subversive of a society that is obsessed with work and tells you to spend your night catching up on office memos and reading reports.

When you are subversive, your actions speak louder than words. They are another way of "speaking truth to power" — the way you interact with others causes them to begin to question and doubt the traditional definitions of success. I like to think of the subversiveness of the Slow Life as a policy of "non-cooperation" with the corporate consumer society. Just as the Danes refused to cooperate with the Nazis when they invaded Denmark — when the Nazis required Jews to wear armbands, everyone started wearing them — we need to practice non-cooperation with contemporary forces of death and destruction.

*When you are subversive, your actions speak louder than words. They are another way of "speaking truth to power" — the way you interact with others causes them to begin to question and doubt the traditional definitions of success.*

## Countercultural

Now let me explain why I included the concept of "countercultural" in this definition. It's because one of the most effective ways to change both the personal and the political is the growth of a counter-culture — a way of life that challenges and undermines the dominant paradigm and shows people a whole new vision of existence. Rather than attacking directly, a counterculture crumbles power and status from within. Counterculture provides a method of change in which people begin to live the values that they are advocating rather than waiting for a sweeping revolution.

The term itself brings to mind the '60s and Theodore Roszak's *The Making of a Counter Culture*. But there have always been countercultures, and it's important for us to realize that the Slow Life meshes well with its long and honored tradition. R.U. Sirius (Ken Goffman) explores the pantheon in his book *Counterculture Through the Ages: From Abraham to Acid House*, describing movements in almost every era: Socrates and his followers, the Enlightenment of the 17th and 18th centuries, the Transcendentalists in the early 19th century, Bohemian Paris in the early 20th century, the beatniks of the '50s and the hippies of the '60s.

The Slow Life fits the roster well. Countercultural movements have certain ongoing themes and characteristics, Goffman notes. Its protagonists are anti-authoritarian and pro-individuality (with the belief in an inner wisdom). They reject conventional ideas of success and challenge conventional thinking; they are egalitarian and irreverent. Countercultural movements protest materialism, hypocrisy, pomposity and phoniness. They are freethinking, iconoclastic and unconventional.

Socrates wandered around just talking to people, in the process inspiring droves of young people who became his followers. Thoreau and Emerson challenged contemporaries to examine lives of quiet desperation. Gertrude Stein popularized salons. Beatniks and hippies drew thousands of young people to poetry, music and conviviality as an alternative to clawing their way up the corporate ladder.

In each age a countercultural movement seems to grow, respond-ing to the deep needs of the era. Today many of our needs center around time poverty. Ask someone how they are and they're likely to answer with one word: "busy." Actually, it's graduated now to "crazed" and "slammed." If they really told the truth — "pre-cardiac" or "cancer-inducive" — maybe they'd wake up to what they're doing to themselves! As it is, they know they want more time for family, for friends, for community, for creativity, for political engagement, for reflection and for spiritual growth. They know they're spinning like a top. What they don't know is how to begin changing it all.

In the Slow counterculture, we try to work less, spend less and rush less. We spend more time with family, friends and community — or pursuing our passions. We watch less television, avoid malls. Families try to eat dinner together at night and limit extracurricular activities for both the parents and the kids. Many home-school their kids (most are not religion-based) or send them to alternative schools.

In the Slow Life, people try to limit their use of cars and walk and bike more. They live in smaller houses, get rid of extra stuff and often rent out part of their homes. They often are involved in alternative health and are searching for a new kind of spirituality. They usually eat organically and eliminate red meat from their diet. Some belong to cohousing groups and work to form community in their neighborhoods. They shop locally and avoid big chains as much as they can. They put their money in socially responsible investments, and, if they have a car, they try to drive a hybrid or biodiesel. Most of all, they try not to rush around, and they take time to sit quietly each day, reflecting on their lives. They don't waste time over regrets and mistakes, but appreciate each day as it goes by. They often invite others over for potlucks and participate in peace and justice activities.

Here are some other themes of the Slow counterculture:

AUTHENTIC KNOWING: Instead of second-hand knowledge, trust personal experience — not talking heads and so-called experts. The consumer society is prone to media "expertise" which exists primarily to sell products. With academic institutions, schools and politics so closely intertwined with big money, Slow counterculturists follow Cuba Gooding's demand in the movie *Jerry Maguire:* "Show me the money!" Tracing the payoffs and financial linkages of hidden persuasion takes time and patience

— going Slow. We have to think for ourselves, seek out alternative media, talk with others and test the truth via personal experience.

ENJOYMENT: Instead of doing things to get ahead, the Slow counterculture puts enjoyment over careerism. In place of dominance and winning, we work with others in a non-competitive manner. We have fun even when it might cost us a raise down the road. We relax playing cards instead of racing our hearts with video games. We walk to the corner grocery instead of driving, strike up a conversation in line instead of complaining and hurrying through the checkout. With Slow, time is not money — time is honey. It takes patience to produce and is best savored in reflection.

THE NATURAL: Instead of accepting the artificial, the Slow counterculture engages with the natural. We read the labels and try to avoid synthetics, chemicals and preservatives. We use water filters; clean our houses with vinegar, lemon juice and baking soda; cut our grass with hand mowers and leave the clippings in place. We hang our clothes outside (when it's not raining!) and buy organic cotton and hemp clothes. We use natural methods of healing and try to avoid prescriptions, painkillers and sleeping pills — medications that take us away from our natural rhythms and bodily balances.

DEMOCRACY: We work for participation, equality and freedom. We resist hierarchy: We work to make life more like a circle of people dancing instead of a ladder of people scaling.

LONG-TERM INSTEAD OF SHORT-TERM: We learn to think in terms of what's good in the long term for us, for the community and for the planet. Our corporations are beholden to short-term profits and act as if tomorrow does not matter if it gets in the way of immediate profits. Not that profit is verboten, but first we must consider consequences for the well-being of people and the planet.

VITALITY AND DIVERSITY INSTEAD OF BLANDNESS AND MONO-CULTURE: We try to avoid mega-chains and giant corporations. Corporate agriculture — genetically altered "super crops" and huge farm "warehouses" that pollute the air and waterways with animal waste for miles around — wants to destroy the diversity of plant and animal life. When diversity is destroyed, we're all at greater risk for survival. It's not just species we consider, either. When mom-and-pop groceries, hardware stores and other outlets go, we lose vitality and a sense of community. When media are conglomerated into three multinational corporations, we lose real news. When independent bookstores are shut down, we have narrower choices in reading material. Instead of Brave New World, we have Bland New World.

CULTURE OF CONNECTION: We focus on connecting with self, nature and the universe. How do we know when we connect? Think of the computer: Unless you get the message "failure to connect," you get a sudden burst of energy, and things start popping to the front. There's light and movement. That's what happens if you connect with life. If you don't connect, you feel dull and dead; if you do, you feel alive and energetic. It's being in tune with life.

Up until now, many of us have worked with the Simplicity movement, but — to reiterate — we haven't necessarily learned to slow down. Hopefully by now we've realized that it's absolutely imperative that we do. But it's not easy.

## The Scamp — the Slow Life Hero

*I am done with great things and big plans, great institutions and big success. I am for those tiny, invisible loving human forces that work from individual to individual, creeping through the crannies of the world like so many rootlets, or like the capillary oozing of water, which, if given time, will rend the hardest monuments of pride.*          — William James

Even though people complain about time constantly, they feel pressured to continue with a frenzied pace. One of the problems is that we just don't have role models or heroes. We need a Slow Superman! A Slackerman! Slower than a popgun bullet! More retro than a locomotive! Able to climb tall buildings one stair at a time! We need a caped hero in the form of a contemporary Thoreau, Gandhi or Socrates.

Most of us grew up dreaming about cowboys, pioneers and Horatio Alger entrepreneurs who went from rags to riches. Problematically, American icons have encouraged people not to come together in caring relationships, but to be winners. Instead of encouraging community, archetypes have nurtured the image of the lone individual conquering a foe — Indians, the frontier, business competitors. All are icons of dominance, conquest and isolation.

Pioneers were rugged individualists who set out to exploit a new land. Although they had many admirable traits, the underlying fact is that they were people who left their community behind. They were people who cut the ties. They were anxious to make it big and were lured by promises of gold. Cowboys are even greater embodiments of the strong, silent type — hours spent alone riding the range, always ready to defend themselves against savages, wild beasts and the elements. But today's culture seems even more influenced by Horatio Alger — the cultural ideal that taught us that money is the most important thing in life, that getting rich will make us happy.

There have always been anti-heroes, and the ones we most often think of are characters in movies — for me, Maude in *Harold and Maude*, Zorba in *Zorba the Greek*, and Viane in *Chocolat*. Having movie characters for heroes may seem a little non-real, but perhaps it's a testament to the media's inability to find — or at least publicize — heroes outside of Hollywood or TV dramatic series.

Maude drops in on funerals, where she meets Harold. She does this because she's planning to die soon and wants to celebrate the ritual of moving on. Harold is there for quite another reason. Despite being rich and comfortable, he feels trapped by a life of emptiness and despair, symbolized by his cold, materialistic mother — for whom he performs ritualistic fake suicides. Harold's mother wants him to get married, so he decides to marry Maude, even though he's only about 20 years old. The denouement is when Harold tells Maude that he wishes he were dead, and she replies, "Yes. I understand. A lot of people enjoy being dead. But they are not dead really. They're just backing away from life." Then she jumps up and exclaims, "Reach out! Take a chance! Get hurt maybe. But play as well as you can. Go team, go! Give me an 'L.' Give me an 'I.' Give me a 'V.' Give me an 'E.' L-I-V-E, LIVE!"

Then, with a wink, she nudges him: "Otherwise you got nothing to talk about in the locker room!" And then she teaches him to dance.

Dancing is a central image in *Zorba the Greek* as well. The repressed Alan Bates character has inherited some money and an abandoned mine in Greece, and he hires Zorba to help him rebuild it. For me, its final scene is the most wonderful in any movie ever. Zorba has created a huge structure that will let them transport trees down the mountain (to be used to prop up the mine). The big day arrives, and everyone is there to watch. Zorba signals to let the logs roll down. The whole structure starts to shake and hum; the logs keep coming down, faster and faster. And then — it all comes crashing down, with everyone running for their lives.

Zorba and Alan Bates are stunned. They stand there speech-less. But then, Zorba starts to laugh. Gradually, Alan Bates does too. Their whole scheme is ruined, and they are laughing! Their money is gone. Their plans are destroyed. And they laugh!

And then, Alan Bates turns to Zorba and says, "Zorba, teach me to dance!" And there they are — above the sunny Aegean Sea, dancing.

*Harold and Maude* ends in a similar way, with Harold dancing on a cliff above the sea. At first you think he has gone over the cliff in his car and committed suicide in mourning for Maude's passing. But then you see him, dancing as Cat Steven's music swells, "If you want to be free, be free …"

Both movies affirm love of life and love of people over the love of money and status. Zorba says to Alan Bates, "I never loved a man more than you." When Harold tells Maude, as she lies dying, that he loves her, she says, "That's wonderful, Harold. Go and love some more." Both of them reject success as embodied in wealth and money. Alan Bates is free from his vision of success as money. Harold is free from his materialistic, status-mongering mother.

Similar themes hold true for *Chocolat*, a more recent addition to Slow Life video. The movie ends with the town jubilant on Easter morning, engaged in games, playing music, eating chocolate and

most of all enjoying one another with conversation and laughter. It
was a small French town revitalized and liberated from its oppressive
mayor by an outsider woman who simply opened a chocolate shop
and began talking with people. "I know just the kind of chocolate you
will like," she would say. Instantly the villagers began to feel recognized and valued.

As Viane talks and listens and affirms each person, they begin
to change. The shy young boy breaks free from his mother, the older
woman stands up to her daughter. The desperate, angry young
woman leaves an abusive husband. All Viane, the chocolatier, does is
listen, laugh and accept.

None of this sits well with the town's repressed priest (the following is from the book, where the priest is the oppressive force —
not, as depicted in the movie, the mayor):

> I see ten or more people in there on some days, some stand-
> ing, some leaning against the padded counter and talking.
> On Sunday and Wednesday afternoons the smell of baking
> fills the damp air, and she leans in the doorway, floury to the
> elbows, throwing out pert remarks at the passersby. I am
> amazed at how many people she now knows by name ... she
> always seems ready with a question or a comment about their
> lives, their problems. Blaireau's arthritis, Lambert's soldier
> son. Narcisse and his prize orchids. She even knows the name
> of Duplessis's dog. Oh, she is wily. Impossible to fail to notice
> her. One must respond or seem churlish. Even I — even I
> must smile and nod, though inside I am seething.

In his plot to destroy all of her chocolates for the Easter festi-
val, the priest loses control and gorges himself on the candy, then
flees town in humiliation.

Viane's winning defense was her ability to talk and listen. The
vision of community she symbolizes will only come into being through
the common, everyday transactions between people — the words we
say to each other, how we say them, the time we take with each other.
Yes, there are big social issues to confront: our long working hours,

our anxiety about losing our jobs, the destruction of the planet. But maybe we can't work on any of those until we pay attention to William James's "tiny, lovable, human forces that work from individual to individual." This is what we need to learn: We must take time to talk, to connect, to build convivial and caring community.

Our movies' anti-heroes aren't just accidents. They are an example of the archetype of the "scamp," an archetype that I think of as a hero for the Slow Life.

The best analysis of the scamp that I've found is by the Chinese writer Lin Yutang in his book, *The Importance of Living*. As portrayed by Lin Yutang, the scamp is someone whose primary focus is the art of living — enjoying life. Yutang sees the scamp as very much a Taoist figure: lighthearted, easygoing, appreciative of whatever life has to offer. With tongue in cheek, Yutang sings the praises of the idler and the loafer. He recommends that you "never be the first in the world," and that we pass time with "a perfectly useless afternoon spent in a perfectly useless manner."

For Yutang, a scamp is someone who pursues not success but "high-mindedness." The scamp is detached from worldly success and tries to avoid the "temptations of fame and wealth and achievement." And the scamp remains committed to his freedom: "It is only with this sense of freedom and nonchalance that one eventually arrives at the keen and intense love of living." The scamp knows how to do nothing — "It is not when he is working in the office but when he is lying idly on the sand that his soul utters, 'Life is beautiful.'"

Yutang contrasts the scamp with a soldier, saying that human dignity is found in the nonconformist, not the "obedient, disciplined and regimented soldier." He links this directly to the state of our democracy, saying,

> In this present age of threats to democracy and individual liberty, probably only the scamp and the spirit of the scamp alone will save us from becoming lost as serially numbered units in the masses of disciplined, obedient, regimented and uniformed coolies. The scamp will be the last and most

formidable enemy of dictatorships. He will be the champion of
human dignity and individual freedom, and will be the last to be
conquered. All modern civilization depends entirely upon him.

The scamp's central quality is that he knows how to enjoy life.
His joie de vivre is embodied, Yutang asserts, in the scamp's attitude
toward food:

> Why do the Westerners talk so softly and look so miserable
> and cedent and respectable at their meals? .... Such is human
> psychology that if we don't express our joy, we soon cease to
> feel it even, and then follow dyspepsia, melancholia, aneuras-
> thenia and all the mental ailments peculiar to the adult life.
> One ought to imitate the French and sigh an "Ah!" when the
> waiter brings a good veal cutlet, and make a sheer animal
> grunt like "Ummm!" after tasting the first mouthful.

(Could Carlo Petrini, the founder of the Slow Food movement, have read these words — written in 1937 — or is this just an
example of a recurrence of perennial wisdom?)

The scamp has dreams, but at the same time he looks at life
with a sense of humor, not letting his sense of perspective get out of
control. Yutang says, "I doubt whether the importance of humor has
been fully appreciated, or the possibility of its use in changing the
quality and character of our entire cultural life — the place of humor
in politics, humor in scholarship and humor in life." He adds:

> Who are the people who start wars? It's not the scamps. It's
> the ambitious, the able, the clever, the scheming, the cautious,
> the sagacious, the haughty, the over-patriotic, the people
> inspired with the desire to "serve" mankind, people who have
> a "career" to carve and an "impression" to make on the world.

In the same vein, Oberlin professor David Orr points out that
we don't need more successful people:

> The plain fact is that the planet does not need more success-
> ful people. But it does desperately need more peacemakers,

healers, restorers, storytellers, and lovers of every kind. It needs people who live well in their places. It needs people of moral courage willing to join the fight to make the world habitable and humane. And these qualities have little to do with success as we have defined it.

I would add that the world also needs more scamps.

"It seems that today the scamp is being displaced by the soldier as the highest ideal of a human being," Yutang adds.

> Instead of wayward, incalculable, unpredictable free individuals, we are going to have rationalized, disciplined, regimented and uniformed, patriotic coolies, so efficiently controlled and organized that a nation of fifty or sixty millions can believe in the same creed, think the same thoughts and like the same food. Clearly two opposite views of human dignity are possible: the one regarding the scamp, and the other regarding the soldier, as the ideal; the one believing that a person who retains his freedom and individuality is the noblest type, and the other believing that a person who has completely lost independent judgment and surrendered all rights to private beliefs and opinions to the ruler or the state is the best and noblest being.

Some of us in the United States are fighting just such a battle between the ideal of the scamp and of the soldier. It is the soldier archetype that the right wing of America lauds. They want to control people, they want people to be disciplined and regimented. They brook no disagreement. But the scamp refuses to be disciplined or to follow orders. The scamp knows that he must be true to himself and to be a "warm, carefree and unafraid soul," as Yutang puts it.

The great short-story writer and poet Raymond Carver described Slow heroism to a T in his poem "Shiftless," which my husband and I heard him read shortly before his death:

> My goal was always to be shiftless. I saw the merit in that.
> I liked the idea of sitting in a chair

in front of your house for hours, doing nothing
but wearing a hat and drinking cola.
What's wrong with that?
…. Once in a while hailing a fat, blond kid like me
and saying, "Don't I know you?"
Not, "What are you going to be when you grow up?"

Scamps and Slow Life Heroes do not have to be famous. It's probably better if they are not — if we are forced to find them in our neighborhoods and classrooms and city streets, in dime stores and bus stations. We have a Slow Hero scamp — a homeless friend named Van who sells the *Real Change* newspaper at our food co-op. Van has a ready smile for every passer-by, not just the ones who come up and pay him a dollar for a newspaper. He's always full of fun and laughter, joking about some news item or a mutual acquaintance. Nothing seems to get him down. He'll stand in rain and sleet and dark, and that smile will light up no matter what the conditions. Van held steady work for a number of years but found he didn't fit in a corporate setting working for a boss he did not like. He doesn't have the conveniences and comforts of most of us, but he is healthy, energetic and, most of all, happy. No one can walk by Van without feeling better about themselves. Van will never be a celebrity or TV personality, but he's a Slow Hero nonetheless.

## Loafing

Van's number one pastime is just hanging out. Above all, the Slow Life is about leisure, idleness and loafing. Americans are uncomfortable with leisure. They look with jaundiced eye at idleness. And they are downright repelled by a suggestion of loafing. I remember once telling someone that I was basically lazy, and she made a point of telling me later (I had only just met her) that I really shouldn't say something like that about myself. She was worried I was putting myself down, missing my point entirely that I felt kind of proud to be lazy. To her it was a cardinal sin! Instead, Raymond Carver had it right: "What's wrong with that?"

Writing *Slow Is Beautiful* has inspired me to become even more of a loafer. Needless to say, it hasn't been a real option while writing a book. But I plan to make up for it! I never expected to be so inspired by the images of idleness and loafing. I had not realized that Walt Whitman had said, "I loaf and invite my soul!" And I was interested to discover a book written in 1934, by then-popular writer Harry Overstreet, called *A Guide to Civilized Loafing*. The title was changed to *A Guide to Civilized Leisure* in less than a year! Overstreet was Slow ahead of his time. He celebrated the importance of loafing — leisure — for a free people, for an openness to life, for "companioning":

> For wherever the individual is, even in small degree, released from the hard pressure of subsistence work, there is the chance that his more essential mind may be stirred into action. It has been realized by the rulers of the world that a thinking people is a dangerous people. It may be true, indeed, that idle hands find mischief, but it is far more likely to be true that when the hands relax from their labor, the tired brain may wonder why life has to be this way. Once it starts wondering, there is no telling how far it may go …. There are two movements of life — the movement of acquisitiveness and the movement of creative sharing. The significance of our free-time activities is that almost inevitably they place us in a sharing mood. Thus in hiking over the countryside, in athletic games, in music, painting, weaving, in the discussion of ideas, we issue from our isolation. We learn the fine art of companioning. And as we learn to companion, we tend to grow the habit of wishing for others the happiness that we ourselves enjoy.

Overstreet talks of learning from children, who still do things just because they want to and are always looking for something that's new and fun:

> There is a picture of the immortal Skeets that illustrates admirably the casual, inconsequential, and yet absorbingly

sequential character of child life. As I remember it, Skeets is standing at the fence, interested in the snow. He gravely pushes off one lump of snow after another, apparently liking the soft thump of it. Then, discovering that he has cleared the fence, he thinks it is a good idea to climb up and walk along the top. Then he jumps down and chases a dog. Pretty soon he sees an automobile, and we next find him being gloriously towed along the road. Then he comes to the top of a hill, finds a board and proceeds to slide down the hillside. And so it goes on from one adventure to another. Finally, we discover him slowly wending his way home again; we see his mother peering anxiously out the door. "Skeets, you're late! Dinner is all ready. We have been waiting for you. Where have you been?"

"Oh, just out for a walk," says Skeets. Life can be like that if we simply let ourselves go.

Who today could even talk about leisure and loafing like that? Who today even sees the human life as being that expansive and wonderful! We've been so diminished by our corporate consumer society.

This is the kind of life our scamp would live — one that has a sense of ease to it, a sense of gracefulness, a sense of delight. Our scamp would rarely blow up out of impatience or frustration, would never strike out at another in an act of road rage, would never give only partial attention in a conversation.

I would like to leave the last word on scamps to a real-life scamp, Kurt Vonnegut, from his essay in *Stories to Live By*. He tells about how his day goes, how he still works on an old typewriter and then calls up a woman who types a fresh copy and then goes out to the stationery store and then to the post office, talking and visiting with people as he goes along.

His wife tells him that he's being silly for not getting a computer — he could just type his story up and send it off and save himself a lot of trouble. No, he retorts: "And I tell you, we are here on Earth to fart around, and don't let anybody tell you any different."

# Bibliography

Adams, Patch. *Gesundheit!* Healing Arts Press, 1993.

Alexander, Christopher. *The Timeless Way of Building.* Center for Environmental Structure Series, 1979.

Bell, Richard, ed., with Barbara Battin. *Seeds of the Spirit: Wisdom of the Twentieth Century.* Westminster John Knox Press, 1995.

Berry, Thomas. *Creative Energy.* Random House, 1996.

Bok, Derek. *Universities in the Marketplace: The Commercialization of Higher Education.* Princeton University Press, 2003.

Buber, Martin. *I and Thou.* Touchstone, 1996.

Bunting, Madeleine. *Willing Slaves: How the Overwork Culture Is Ruling Our Lives.* Harper Perennial, 2004.

Cahill, Thomas. *How the Irish Saved Civilization.* Nan A. Talese/ Doubleday, 1995.

Callahan, David. *The Cheating Culture: Why More Americans Are Doing Wrong to Get Ahead.* Harcourt Books, 2004.

Carver, Raymond. *Ultramarine.* Random House, 1986.

Cox, Harvey. *Feast of Fools.* HarperCollins, 2000.

Csikszentmihalyi, Mihaly. *Finding Flow: The Psychology of Engagement with Everyday Life.* Basic Books, 1997.

Csikszentmihalyi, Mihaly. *Flow: The Psychology of Optimal Experience.* Harper & Row, 1990.

Daniels, Bruce. *Puritans at Play: Leisure and Recreation in Colonial New England.* Palgrave MacMillan, 2005.

de Botton, Alain. *Status Anxiety.* Vintage, 2005.

de Graaf, John, ed. *Take Back Your Time: Fighting Overwork and Time Poverty in America*. Berrett-Koehler Publishers, Inc., 2003.

Deikman, Arthur. *The Wrong Way Home: Uncovering the Patterns of Cult Behavior in American Society*. Beacon Press, 1990.

Drennan, Robert E., ed. *The Algonquin Wits: Bon Mots, Wisecracks, Epigrams and Gags*. Replica Books, 1999.

Easwaran, Eknath. *The Compassionate Universe*. Blue Mountain Center of Meditation, 1989.

Eliot, George. *Middlemarch*. Oxford University Press, 1996.

Field, Joanna. *A Life of One's Own*. Virago, 1986.

Franck, Frederick. *Art As a Way: A Return to the Spiritual Roots*. Crossroad, 1981.

Fromm, Erich. *Escape from Freedom*. Henry Holt, 1941.

Fromm, Erich. *The Sane Society*. Ballantine Books, 1955.

Gini, Al. *The Importance of Being Lazy: In Praise of Play, Leisure, and Vacations*. Routledge, 2003.

Goffman, Ken (R.U. Sirius) and Dan Joy. *Counterculture Through the Ages: From Abraham to Acid House*. Villard Books, 2004.

Gottlieb, Roger. *A Spirituality of Resistance: Finding a Peaceful Heart and Protecting the Earth*. Crossroad Publishing Company, 1999.

Harris, Joanne. *Chocolat*. Penguin Books, 1999.

Heinberg, Richard. *Power Down: Options and Actions for a Post-Carbon World*. New Society Publishers, 2004.

Heschel, Abraham Joshua. *Man Is Not Alone*. Strauss & Giroux, 1951.

Heschel, Abraham Joshua. *Moral Grandeur and Spiritual Audacity*. Farrar, Straus and Giroux, 1996.

Heschel, Abraham Joshua. *The Wisdom of Heschel*. Farrar, Straus and Giroux, 1970.

Honore, Carl. *In Praise of Slowness: How a Worldwide Movement Is Challenging the Cult of Speed*. HarperSanFrancisco, 2004.

Horney, Karen. *The Neurotic Personality of Our Time*. W.W. Norton & Co., 1937.

Huizinga, Johan. *Homo Ludens*. Beacon Press, 1950.

Hunnicutt, Benjamin. *Kellogg's Six-Hour Day*. Temple University Press, 1996.

Jamison, Kay Redfield. *Exuberance: The Passion for Life*. Alfred A. Knopf, 2004.

Jaspers, Karl. *Socrates, Buddha, Confucius, Jesus: From the Great Philosophers, Vol. I*. Harcourt Brace, 1962.

Kasser, Tim. *The High Price of Materialism*. A Bradford Book, 2002.

Kasser, Tim, ed., with Allen D. Kanner. *Psychology and Consumer Culture: The Struggle for a Good Life in a Materialistic World*. American Psychological Association, 2004.

Kohn, Alfie. *No Contest: The Case Against Competition*. Houghton Mifflin, 1986.

Labier, Douglas. *Modern Madness: The Hidden Link Between Work and Emotional Conflict*. Addison-Wesley, 1986.

Lakoff, George. *Don't Think Of An Elephant!* Chelsea Green, 2004.

Lane, Robert E. *The Loss of Happiness in Market Democracies*. Yale University Press, 2000.

Larrabee, Eric, ed., with Rolf Meyersohn. *Mass Leisure*. The Free Press, 1958.

Layard, Richard. *Happiness: Lessons from a New Science*. Penguin Press, 2003.

Lifton, Robert. *Explorations in Psychohistory: The Wellfleet Papers*. Touchstone, 1975.

Lindbergh, Anne Morrow. *Gift from the Sea: 50th Anniversary Edition*. Pantheon, 1992.

Marmot, Michael. *The Status Syndrome: How Social Standing Affects Our Health and Longevity*. Owl Books, 2004.

Maslow, Abraham. *Motivation and Personality*. Harper & Row, 1970.

Mayer, Milton. *They Thought They Were Free: The Germans, 1933–1945*. Phoenix Books, 1955.

Melville, Herman. "Bartleby the Scrivener: A Story of Wall Street," in *Great Short Works of Herman Melville*. Perennial Classics, 2004.

Merton, Thomas. *Conjectures of a Guilty Bystander*. Doubleday, 1966.

Moore, Thomas. *Care of the Soul: A Guide for Cultivating Depth and Sacredness in Everyday Life*. HarperCollins, 1992.

Mulvey, Deb, ed. *We Had Everything But Money: Priceless Memories of the Great Depression*. Reminisce Books, 1992.

Myers, David G. *The Pursuit of Happiness: Spiritual Hunger in an Age of Plenty*. Yale University Press, 2000.

Needleman, Jacob. *Time and the Soul: Where Has All the Meaningful Time Gone — And Can We Get It Back?* Berrett-Koehler Publishers, 2003.

Nettle, Daniel. *Happiness: The Science Behind Your Smile*. Oxford University Press, 2005.

Newman, Katherine S. *Rampage: The Social Roots of School Shootings*. Basic Books, 2004.

O'Hara, Bruce. *Enough Already! Breaking Free in the Second Half of Life*. New Star Books, 2004.

Oldenburg, Ray. *The Great Good Place*. Marlowe & Co., 1989.

O'Reilly, James, ed., with Sean O'Reilly and Larry Habegger. *Stories to Live By: Wisdom to Help You Make the Most of Every Day*. Travelers' Tales, 2005.

Orr, David. *Ecological Literacy: Education and the Transition to a Postmodern World*. State University of New York Press, 1992.

Overstreet, Harry. *A Guide to Civilized Leisure*. W.W. Norton & Co., 1934.

Petrini, Carlo. *Slow Food: The Case for Taste*. Columbia University Press, 2001.

Pieper, Josef. *Leisure: The Basis of Culture*. St. Augustine's Press, 1998.

Pizzigati, Sam. *Greed and Good*. Apex Press, 2004.

Plato. *The Last Days of Socrates*. Penguin Books, 1954.

Postman, Neil and Charles Weingartner. *Teaching as a Subversive Activity*. Dell, 1969.

Putnam, Robert. *Better Together: Restoring the American Community*. Simon & Schuster, 2003.

Putnam, Robert. *Bowling Alone*. Simon & Schuster, 2000.

Putney, Snell and Gail Putney. *Adjusted American: Normal Neurosis in the Individual and Society*. HarperCollins, 2000.

Roszak, Theodore. *The Making of a Counter Culture*. Doubleday, 1968.

Roszak, Theodore. *Where the Wasteland Ends*. Anchor Books, 1973.

Schor, Juliet B. *The Overworked American: The Unexpected Decline of Leisure*. Basic Books, 1991.

Schumacher, E.F. *Small Is Beautiful*. Harper & Row, 1989.

Schwartz, Barry. *The Paradox of Choice: Why More Is Less*. HarperCollins, 2004.

Seligman, Martin. *Authentic Happiness: Using the New Positive Psychology to Realize Your Potential for Lasting Fulfillment*. Free Press, 2002.

Shawn, Wallace and André Gregory. *My Dinner with André*. Grove Press, 1981.

Slater, Philip. *The Pursuit of Loneliness*. Beacon Press, 1970.

Slater, Philip. *Wealth Addiction*. Dutton, 1980.

Spence, Gerry. *Give Me Liberty! Freeing Ourselves in the Twenty-First Century*. St. Martin's Griffin, 1999.

Swimme, Brian and Thomas Berry. *The Universe Story: From the Primordial Flaring Forth to the Ecozoic Era: A Celebration of the Unfolding of the Cosmos*. HarperCollins, 1992.

Twain, Mark. *Tom Sawyer*. Penguin Books, 1986.

Underhill, Evelyn. *Practical Mysticism*. Ariel Press, 1914.

Washburn, Jennifer. *University Inc.: The Corporate Corruption of Higher Education*. New America Books/Basic Books, 2005.

Weber, Max. *The Protestant Ethic and the Spirit of Capitalism*. Penguin Books, 1970.

Whybrow, Peter C. *American Mania: When More Is Not Enough*. W. W. Norton & Co., 2005.

Yutang, Lin. *The Importance of Living*. William Morrow, 1937.

Yutang, Lin. *Lin Yutang on the Wisdom of America*. John Day, 1950.

# *Endnotes*

## Chapter 1: Toward a Philosophy of Slow

p. 9: "In this book, Fast and Slow do more .." Carl Honore, *In Praise of Slowness*, p. 14.

p. 11: "Culture of Connection .." Philip Slater, "Connected We Stand," *Utne Reader*, April–May, 2003, www.utne.com/cgi-bin/texis/scripts/utne-search/search.html?query=connection+slate r&x=0&y=0 (April 1, 2006)

## Chapter 2: The Truth About Happiness

p. 13: "Amidst the satisfaction people feel .." Robert E. Lane, *The Loss of Happiness in Market Democracies*, p. 3.

p. 17: "$34 million lottery purchased .." *New York Times*, "Instant Millions Can't Halt Winners' Grim Slide," December 5, 2005, A1.

p. 19: "More than ever, we have big houses .." David G. Myers, www.gbgm-umc.org/ncnyenvironmentaljustice/articles.htm# Wealth,%20Well-Being,%20and%20the%20NAD [online]. [Cited April 1, 2006].

p. 23: "The consequences of believing that the wealthy .." Tim Kasser, *The High Price of Materialism*, p. 54.

p. 24: "We have thus far seen three ways .." ibid., p. 72.

p. 24: "Materialism derives from .." ibid., p. 76.

p. 25: "Such motivations reflect .." ibid., p. 84.

p. 26: "Most of the world's population .." ibid., pp. ix–x.

p. 26: "My hypothesis is that there is a kind of famine .." Lane, p. 9.

p. 27: "The death of a culture is not usually encountered .." ibid., p. 10.

p. 30: "Positive emotions .." This list adapted from Martin Seligman, *Authentic Happiness*, pp. 125–161.

p. 32: "Richard Davidson, a professor .." http://psyphz.psych.wisc.edu/ web/News/Time_Jan06.html [online]. [Cited April 1, 2006].

p. 34: "Satisficers" is a term used by Barry Schwartz, *The Paradox of Choice: Why More Is Less*.

p. 36: " .. created an accelerated .." Peter Whybrow, *American Mania*, pp. 3-4.

p. 36: "Prolonged exposure .." ibid., p. 15.

p. 39: "People who work part-time, control their own lives .." Daniel Nettle, *Happiness: The Science Behind Your Smile*, p. 179.

p. 40: "Prisoner #151.." Arthur Waskow, www.pjvoice.com/v5/ 5010rabbi.html [online]. [Cited April 1, 2006].

p. 42: "For Epicurus .." Bruce O'Hara, *Enough Already! Breaking Free In the Second Half of Life*, p. 105.

## Chapter 3: Reversing the Spell of Status

p. 43: "The fact is, while most people think of ordinariness .." Eknath Easwaran, *The Compassionate Universe*, p. 22.

p. 44: " .. out of 25 industrialized Western nations .." Sam Pizzigati, *Greed for Good*, pp. 326. Subsequent data on health and wealth adapted from Pizzigati, pp. 311–351.

p. 45: "How foolish this question sounds to American ears .." ibid., p. 318.

p. 46: Government study cited in "Boomers May Put Brakes on Longevity," *Seattle Times*, December 9, 2005, A1.

p. 46: " .. Sir Michael Marmot .." reference is to his book, *The Status Syndrome*.

p. 48: "Average hourly earnings of non-supervisory workers .." Paul Krugman, "The Joyless Economy," *New York Times*, December 6, 2005, A24.

p. 49: "an imbalance between .." Plutarch, http://en.thinkexist.com/ quo-tation/an_imbalance_between_rich_and_poor_is_the_oldest/ 218004.html [online]. [Cited April 1, 2006].

p. 49: "Excess and deficiency .." Confucius, www.questia.com/PM.qst?a= o&d=5000167420 [online]. [Cited April 1, 2006].

p. 49: "They all said .." Arnold Toynbee, www.questionsquestions.net/docs04/ 911truthstatement.html [online]. [Cited April 1, 2006].

p. 49: "Our incomes are like our shoes .." Charles Colton,
www.brainyquote. com/quotes/quotes/c/charlescal156469. html
[online]. [Cited April 1, 2006].

p. 49: "We can either have democracy .." Louis Brandeis, www.swans.com/
library/art8/gowans31.html [online]. [Cited April 1, 2006].

p. 49: "As the gap between rich and poor has widened .." *Wall Street
Journal*, "As Rich-Poor Gap Widens in U.S., Class Mobility
Stalls," May 13, 2005, p A1.

p. 50: "Plutocracy should be called the great national crime .." Milford
Howard, cited in Pizzigati, *Greed for Good*, p. xix.

p. 52: "Standing witness to hidden lives, novels .." Alain de Botton,
*Status Anxiety*, p. 131.

p. 52: "Her finely-touched spirit had its fine issues .." George Eliot,
*Middlemarch*, p. 834.

p. 53: "Jokes become attempts to cajole .." de Botton, *Status Anxiety*, p.
164. Subsequent citations of Flaubert and Stendhal also are found
in de Botton.

p. 54: "Whatever the excesses of the outer wings of bohemia .." ibid., p.
291.

p. 54: "Mansionization" episode, CBS *60 Minutes*, November 27, 2005.

## Chapter 4: "Fast" and the Consumer Society

p. 57: "Americans have mastered .." Breyten Breytenbach, quoted by
Terry Tempest Williams in interview by Scott London, www.scott
london. com/interviews/williams.html [online]. [Cited April 1,
2006].

p. 58: "What happened here .." Milton Mayer, *They Thought They Were
Free*, p. 166.

pp. 61–62: US banned carcinogens turning up in foreign countries. Ref.
"The Corporate Crime of the Century," *Mother Jones*, www.moth-
erjones.com/news/feature/1979/11/dowie.html [online]. [Cited
April 1, 2006].

p. 63: "Academic administrators refer to students .." This is summary of
points made in Jennifer Washburn's *University Inc.: The Corporate
Corruption of Higher Education*.

p. 64: "The past quarter-century .." Paul Krugman, "Drugs, Devices and
Doctors," *New York Times*, December 16, 2005, A35.

p. 67: "Modern culture is economically based on the principle of individual competition .." Karen Horney, *The Neurotic Personality of Our
Time*, pp. 166–168.

p. 68: "Alfie Kohn, an ardent fighter .." Alfie Kohn, *No Contest: The Case Against Competition.*

## Chapter 5: Work Slowdown

p. 78: " ..willing slaves .." Madeleine Bunting, *Willing Slaves: How the Overwork Culture Is Ruling Our Lives.*

p. 79: "Our drive to have the kind of work that makes us feel important is very dangerous .." Roger Gottlieb, *A Spirituality of Resistance.* This and subsequent quotes in this chapter are from p. 69.

p. 84: "Americans are working 20 percent longer .." John de Graaf, ed., *Take Back Your Time,* in conversation.

p. 83: "93 percent of Americans .." Center for New American Dream, www.newdream.org/newsletter/survey.php [online]. [Cited April 1, 2006].

p. 83: Harris survey cited by John de Graaf, www.yesmagazine.org/article. asp?ID=1208 [online]. [Cited April 1, 2006].

p. 83: ".. Harvard School of Public Health .." www.simpleliving.net/time-day/ time_to_care_call.asp [online] [Cited June 18, 2006].

p. 85: "In America's demand-based and time-driven .." Whybrow, *American Mania,* p. 7.

## Chapter 6: the Subversiveness of Joie de Vivre

p. 91: "Yes we're bored .." Wallace Shawn and André Gregory, *My Dinner With André,* pp. 91–93.

p. 91: "We teach children how to measure, how to weigh .." Abraham Joshua Heschel, http://bethor.org/articles/marxcol2.html [online]. [Cited April 1, 2006].

p. 92: "Anything worth doing .." G. K. Chesterton, www.aphids.com/cgi-bin/ quotes.pl?act=ShowListingsForCat&Category=C [online]. [Cited April 1, 2006].

p. 92: "All the earth is gay .." William Wordsworth, "Intimations of Immortality," www.bartleby.com/145/ww331.html [online]. [Cited April 1, 2006].

p. 95: 'No-Eyes' has fixed his attention .." Evelyn Underhill, *Practical Mysticism,* pp. 29–30.

p. 96: "I went to the woods .." Henry David Thoreau, *Walden,* http://home. supernet.com/~rhymer/walden94.html [online]. [Cited April 1, 2006].

p. 97: "Surely joy is the condition of life." Thoreau, www.proz.com/ kudoz/1032687 [online]. [Cited April 1, 2006].

p. 98: "Thirteen billion years ago, the universe began as hydrogen .." Brian Swimme, www.natcath.com/NCR_Online/archives/081001/081001a. htm [online]. [Cited April 1, 2006].

p. 98: "Awareness of an all-pervading mysterious energy articulated .." Thomas Berry, *Creative Energy*, pp. 1–2.

p. 99: "Whether we like it or not, our lives will leave a mark on the universe .." Mihaly Csikszentmihalyi, *Finding Flow*, p. 131.

p. 99: "We are discovering how all forms of life depend .." ibid., p. 142.

p. 99: "The aim of life is the unfolding of man's creative powers .." Erich Fromm, *The Sane Society*, p. 233.

p. 101: "You know of the disease in Central Africa called sleeping sickness .." Albert Schweitzer, www.gurze.net/site12_5_00/newsletteredt4. htm [online]. [Cited April 1, 2006].

p. 102: "Nothing great was ever achieved without enthusiasm .." Ralph Waldo Emerson, www.transcendentalists.com/emerson_quotes.htm [online]. [Cited April 1, 2006].

p. 102: "Happy is he who bears a god .." Louis Pasteur, http://en.wikiquote.org/wiki/Louis_Pasteur [online]. [Cited April 1, 2006].

p. 102: "A passion for life is life's .." Kay Redfield Jamison, *Exuberance: The Passion for Life*, p. 308.

p. 103: ".. What happens, though, when .." ibid., p. 297.

p. 104: ".. The energy, enthusiasm .." ibid., p. 100.

p. 103: "The US comprises only 4 percent .." www.swans.com/library/dossiers/energy01.html [online]. [Cited April 1, 2006].

p. 105: "The choice is always ours .." Aldous Huxley, http://www.int-edu.ru/lbp/article/TRIBUTEtoALS.pdf [online]. [Cited April 1, 2006].

p. 105: "The fairest thing we can experience .." Albert Einstein, www.einsteinandreligion.com/ [online]. [Cited April 1, 2006].

p. 106: "There are two ways to live your life .." Albert Einstein, www.heartquotes.net/Einstein.html [online]. [Cited April 1, 2006].

p. 106: "The beginning of our happiness .." Abraham Heschel, *God in Search of Man*, p. 46.

p. 106: "To thine own self be true .." William Shakespeare, *Hamlet*, www.saliu.com/bbs/messages/839.html [online]. [Cited April 1, 2006].

p. 107: "I begin to shed .." Anne Morrow Lindbergh, *Gift from the Sea*, p. 20.

p. 107: "The revelation of the mystery .." Frederick Franck, *Art As a Way*, p. 68.

p. 109: "Men are very generally spoiled by being so civil .." Henry David Thoreau, ccms.ntu.edu.tw/~karchung/poemsS01B.doc [online]. [Cited April 1, 2006].

p. 111: "Quality which has no name .." Christopher Alexander, *The Timeless Way of Building*, p. 48. The subsequent quote, "Our letting go is stifled .." also p. 48. And "when we forget ourselves…" is from p. 50.

p. 112: "A man is alive when he is wholehearted .." ibid., p. 105.

p. 113: "The fact is, a person is so far formed .." ibid., p. 106.

p. 116: "We are pleasantly sedated by the flatness and predictability of modern life .." Thomas Moore, *Care of the Soul*, p. 118.

p. 117: Johan Huizinga, *Homo Ludens*. This discussion of play summarizes points throughout the book.

p. 119: "Work-up" may not even exist any more as an expression. It refers to working your way up to the plate in baseball.

p. 120: "Wearing a rubber nose .." Patch Adams, *Gesundheit!*, pp. 67–85.

p. 121: "You must laugh 10 times during the day .." Nietzsche, *Thus Spake Zarathustra*, www.literaturepage.com/read/thusspakezarathustra-31.html [online]. [Cited April 1, 2006].

p. 121: "The old man laughed loud and joyously .." Mark Twain, *Tom Sawyer*, p. 180.

p. 122: "In conversation, humor is worth more than wit .." George Herbert, www.brainyquote.com/quotes/authors/g/george_herbert.html [online]. [Cited April 1, 2006].

p. 122: "Beatrice, I've told you a hundred times .." Robert E. Drennan, ed., *The Algonquin Wits*, p. 32.

p. 123: "Among those whom I like or admire, I can find no common denominator .." W. H. Auden, www.quoteworld.org/quotes/701 [online]. [Cited April 1, 2006].

p. 124: "When we begin to take our failures non-seriously .." Katherine Mansfield, http://en.thinkexist.com/quotation/when_we_begin_to_take_our_failures_non-seriously/213075.html [online]. [Cited April 1, 2006].

p. 125: "In 1925, Harold Ross was struggling .." www.princeton.edu/~howarth/380/ross.html [online]. [Cited April 1, 2006].

p. 127: "Carnivals of protest create their own bubble of consciousness .." "The 'American Street' Speaks: Will the Democratic Party

Listen?" *Salon*, http://dir.salon.com/story/opinion/feature/2005/09/29/ protests/print.html [online]. [Cited April 1, 2006].

p. 127: "Unmasking the pretense of the powerful always makes their power seem less irresistible .." Harvey Cox, *Feast of Fools*, p. 5.

p. 131: "Lawful recreations .." Increase Mather quoted in Bruce Daniels, *Puritans At Play*, p. 17. Later quote, "often spend more time therein .." also p. 17.

p. 133: "Sabbath laws forbade .." ibid., p. 75.

p. 133: "Social custom proscribed .." ibid., p. 76.

p. 134: "I did not wish to live what was not life .." Thoreau, http://quotes.prolix.nu/Authors/?Henry_David_Thoreau [online]. [Cited April 1, 2006].

p. 136: "One recounts .." *New York Times*, "Army Details Scale of Abuse in Afghan Jail," March 12, 2005, A1.

p. 136: " ..other tells .." "Bush Picks Adviser to Repair Tarnished U.S. Image Abroad," *New York Times*, A2.

p. 136: "Reality is fabulous .." Thoreau, www.vcu.edu/engweb/ transcendentalism/authors/thoreau/walden/chapter02.html [online]. [Cited April 1, 2006].

p. 136: "In everyone there is some longing .." Richard Bell, ed., with Barbara Battin, *Seeds of the Spirit: Wisdom of the Twentieth Century*, p. 62.

p. 136: "But when the transcendent energies waste .." Theodore Roszak, *Where the Wasteland Ends*, p. xxi.

p. 137: "The stirring in our hearts when watching .." Abraham Joshua Heschel, *Moral Grandeur and Spiritual Audacity*, p. 4.

## Chapter 7: Visionary Leisure

p. 139: "You don't need to leave your room .." Kafka, www.karenmcquestion. com/archived_quotes.htm [online]. [Cited April 1, 2006].

p. 139: "The capacity for reflection comes from a state of mind .." Lin Yutang, *Lin Yutang on the Wisdom of America*, p. 239.

p. 140: ".. grateful for what I am and have .." Henry David Thoreau, www.kirjasto.sci.fi/thoreau.htm [online]. [Cited April 1, 2006].

p. 147: "Can the world of man be exhausted .." Josef Pieper, *Leisure, The Basis of Culture*, p. 33. Subsequent quotations through p. 154 are from Pieper, pp. 12–42.

p. 152: "putting-oneself-into-relation .." ibid., p. 85.

p. 152: "The highest state to which humanity .." Goethe, quoted in Pieper, p. 105.

p. 152: "It therefore belongs to the nature of philosophy .." ibid., p. 113.

p. 154: "Is the stress of time, the famine of time .." Joseph Needleman, *Time and the Soul*, p. 149.

p. 154: "The problem of time in our world .." ibid., p. 154.

p. 155: "The morality of work is the morality of slaves .." Bertrand Russell, *In Praise of Idleness*, www.whywork.org/rethinking/leisure/russell. html [online]. [Cited April 1, 2006].

p. 155: "Gradually, however, it was found possible to induce many of them .." ibid.

p. 156: "capacity for light-heartedness and play .." and "In a world where no one is compelled .." ibid.

p. 158: "workers would be liberated .." Benjamin Hunicutt, www.context. org/ICLIB/IC37/Hunnicut.htm [online]. [Cited April 1, 2006].

p. 160: "What is all this progress? .." H.G. Wells, *Things to Come* (1936).

## Chapter 8: Slow Together: Exhuberant Community

p. 163: "Then I saw a story .." "The Tyranny of the Book Group," *Wall Street Journal*, January 15, 1999, W1.

p. 169: "Truth comes to us in dialogue .." Karl Jaspers, *Socrates, Buddha, Confucius, Jesus: From the Great Philosophers*, Vol. I, p. 4.

p. 170: "Grey duvet," James Scarlett-Lyon, in conversation.

p. 176: "Entertaining friends .." Statistical data from Robert Putnam, *Bowling Alone*, pp. 192–202.

p. 176: "We must learn to view the world through a social capital lens .." Lew Feldstein, www.bettertogether.org/ [online]. [Cited April 1, 2006].

p. 177: "This book is the true story of how things were in the Great Depression .." Deb Mulvey, ed., *We Had Everything But Money: Priceless Memories of the Great Depression*, p. 8.

p. 180: "We not only survived .." ibid., p. 16.

p. 180: "It made us appreciate .." ibid., p. 24.

p. 180: "There may have been .." ibid., p. 25.

p. 180: "I'll never forget .." ibid., p. 26.

p. 180: "The Depression was terrible .." ibid., p. 27.

p. 185: "The mundane world subdues us .." Ray Oldenburg, *The Great Good Place*, p. 58.

p. 190: "In a survey taken by .." http://archives.cnn.com/ 2002/US/04/02/rude.americans/index.html [online]. [Cited April 1, 2006].

p. 193: "Social life revolves around faith .." Katherine Newman, *Rampage: The Social Roots of School Shootings*, p. 114.

## Chapter 9: Slow Is Beautiful

p. 197: "We have lost our sense of time .." Carlo Petrini, www.fastcompany. com/magazine/34/slowfood.html [online]. [Cited April 1, 2006].

p. 199: "There is a pervasive form of contemporary violence .." Thomas Merton, *Conjectures of a Guilty Bystander*, p. 86.

p. 203: "The sublime may be sensed in things of beauty .." Abraham Heschel, *The Wisdom of Heschel*, p. 123.

p. 211: "There is a time when the operation of the machine .." Mario Savio, December 3, 1964, Berkeley Free Speech Movement www.fsm-a.org/stacks/mario/mario_speech.html [online]. [Cited April 1, 2006].

p. 217: "I am done with great things and big plans .." William James, http://tasmaniantimes.com/index.php/weblog/C44/ [online]. [Cited April 1, 2006].

p. 220: "I see ten or more people in there on some days .." Joanne Harris, *Chocolat*, p. 79.

p. 221: " ..never be the first in the world .." Lin Yutang, *The Importance of Living*, p. 2.

p. 221: "In this present age of threats to democracy .." ibid., p. 12.

p. 222: "Why do the Westerners talk so softly .."ibid., p. 47.

p. 222: "I doubt whether the importance of humor .." ibid., p. 77.

p. 222: "Who are the people who start wars? .." ibid., p. 78.

p. 222: "The plain fact is that the planet does not need .." David Orr, *Ecological Literacy*, p. 12.

p. 223: "Instead of wayward, incalculable, unpredictable .." Yutang, p. 84.

p. 223: "Shiftless," Raymond Carver, *Ultramarine*, p. 59.

p. 225: "For wherever the individual is, even in small degree .." Harry Overstreet, *A Civilized Guide to Leisure*, p. 26; "There is a picture of the immortal Skeets .." ibid., pp. 210–211.

p. 226, "And I tell you .." Kurt Vonnegut, "Kurt's View," in *Stories to Live By*, ed. James O'Reilly et al., p. 82.

# Index

*A*

advertising, 11, 18, 24, 28, 57-58, 63 184. *See also* commercialization
Alexander, Christopher, 110-113
authenticity, 106-114, 215-16

*B*

Bentham, Jeremy, 14, 37
Berry, Thomas, 97-101
Bohemia, 53-54
Bok, Derek, 65-66
Bush, George, 6, 16, 83, 88, 127, 133, 134, 210

*C*

Callahan, David, 134
commercialization, 61-66, 185, 212
community, 10-11, 39, 40, 164, 186-92
        *See also* the Great Good Place
competition, 11, 28, 29, 66-71, 84-85, 119, 123, 126, 182
connections, 99, 112, 133, 138, 146-47, 152-53, 154
consumerism, 11, 21-22, 25, 56-57, 60, 81, 143, 161, 203-204, 212
contemplation. *See* reflection
conversation, 167-70, 172, 189-92
conviviality, 192
core strengths, 30-33

corporatism, 64, 68-71, 82, 86, 151, 186, 216-17.
        *See also* commercialization; consumerism
counterculture, 214-17
Csikszentmihalyi, Mihaly, 17, 101
culture, 27, 53, 67-68, 72, 74, 117, 160
culture of connection, 11-12, 73, 204, 217

*D*
Davidson, Richard, 32
de Botton, Alain, 51-54
de Graaf, John, 9, 83
democracy, 68, 133-34, 218
depression, 3, 13, 14, 19, 20, 25, 27, 30, 33, 38, 85, 165
Depression, The Great, 158, 159, 160, 161, 177-78, 180-81
disease, 16, 25, 45, 46, 65, 84. *See also* depression; health

*E*
EcoVillage, 173-176
education, 28, 51-52, 62-66, 68-69, 74-76, 151-52, 211-12
environment, the, 3,8, 21, 80, 99, 165, 216

*F*
family, 17, 22, 27, 36, 38, 42, 83, 159, 200, 215
food, 6-7, 73, 114-15. *See also* Slow Food
Field, Joanna. *See* Milne, Marion
Fromm, Erich, 60, 99, 161

*G*
Gottlieb, Roger, 78-82
Great Good Place, the, 181-86

*H*
happiness, 3, 13-42, 44-45, 46, 82-83, 85, 184. *See also* joie de vivre
health, 14, 15, 24, 28, 33, 37, 44-45, 70, 109, 118, 120-21, 159, 202. *See also* disease
Heinberg, Richard, 6
Honore, Carl, 9
Horney, Karen, 67-68
Huizinga, Johan, 117-19
Hunnicutt, Benjamin, 158-60

*J*
Jamison, Kay Redfield 102-104, 117
Japanese, 44-45
joie de vivre, 10-11, 96-98, 102-104, 105, 198
        undermining of, 132-39. *See also* laughter

## K
Kasser, Tim, 20-26, 47, 55, 117
Kellogg, W.K., 157-158
Kohn, Alfie, 68
Krugman, Paul, 48, 64

## L
Labier, Douglas, 85
Lane, Robert E., 13-14, 26-30, 93
Laughter, 120-128, 200
Layard, Richard, 14, 37-38
leisure, 10-11, 82, 139-61, 190, 198, 203, 213, 224-26. *See also* play
Lindbergh, Anne Morrow, 107
local currency, 73

## M
Marmot, Sir Michael, 46-47
marriage, 25, 33, 38, 123-24
Maslow, Abraham, 17, 160
materialism, 16-26, 28-29, 55. *See also* commercialization
Melville, Herman, 86-88
Milne, Marion, 200
Moore, Thomas, 116
Myers, David G., 19

## N
Needleman, Joseph, 153-54
Nettle, Daniel, 35-41
Newman, Katherine, 193-94

## O
O'Hara, Bruce, 41-42
Oldenburg, Ray, 181-84
Overstreet, Harry, 225

## P
peak oil, 6, 67, 74
Petrini, Carlo, 197
Pieper, Josef, 147-153
Pizzigati, Sam, 45-48
play, 116-120, 156, 198. *See also* leisure
psychic numbing, 100-101
Putnam, Robert, 29, 175-76, 192-93, 207
Putney, Snell and Gail, 106-107

*R*

*Real Change*, 100, 115
reflection, 39, 145, 146, 148, 149, 198, 200-201
relationships, 11, 17, 23, 26-28, 29, 30, 42, 86, 122-23, 135, 198.
       *See also* community
religion, 51, 82, 89, 97, 98, 104-105, 113, 130-32, 164, 193-94
Russell, Bertrand, 155-57
Ryan, Richard, 21, 26

*S*

scamp, the, 221-24
Schor, Juliet, 21
Schumacher, E.F., 11
Schwartz, Barry, 34
self-esteem, 20, 22-23, 25, 27, 28, 113, 125
Seligman, Martin, 30-35
Silicon Valley, 4-5
Slater, Philip, 11-12
Slow Food, 7-10, 199, 205, 209, 222
Slow Life, 8-12, 39, 70, 104, 149, 152, 197-224
social capital, 5, 45, 176, 180, 191
social change, 104, 164-95, 205-11
social cohesion, 45-47
social inventions, 71-72
Stanford University, 4-5, 78, 186-87, 189
status, 3-4, 37-38. 43-55, 80, 144, 150, 182, 186-87
stress, 43, 46, 47, 85, 183, 202
Swimme, Brian, 99-103

*T*

Take Back Your Time Movement, 41, 83, 198, 210
television, 8, 11, 21-22, 132-33, 135, 159, 184, 185

*U*

Underhill, Evelyn, 95-96, 152

*V*

voluntary simplicity, 50-51, 76-77
Vonnegut, Kurt, 190, 226

*W*

Washburn, Jennifer, 63
Waskow, Arthur, 40
wealth divide, 37, 44, 45, 48-49, 50-51, 182, 186-87
Whybrow, Peter, 2-3, 14, 18, 36-37, 84-85, 104, 143-44
workplace, the, 30, 47, 70-71, 73-89, 143-44, 156-61, 168

# *About the Author*

RON ANTON ROCZ

CECILE ANDREWS is a community educator who works to build civic engagement and to encourage people to live more simply and slowly — creating lives that are more sustainable, joyful, and just. She is the author of *The Circle of Simplicity: Return to the Good Life* and has contributed to, among others, *Take Back Your Time: Fighting Overwork and Time Poverty in America, Simpler Living, Compassionate Life,* and *Stories to Live By.*

She has her doctorate in education from Stanford University where she was also a visiting scholar, and has been an adjunct professor at Seattle University and a community college administrator. She is a cofounder of the Phinney EcoVillage, an informal project to build community and sustainability in her north Seattle neighborhood.

Cecile's work has been featured in the PBS video "Escape from Affluenza" and the TBS video "Consumed by Consumption" (featuring Cecile, Ed Begley Jr., and Phyllis Diller), CBSNews "Eye on America", *New York Times, Los Angeles Times, Esquire,* and various PBS and NPR programs. Cecile has written a column for the *Seattle Times.* For more information, visit www.cecileandrews.com

If you have enjoyed *Slow is Beautiful*, you might also enjoy other

# BOOKS TO BUILD A NEW SOCIETY

Our books provide positive solutions for people who want to
make a difference. We specialize in:

Sustainable Living • Ecological Design and Planning
Natural Building & Appropriate Technology • New Forestry
Environment and Justice • Conscientious Commerce
Progressive Leadership • Resistance and Community • Nonviolence
Educational and Parenting Resources

## New Society Publishers
### ENVIRONMENTAL BENEFITS STATEMENT

New Society Publishers has chosen to produce this book on recycled paper
made with 100% post consumer waste, processed chlorine free, and old
growth free.

For every 5,000 books printed, New Society saves the following resources:[1]

| | |
|---:|---|
| 26 | Trees |
| 2,327 | Pounds of Solid Waste |
| 2,560 | Gallons of Water |
| 3,339 | Kilowatt Hours of Electricity |
| 4,230 | Pounds of Greenhouse Gases |
| 18 | Pounds of HAPs, VOCs, and AOX Combined |
| 6 | Cubic Yards of Landfill Space |

[1]Environmental benefits are calculated based on research done by the Environmental Defense
Fund and other members of the Paper Task Force who study the environmental impacts of the
paper industry.

*For a full list of NSP's titles, please call 1-800-567-6772 or check out our web site at:*

**www.newsociety.com**

NEW SOCIETY PUBLISHERS